WOMEN AND FILM:
A Bibliography

by

Rosemary Ribich Kowalski

The Scarecrow Press, Inc.
Metuchen, N.J.   1976

Library of Congress Cataloging in Publication Data

Kowalski, Rosemary Ribich.
  Women and film.

    Bibliography: p.
    Includes index.
    1. Women in the motion picture industry--Bibliography.
I. Title.
Z5784. M9K68   [PN1995. 9. W6]   016. 79143   76-25051
ISBN 0-8108-0974-5

TO
MY SONS,
Bob, Mike and Steve

CONTENTS

Introduction   vii

1. Women as Performers
   A. Reference and Historical Works   1
   B. Specific Works   15

2. Women as Film-makers
   A. Reference and Historical Works   90
   B. Catalogues   99
   C. Specific Works   103

3. Images of Women
   A. Reference and Historical Works   175
   B. Catalogues   179
   C. Specific Works   182

4. Women Columnists and Critics   227

Subject Index   243

INTRODUCTION

I began this bibliography as a class assignment for "Library Research Methods." The instructor said: "Choose a topic which you think is interesting and which could develop into a thesis."

Being rather new to women's studies and film studies, and wanting to find out as much as possible about both, I decided to collect as much information as possible about the contributions women have made in the field of film.

My biggest problem was my own lack of knowledge on the subject and so, when I began, I made certain assumptions. One, I feared I could not find too much information on "Women and Film." Two, I really had no clear idea just what the term meant. When I began, therefore, I collected any and all manner of data even vaguely related to my topic. As I worked, information on "Actresses" began accumulating steadily, while "other" information--I had not categorized it yet--built at a far slower pace. Fearing I would not find "anything," I kept the material on actresses, just in case.

By the time I had completed the assignment for my class, I had a very clear idea of what "Women and Film" meant and, as is evident in this bibliography, it is a very broad phrase. It refers to any and all aspects of women's contributions to the development of film.

My early fear that I would not find much was completely erroneous, as witness this enlarged version of my original project. And I realize as I write this that there is more to be discovered and that new material is accumulating at a rapid rate. But I had to stop somewhere.

My all-inclusive approach--collecting anything and everything about women in film from its beginnings to the present--necessitated perusing a variety of materials from the last seventy-five years or so. The research, while time-consuming, was never boring for I discovered much more than I expected to find. It was exciting learning who the contributors were and are, what kind of contributions they made and are making, and realizing that women have tenaciously held a place, albeit a tiny one, in the field of film since its inception.

The bibliography is divided into four major sections: Women as Performers, Women as Film-makers, Images of Women Presented on the Screen, and Women as Columnists and Critics.

My original lack of interest in including "Actresses" yielded to the realization that this area in film-making is the one in which women have made the most obvious contribution to film. To ignore them is to ignore one of the few fields in film--or anywhere--in which women have as large a representation as men. Material on actresses is voluminous. I have necessarily limited this section to books which are devoted exclusively to one actress or which make mention of a number of particular actresses, and to articles which were listed in early film indexes or which have appeared in the last five years in major women's or film periodicals. Articles in between these two periods are very adequately covered in Mel Schuster's bibliography of <u>Motion Picture Performers</u> which is listed, and the specific names of actresses he has information on are noted in the index to this bibliography.

In the section "Women as Film-makers," I have included articles and books by or about women who in one way or another contributed to the aesthetic or technical aspects of film-making as producers, directors, editors, screenwriters, etc. Very little information was found on women (or men for that matter) cinematographers, art directors, choreographers, costume designers, make-up artists, musicians, etc.--fields which are vital to film-making and in which women are represented but which seem to have attracted few writers.

The articles in the section "Images of Women" are of extreme importance to Women's Studies scholars. Film as one means of socialization is being carefully scrutinized for its effects on women and the increase in the number of articles on this topic in the last several years is very evident. The images of women projected on the screen have been primarily from a male viewpoint. Women, and men with more "sensitive" attitudes, are needed to project new images if changes in the status or roles of women and men are to occur. It is obvious that more women film-makers are needed

to project new images for women, and it is equally obvious
that careful study needs to be made of the images that have
been depicted so far. Women and men must understand what
images are being reinforced and why and how this is done.
Only then will it be possible to begin developing new ones.

The section on "Columnists and Critics" was included,
initially, because the material surfaced during the research.
It is interesting for several reasons. Serious discussion of
film has been almost the exclusive property of men, while
"Hollywood" publicity and gossip was most effectively con-
veyed by women such as Hedda Hopper and Louella Parsons.
The implications are obvious. But it is equally interesting to
note the emergence of "feminist" critics in the last several
years. While their debate over the question "What is women's film?" continues, one realizes the importance of their
perspective in the use of film as a socializing tool. Their
voices should and will have an effect on the images depicted
by film-makers and actresses.

In order to facilitate the reader's use of this bibliography, I have separated certain works in each section. Reference tools or surveys of a historical nature are listed first;
lists or catalogues of films are included here as well. The
more specific works follow.

If some annotations in this bibliography seem particularly long, it is because the articles so annotated were deemed
to be of importance in identifying women who have made significant contributions to film, and note was made of them so
that the reader could familiarize himself/herself with the
names and pursue further research more easily. My assump-
tion was that the reader might know as little as I did when I
began.

Some articles are listed in more than one section where
this seemed appropriate.

In addition, a subject and name index has been provid-
ed to aid the reader in identifying all items which may be related to his/her topic.

I wish to thank Sharon Lossing for her invaluable as-
sistance in compiling this bibliography. I also wish to thank
Marvin Felheim and the many friends whose acts of kindness
and words of encouragement sustained me throughout this project.

R. R. K.

Chapter 1

WOMEN AS PERFORMERS

A. Reference and Historical Works

1 Alicoate, Charles A., ed. The Film Daily Yearbook, 1929-1968. New York: Film Daily, Inc.

2 The American Film Institute Catalogue, Feature Films 1921-1930. New York and London: R. R. Bowker, 1971.

3 Annuario del Cinema Italiano, 1966-1967. Rome: Ferrau, Cenedizioni.

4 Balshafer, Fred and Arthur C. Miller. One Reel a Week. Berkeley and Los Angeles: University of California Press, 1967.
    Reminiscences by two early cameramen and their work in early studios. References to actresses and other film women (Lois Weber, director) but any information must be culled by reading whole text.

5 Barry, Iris. Let's Go to the Movies. New York: Arno Press, 1972.
    Includes interesting chapters on images of women and messages for women in film (Chap. IV), Mary Pickford (Chap. VII), the innocent heroine and wicked vamp as film types (Chap. IX). Original printing was 1926.

6 Baxter, John. Hollywood in the Sixties. New York: A. S. Barnes and Co., 1972.

6a _____. Hollywood in the Thirties. New York: A. S. Barnes, 1968.

7 Best, Marc. Those Enduring Young Charms. South Brunswick: A. S. Barnes and Co., 1971.

Pictorial essay on child performers. The text
reads like a fan magazine but included are some old
favorites such as Shirley Temple, Natalie Wood, Deanna
Durbin.

8   Billings, Pat and Allen Eyles. Hollywood Today. New
York: A. S. Barnes and Co., 1971.

9   Blum, Daniel. A Pictorial History of the Silent Screen.
New York: Putnam, 1953.

10 Bond, Frederick W. The Negro and the Drama, the
Direct and Indirect Contribution which the American
Negro Has Made to Drama and the Legitimate Stage.
College Park, Maryland: McGrath Publishing Co.,
1969.
        "Negro Drama in Moving Pictures and Radio" (Chap.
10).

11 Boussinot, Roger, ed. L'Encyclopédie du Cinéma.
Paris: Bordas, 1967.
History of French cinema.

12 Brownlow, Kevin. The Parade's Gone By. New York:
Knopf, 1968.

13 Bull, Clarence Sinclair with Raymond Lee. The Faces
of Hollywood. New York: A. S. Barnes and Co.,
1969.

14 Burton, Jack. The Blue Book of Hollywood Musicals.
Watkins Glen, N.Y.: Century House, 1953.
        Year-by-year account of Hollywood musicals, 1927-
1952. Lists songs and singers. Indexed by movie, so
must read in entirety to find women's credits (1936,
"The Way You Look Tonight," Academy Award, Dorothy
Fields and Jerome Kern). Indexed by song titles only,
not composers or lyricists. Some names: Mabel Wayne,
Evelyn Lyn, Dolly Morse, Dorothy Shay, Dorothy Fields,
Diane Manners, Ann Canova, Vera Bloom, Doris Fisher,
Sylvia Fine, Judy Canova, Grace Hamilton. Names fore-
most singing and dancing stars.

15 Cameron, Ian Alexander. Dames. New York: Praeger,
1969.
        Published in London as Broads.

16 Clode, E. J. My Strange Life; the Intimate Life Story

of a Moving Picture Actress. New York, 1915.
Illustrated with the photographs of America's most
famous motion picture actresses.

17 Curtis, Anthony, ed. The Rise and Fall of the Matinee
Idol: Past Deities of Stage and Screen, their Roles,
their Magic, their Worshippers. New York: St.
Martin's Press, Inc., 1974.
Collected essays about the cult that surrounded the
gods and goddesses of stage and screen. American Cinematographer reviewer says "the literary quality of the
writing does not offset the book's absolute vapidness."

18 Daniel Blum's Screen World, 1949- . Vol. 1- , 1949- .
Lists films released during the year with stills and
credits.

19 Dickinson, Thorold and Catherine de la Roche, eds.
Soviet Cinema. London: Falcon Press, 1948.

20 Dietz, Howard. Dancing in the Dark. New York:
Quadrangle, 1974.
Autobiography of popular lyricist and chief of MGM's
publicity dept. Includes many references to stage, screen
and society personalities.

21 Dimmitt, Richard Bertrand. An Actor Guide to the Talkies. Metuchen, N.J.: Scarecrow Press, 1967. 2v.
Lists films produced from January, 1949 to December, 1964, and credits them under specific actor or
actress's name. A good source for discovering some of
the films a performer appeared in.

22 Durgnat, Raymond. The Crazy Mirror. London: Faber,
1969.
Traces the history of comedy with references to
comediennes woven into the text. Index for performers
includes a filmography for each which also lists director,
producer, screenwriter and other contributors.

23 Eyler, Allen. American Comedy Since Sound. New
York: A. S. Barnes and Co., 1970.
Comments and filmographies on comedians, comedy
teams, actors, directors and supporting players.

24 Fordin, Hugh. The World of Entertainment. Garden City,
N.Y.: Doubleday and Co., Inc., 1975.
Description and discussion of Hollywood's greatest
musicals and musical stars.

25 Fox, Charles Donald. Mirrors of Hollywood. New
     York: Charles Renard Corp. , 1925.
     Brief biographies of favorite film folk with fore-
     word by Will W. Hays.

26 Gabor, Mark. The Pin-Up: A Modest History. New
     York: Universe Books, Inc. , 1973.
     A gallery of cheesecake from the fin de siècle pos-
     ter to today's literate sex magazine. Starlets and act-
     resses are included in the collection, such as Monroe,
     Mansfield, Grable, Loren, Hayworth, E. Taylor.

27 Gillman, Barbara. Photoplay Treasury. New York:
       Crown Publishers, Inc. , 1973.
     A sampling of articles from Photoplay magazine,
     the granddaddy of fan magazines. Hollywood at work
     and play, back to the early 'teens of the 20th century.
     Gives perspective on social attitudes and early tech-
     niques.

28 Goldwyn, Samuel. Behind the Screen. New York:
       George H. Doran, 1923.
     Mr. Goldwyn includes in his reminiscences anec-
     dotes about many women performers including Pickford,
     Mary Garden, Pola Negri, the Talmadge sisters, Alice
     Terry, Geraldine Farrar, Fanny Ward, Mae Murray,
     Maxine Elliott and Pauline Frederick.

29 Goodman, Ezra. The Fifty-Year Decline and Fall of
       Hollywood. New York: Simon and Schuster, 1961.
     Publicist punctures the images of a number of
     showbusiness greats and discloses the tarnish beneath
     the tinsel.

30 Gow, Gordon. Hollywood in the Fifties. New York:
       A. S. Barnes and Co. , 1971.

31 Graham, Peter John. A Dictionary of the Cinema.
       London: Zwemmer; New York: A. S. Barnes and
       Co. , 1968.

32 Graham, Sheilah. Confessions of a Hollywood Colum-
       nist. New York: Wm. Morrow and Co. , 1969.
     Discusses actors, correspondence, reminiscences.
     Various chapters on individuals, including Barbra Strei-
     sand, Katherine Hepburn and Spencer Tracy, Marilyn
     Monroe, Elizabeth Taylor, Sophia Loren, Jane Fonda,

Greta Garbo. Gossipy.

33 Griffith, Linda Arvidson (Mrs. D. W.). When the Movies Were Young. New York: E. P. Dutton and Co., 1925.
Traces the history of early American film with particular emphasis on Griffith. Included are some chapters on Griffith's actresses.

34 Griffith, Richard. The Movie Stars. Garden City, N.Y.: Doubleday, 1970.
Analysis and photos of many Hollywood stars.

35 _____. The Talkies. New York: Dover Publications, 1971.
Reprints of articles and illustrations from Photoplay magazine, 1928-1940. Fascinating articles primarily about stars but also about some of the people behind the scenes (Dorothy Arzner); includes the effect of Hollywood on its fans.

36 Halliwell, Leslie. The Filmgoer's Companion. New York: Hill and Wang, 1974.
A collection of facts about films and people who make them. In dictionary format.

37 Hardy, Forsyth. Scandinavian Film. London: Falcon Press, 1952.

38 Herman, Hal C., ed. How I Broke into the Movies. Hollywood, 1930.
Signed autobiographies by sixty famous screen stars.

39 Hibben, Nina. Eastern Europe. New York: A. S. Barnes and Co., 1969.
History of Eastern European cinema.

40 Higham, Charles and Joel Greenberg. Hollywood in the Forties. New York: A. S. Barnes and Co., 1968.
(International Film Guide Series)

41 Hopper, Hedda. From Under My Hat. New York: Doubleday, 1952.

42 _____. The Whole Truth and Nothing But. New York: Doubleday, 1963.

43   Hoyne, Donald, ed.   The Autobiography of Cecil B. De-
     Mille.   New Jersey: Prentice-Hall, Inc., 1959.
           References to some actresses scattered throughout
     the book.

44   Hughes, Langston and Milton Meltzer.   Black Magic: A
     Pictorial History of the Negro in American Entertain-
     ment.   Englewood Cliffs, N. J.:   Prentice-Hall, 1967.

45   International Motion Picture Almanac, 1933-1972.   New
           York: Quigley Publications.

46   Irwin, Wm. Henry.   The House That Shadows Built.
     Doubleday-Doran, 1928.
           Story of Adolph Zukor and the rise of motion pic-
     ture industry.   Includes "Exit Mary Pickford" and scat-
     tered references to actresses throughout.

47   Jacobs, Lewis.   The Rise of American Film.   New York:
     Teachers College Press, 1969.

48   Jerome, Victor Jeremy.   The Negro in Hollywood Films.
     New York: Masses and Mainstream, 1950.
           A "Marxist indictment of American films of the
     40's dealing with racial themes."   The author believes
     that the stereotyped portrayals of Black characters
     would help perpetuate the American Black condition.

49   Kanin, Garson.   Hollywood: Stars and Starlets, Tycoons
     and Flesh-Peddlers, Moviemakers and Moneymakers,
     Frauds and Geniuses, Hopefuls and Has-Beens, Great
     Lovers and Sex Symbols.   New York: Viking Press,
     Inc., 1974.

50   Knight, Arthur.   The Liveliest Art.   New York and Tor-
     onto: The New American Library, 1957.

51   _____ and Hollis Alpert.   Playboy's Sex in Cinema.
     3 vols.   Chicago: Playboy Press, n. d.

52   Kobal, John.   Fifty Super Stars.   New York: Crown
     Publications, 1974.

53   _____.   Gotta Sing, Gotta Dance.   New York: Ham-
     lyn, 1970.
           Discussion of Hollywood musicals and their stars.

54 _____. Romance and the Cinema. London: Studio
Vista, 1973.

55 Lahue, Kalton C. Bound and Gagged: the Story of Silent Serials. South Brunswick, N. J. : A. S. Barnes
and Co. , 1968.
Discusses many of the stars of the early silent
serials, Pearl White, Ruth Roland, Allene Ray, Ethlyne
Clair, etc. , but primarily pictorial.

56 _____ and Sam Gill. Clown Princes and Court Jes-
ters: Some Great Comics of the Silent Screen. New
York: A. S. Barnes and Co. , 1970.
Analysis and photographic illustration of acts of
each of 50 male and female comics including Dorothy
Devore, Louise Fazenda, Gale Henry, Alice Howell,
Mable Normand, Fay Tincher and members of Our Gang.

57 Landays, Eileen. Black Film Stars. New York: Drake
Publishers, Inc. , 1974.
Chronicles lives and careers of thirty outstanding
Negro performers from the movies' early years. A
well-researched and lively book.

58 Levin, Martin, ed. Hollywood and the Great Fan Magazines. New York: Arbor House, 1970.
An anthology of the best of Photoplay, Motion Picture and Silver Screen articles. Mostly from the thirties, some from the twenties and forties. No index, so
must scan the whole for articles on women. Articles
read as though they are the products of a studio publicity department.

59 Lowrey, Carolyn. The First One Hundred Noted Men
and Women of the Screen. New York: Moffatt, Yard
and Co. , 1920.

60 Lyons, Timothy J. The Silent Partner: The History of
the American Film Manufacturing Co. , 1910-1921.
V. 7. New York: Arno Press, 1974.

61 McClelland, Doug. The Unkindest Cuts. South Brunswick and New York: A. S. Barnes and Co. , 1972.
Discusses some of the most memorable cuts made
in motion pictures. Chapter 2, "In a Class by Herself,"
about Ethel Griffies, discusses this oldest working English

actress, famous as "battle-axe" in many Hollywood films
of the 30's and 40's. Chapter 3, "A Mother's Hisses,"
discusses character actress Anne Revere, famous in
mother roles, and her cuts as a result of her appearance
before the House Unamerican Activities Committee in
1951. Chapter 7, "The Lady in a Cage ...," is on
cuts of Ann Sothern, Eva Marie Saint, Claire Bloom.
The references to women throughout are very interesting.

62 McClure, Arthur F. and Ken D. Jones. Star Quality.
    New Jersey: A. S. Barnes and Co., 1975.
        Seventy-nine screen performers and featured players
    who never achieved real stardom but commanded popular
    appeal are reviewed in concise biographical sketches and
    an abundance of photos.

63 McVay, J. Douglas. The Musical Film. London:
    Zwemmer; New York: Barnes, 1967.

64 Maltin, Leonard. Movie Comedy Teams. With Introduc-
    tion by Billy Gilbert. New York: New American Li-
    brary, 1970.

65 Manvell, Roger and Heinrich Fraenkel. The German
    Cinema. New York: Praeger Publications, 1971.
    (See entry under Film-makers.)

66 Mapp, Edward. Blacks in American Films: Today and
    Yesterday. Metuchen, N. J.: Scarecrow Press, 1972.
        Discusses Black performers and their roles.

67 Meyers, Warren B. "Who Is That?" New York: Per-
    sonality Posters, 1967.
        The late late viewer's guide to the old old movie
    players.

68 Michael, Paul. The Academy Award: A Pictorial His-
    tory. New York: Crown Publishers, 1968.

69 _____. The American Movies Reference Book: The
    Sound Era. Englewood Cliffs, N. J.: Prentice-Hall,
    1969.
        Six sections: history, players, films (including
    credits), directors, producers, the Academy Awards.

70 Morin, Edgar. The Stars. New York: Grove Press,
    1960.

71 The New York Times Film Reviews 1913-1968 and Index.
    6 vols. New York: New York Times and Arno Press,
    1970.

72 Noble, Peter, ed. The British Film and Television
    Yearbook, 1947-1968. London: British Yearbook.

73 _____. The Cinema and the Negro, 1905-1948. Lon-
    don: 1948. 21 pp. (Special supplement to Sight and
    Sound, Index Series, No. 14.)
        Index to the work of Negro actors in the cinema:
    the important productions of the previous fifty years con-
    taining parts for Negroes or touching on racial themes
    generally. American, British, continental (French, Ger-
    man, Russian) films. Listed by name of film in chrono-
    logical order. Must scan for women.

74 Null, Gary. Black Hollywood: The Negro in Motion Pic-
    tures. New York: Citadel Press, 1974.

75 Osborne, Robert. The Academy Awards Illustrated. La
    Habra, Calif.: Ernest Schworck, 1969.
        History, 1927-68. Only five major awards listed,
    including best actress and supporting actress (and actor,
    supporting actor, best picture). Includes winner and
    other nominees.

76 _____. Best Actress--Academy Awards. La Habra,
    Calif.: E. E. Schworck, 1970.
        Paperback. Full volume is recommended.

77 Parish, James Robert and Ronald L. Bowers. The MGM
    Stock Company: The Golden Era. New York: Arling-
    ton House Publishers, 1973.
        Minibiographies of 145 MGM performers during
    MGM's lush years.

78 Parsons, Louella. The Gay Illiterate. Garden City,
    N.Y.: Doubleday, Doran, 1944.
        Memoirs of "most powerful" woman columnist in
    Hollywood, about herself and people she knew.

79 _____. Tell It to Louella. New York: G. P.
    Putnam's Sons, 1961.
        Memoirs about the people she knew.

80 Pickard, R. A. E. Dictionary of 1000 Best Films.

New York: Association Press, 1971.
(See listing under Film-makers.)

81   Pickard, Roy.   A Companion to the Movies.   New York:
     Hippocrene Books, Inc. , 1972.
     The book is divided into film genres.   The most
important films in each genre are described and credits
listed, followed by a Who's Who in that genre (actors,
directors, writers, producers, comedy, fantasy, thrillers
and crime, Westerns, musicals, romance, epics, war,
swashbucklers, adventure).   No women are listed in
"Famous films and their cameramen" or "Musical scores."
Under "Original screenplays" are listed Ruth Gordon and
Garson Kanin, Betty Comden and Adolph Green, Adrien
Joyce, Charles Bennett and Joan Harrison, Wm. and
Tonia Rose, Mae West and W. C. Fields, Edward and
Edna Anholt, Alan Campbell, Robert Carson and Dorothy
Parker, Penelope Gilliatt.

82   Pines, Jim.   Blacks in the Cinema: The Changing Image.
     London: Education Dept. , British Film Institute, 1971.
     Historical assessment of stock-type figures in rela-
tion to cultural aspects of the Black community and
American society.   Definition of the role mass cultural
media have played in Black political and cultural affairs.
Contains a filmography of most important films made
about Blacks from 1950, plus others from the 20's, 30's
and 40's.

83   Pleasants, Henry.   The Great American Popular Singers.
     New York: Simon and Schuster, 1974.
     Celebrated vocalists who made American popular
songs the folk music of the Western world from Al Jolson
to Barbra Streisand.

84   Ramsaye, Terry.   A Million and One Nights.   New York:
     Simon and Schuster, 1926.   2 vols.
     A history of the motion picture, begun in 1920 as
a series of twelve articles for Photoplay, which was ex-
tended to thirty-six and then to book form.   An impres-
sively detailed account of the development of motion pictures.   With careful reading one can glean the names of
women participants in the early days of film (Florence
Turner, 1906, one of the first wardrobe mistresses for
Vitagraph).   More easily accessible are the chapters on
film actresses (Mary Pickford, the Gish sisters, Theda
Bara) and partial chapters (Florence Laurence, Mae

Marsh, the Talmadges, Nazimova, Swanson).

85 Reed, Langford and Hetty Spiers, eds. Who's Who in
    Filmland. 3rd ed. London: Chapman and Hall, Ltd.,
    1931.
        A biographical yearbook of over 2,450 men and
    women of the screen.

86 Robinson, David. Hollywood in the Twenties. London;
    New York: A. S. Barnes and Co., 1968.
        Depicts the decade of the 20's in film. Special
    note is made of its idols which include Pickford, Garbo,
    L. Gish, Mae Marsh, Mable Normand, Pearl White,
    Swanson, etc. Also paragraphs on directors Frances
    Marion, Dorothy Arzner and Gish.

87 Rosenberg, Bernard and Harry Silverstein, eds. The
    Real Tinsel. New York: The Macmillan Co., 1970.
        Personal accounts of people in the business: actres-
    ses Blanche Sweet, Mae Marsh, Dagmar Godowsky, Wini
    Shaw and writer Anita Loos.

88 Ross, Murray. Stars and Strikes: Unionization in Holly-
    wood. New York: AMS Press, Inc., 1941.

89 Ross, Theodore T. Film and the Liberal Arts. New
    York: Holt, Rinehart and Winston, 1970.
        Contains some material on Blacks in motion pic-
    tures.

90 Rosten, Leo C. Hollywood: the Movie Colony, the Mo-
    vie Makers. New York: Harcourt, Brace, 1941.

91 Rotha, Paul and Richard Griffith. The Film Till Now:
    A Survey of World Cinema. 4th rev. ed. London:
    Spring Brooks, 1967.
        Fine history with references to women scattered
    throughout.

92 Sadoul, Georges. Dictionary of Films. Berkeley: Univ.
    of California Press, 1972.
        Alphabetical listing of 1,200 films from various
    countries with film credits including date. Lists direc-
    tor, photographer, art director, editors, cast and pro-
    ducer. Must scan for females.

93 Schickel, Richard. Movies; the History: an Art and an

Institution. New York: Basic Books, 1964.

94 _____. The Stars. New York: The Dial Press,
1962.
A pictorial survey from 1920-1960 with some
omissions. Divided into sections by period and types.
Again, the same outstanding personalities are discussed
(Pickford, Bara, Swanson, Garbo, Davis, Hepburn,
Hayworth, Bergman, Monroe, Taylor, etc.).

95 Schumach, Murray. The Face on the Cutting Room
Floor. New York: Da Capo Press, Inc., 1964.
Story of movie and television censorship.

96 Schuster, Mel. Motion Picture Performers: A Bibliography of Magazine and Periodical Articles, 1900-
1969. Metuchen, N.J.: Scarecrow Press, 1971.
Names of actresses included in this volume are
listed in the index to this bibliography. A supplement
to Schuster's book was published early in 1976.

97 Scott, Evelyn F. Hollywood When Silents Were Golden.
New York: McGraw-Hill, 1972.
Reminiscences of daughter of Beulah Marie Dix,
novelist, playwright and screenwriter. Also mentions
other early female technicians. No index, so difficult
to locate any pertinent names. Evelyn Scott, at MGM
since 1952, is a story analyst for various studios.
Arrived July 2, 1916 to visit Beatrice de Mille,
mother of William and Cecil. Bibi had been an agent
for Beulah Marie Dix Flebbe. Bibi and the boys worked at Lashey Studio. Bibi had promoted Avery Hopwood.
Beulah's co-workers were Frances Marion (ex-
newspaperwoman), Eve Unsell, Jeanie Macpherson (did
majority of Cecil's scripts), Anne Bauchens (Cecil's
chief film editor), Dorothy Arznor (from cutter to director), Clarr Beranger (writer who married William
after he divorced Anna), Jeanie Macpherson (scenarist),
Ruth Roland (from actress to producer), and screenwriters Adela Rogers St. John and Clare Booth Luce.

98 Sennett, Ted. Lunatics and Lovers. New Rochelle,
N.Y.: Arlington House, 1973.
(See entry under "Images.")

99 Sherwood, Robert E., comp. "Who's Who in the Movies," in The Best Moving Pictures of 1922-23.

Boston: Small, Maynard, 1923.

100 Shipman, David. The Great Movie Stars: The Golden
Years. New York: Crown, 1970.
Encyclopedia-like text of 181 major motion picture
stars who achieved stardom before and during World
War II. Special emphasis on the 30's. Lists all feature films they appeared in between 1920-45 and gives
a brief biographical sketch.

101 _____. The Great Movie Stars: The International
Years. New York: Angus & Robertson, Ltd., 1972.
A pictorial survey of world cinema stars in post-
war years. Given in alphabetical order with biographical notes and photos.

102 Slide, Anthony. Early American Cinema. New York:
A. S. Barnes and Co., 1970.
Gives many references to women in early films.
A discussion of early movie companies. There is a
chapter on Pearl White and the Serial Queens.

103 Smith, Sharon. Women Who Make Movies. New York:
Hopkinson and Blake, 1974.
(See entry under "Film-makers.")

104 Springer, John. All Talking, All Singing, All Dancing.
New York: Citadel Press, 1966.
About movie musicals. Lists film songs and com-
posers of various "periods." Includes chapter on the
Dancing Ladies and the Blonds and those stars of Holly-
wood musicals.

105 _____ and Jack Hamilton. They Had Faces Then.
Secaucus, N.J.: Citadel Press, 1974.
Pictures and brief biographies of superstars, stars
and starlets of the 1930's.

106 Stewart, John, compiler. Filmarama. Vol. I, The
Formidable Years, 1893-1919. Metuchen, N.J.:
Scarecrow Press, Inc., 1975.
Alphabetical listing of screen personalities and a
listing of the films in which they appeared.

107 Stuart, Roy, ed. Immortals of the Screen. New York:
Bonanza Books, 1965.

108   Taylor, John Russell. The Hollywood Musical. London: Secker and Warburg, 1971.

109   Thomas, Lawrence. The MGM Years. New York: Columbia House; distributed by Arlington House, 1972.

110   Truitt, Evelyn Mack. Who Was Who on Screen. New York: R. R. Bowker Co., 1974.
       6000 screen personalities (American, British and French stars, supporting players and screen personalities) who died between 1920-1971. Gives a brief biographical sketch and filmography of each.

111   Twomey, Alfred E. and Arthur F. McClure. The Versatiles: A Study of Supporting Actors and Actresses in the American Motion Picture, 1930-1955. New York: A. S. Barnes and Co., 1969.
       An alphabetical listing (if interested in any one actress you must know her name or browse through the whole book). Picture of each. The biographical section gives a paragraph and photo of each player. The nonbiographical section gives only names and photographs.

112   Vallance, Tom. The American Musical. New York: Barnes, 1970.
       An encyclopedia with 500 entries. Gives major personalities and artisans with capsule career description.

113   Von Sternberg, Josef. Fun in a Chinese Laundry. New York: Macmillan Co., 1965.
       Gives references to actresses throughout.

114   Wagner, Robert Leicester. Film Folk. New York: The Century Co., 1918.

115   Warner, Jack L. with Dean Jenning. My First Hundred Years in Hollywood. New York: Random House, 1965.
       The autobiography of a studio executive, but includes sections on female stars Davis and Garland.

116   Weaver, John T. Forty Years of Screen Credits, 1929-1969. Metuchen, N. J.: Scarecrow Press, 1970. 2 vols.

Primarily actors and actresses, but if they held
another capacity in film that is also noted.

117   . Twenty Years of Silents, 1908-1928.
        Metuchen, N. J. : Scarecrow Press, 1971.
        Credits actors primarily, but separates perform-
    ers by sex in a section on "vital statistics."

118   Weitzel, Edward Winfield. Intimate Talks with Movie
        Stars. New York: Dale, 1921.
            124 pp. illustrated (portraits).

119   Williamson, (Mrs.) Alice Murial (Livingston). Alice in
        Movieland. New York: Appleton, 1928.
            Scattered references to actresses throughout.

120   Zierold, Norman J. The Child Stars. New York:
        Coward-McCann, Inc. , 1965.
            Includes chapters on Shirley Temple, Jane Withers,
        Judy Garland, Deanna Durban and others.

B. Specific Works

121   Abrams, L. "Four Interviews I Never Got with Dustin
        Hoffman, Marlon Brando, Julie Christie, and Barbra
        Streisand. " Inter/View 37 (October, 1973):12-13.
            The difficulties of getting interviews with film
        stars.

122   "Actresses Must Be Young. " Moving Picture World 18
        (December 27, 1913):1556.

123   Ager, Cecilia. "Edna May Oliver Likes Hollywood. "
        Variety 105(December 29, 1931):4

124   Albert, Katherine. "Claire Windsor Talks of Herself. "
        Cinema Art 5(December, 1926):28-9.

125   Albertson, Lillian. Motion Picture Acting. New York:
        Funk and Wagnalls Co. , 1947.

126   Alden, Mary. "The Woman Making Up for the Screen, "
        in Opportunities in the Motion Picture Industry. Los
        Angeles: Photoplay Research Society, 1922.
            Directions on make-up for actresses by veteran

character actress, Mary Alden, who played the mulatto
in "Birth of a Nation."

127 Alexandrescu, M. "B. B. --Contestata de Bardot."
     Cinema (Bucharest) 11, 4(April, 1973):36.
         Brigitte Bardot objects to the myth which she has
     acquired.

128 "Alice White." Films in Review 18, 5(May, 1967):318-
     19.
         Filmography of the actress.

129 Allen, Robert C. "Asta Nielsen: the Silent Muse."
     Sight and Sound 42, 4(Autumn, 1973):205.
         Article on famous Danish silent screen actress.
     One of the greatest international stars of the 10's and
     20's. Her career is reviewed.

130 Alpert, Hollis. The Barrymores. New York: Dial
     Press, 1964.
         Ethel, John, Lionel; woven into text is discussion
     of their films.

131 Ames, Aydelott. "Mary Miles Minter." Films in Re-
     view 20, 8(October, 1969):473-95.
         A filmography and discussion of the career of this
     silent screen heroine.

132 Anderson, E. "Marion Davies." Films in Review 23, 6
     (June-July, 1972):321-53.
         Bio-filmographic information on the actress.

133 "Angela Lansbury." Films in Review 14, 2(February,
     1963):123-24.
         A filmography.

134 "Anita Ekberg." Films in Review 14, 10(December,
     1963):636-37.
         A filmography of the Swedish actress.

135 "Anna May Wong." Films in Review 19, 10(December,
     1968):661-63.
         Reminiscences.

136 "Anne Morrison Chaplin: Obituary." New York Times
     (April 9, 1967):92.
         Actress and screenwriter.

137   Apon, A. "Sylvana Mangano." Skrien (Amsterdam) 28
       (January, 1972):16-18.
          Sylvana Mangano as a figurative symbol, illustrated
       by an introduction by Pasolini to "Oedipus Rex." A
       filmography.

138   Ardmore, Jane. The Self-Enchanted Mae Murray:
       Image of an Era. New York: McGraw-Hill, 1959.
       Biography.

139   Arinbasarova, N. "Preodolet' razobscennost'."
       Iskusstvo Kino (Moscow) 8(August, 1973):130-33.
          Natal'ja Arinbasarova, a young actress, describes
       her work and problems.

140   Armstrong, Michael. "Fortune--Youth's Eyes." Films
       and Filming 16, 11(August, 1970):26-27.
          The trend is to unknown teen-age actors and
       actresses.

141   Astor, Mary. A Life on Film. New York: Delacorte
       Press, 1971.

142   _____. My Story: An Autobiography. Garden City,
       N.Y.: Doubleday, 1959.

143   Azernikova, E. "O noua generatie Bondarčuk."
       Cinema (Bucharest) 11, 3(March, 1973):10.
          Roles played by the actress Natalija Bondarčuk.

144   Badescu, A. "Artistul tot mai cetateon." Cinema
       (Bucharest) 11, 4(April, 1973):8-11.
          Militant political activity on the part of actors
       Jane Fonda, Marlon Brando, Gian Maria Volonti and
       directors Bertolucci and Petri.

145   Badescu, M. "O romanca pe mapamond: Narghita."
       Cinema (Bucharest) 11, 8(August, 1973):36-37.
          The career of Narghita, Rumanian singer and
       actress.

146   Bailey, Pearl. The Raw Pearl. New York: Harcourt,
       1968.
       Autobiography.

147   Bainbridge, John. Garbo. New York: Holt, Rinehart
       and Winston, 1971.

Biography of the woman who failed to follow conventions of society; a legend in her own lifetime.

148   _____. "Garbo is 65." Look 34, 18(September 8, 1970):48-50, 52, 54, 56, 59.

149   Baker, Peter. "All About Bette." Films and Filming 2, 8(May, 1956):7-9.
On Bette Davis.

150   _____. "The Monroe Doctrine." Films and Filming 2, 12(September, 1956):12.
The career of Marilyn Monroe.

151   _____. "A Star Without the Limelight." Films and Filming 2, 6(March, 1956):5.
An interview with Claire Bloom, actress. Thoughts on her career.

152   Ball, Eleanor. "Lady Peel Comes to the Movies." Cinema Art 5(December, 1926):32-3
About Beatrice Lillie.

153   _____. "Laugh Them Off." Cinema Art 5(May, 1926):20-1, 50.
About Margaret Livingston.

154   Bankhead, Tallulah. Tallulah: My Autobiography. New York: Harper and Bros., 1952.
Her film career--"Duels with the Screen."

155   Bara, Theda. "How I Became a Film Vampire." Forum 61(June, 1919):715-17 and 62(July, 1919): 82-93.

156   "Barbara Bates." Films in Review 20, 7(August-September, 1969):456.
A filmography of the American leading lady.

157   Bard, Ben. "Finding What They've Got." Films and Filming 4, 10(July, 1958):10, 30.
Director of New Talent for 20th Century Fox: how he trains new actresses and actors.

158   Barker, Felix. The Oliviers, a Biography. Philadelphia: Lippincott, 1953.
On Sir Laurence Kerr Olivier (1907-) and Vivien Leigh (1913-).

159   Barrymore, Diane and Gerold Frank. <u>Too Much Too</u>
       <u>Soon.</u> New York: Holt, 1957.

160   Barrymore, Ethel. <u>Memories, an Autobiography.</u> New
       York: Harper, 1955.

161   "Barrymore, Ethel. " <u>Moving Picture World</u> 20(April 4,
       1914):79.

162   "B. B. Mythe ou femme?" <u>Cinéma</u> (Paris) 176(May,
       1973):15.
            Criticism of a television interview with Brigitte
       Bardot.

163   Bean, Robin. "Will There Be Film Stars in 1974?"
       <u>Films and Filming</u> 10, 10(July, 1964):9-14.
            Predictions about young actors and actresses.

164   Beatty, Jerome. <u>Shirley Temple.</u> Akron, Ohio; New
       York: The Saalfield Publishing Co., 1935.
       (Authorized ed.)

165   Beauvoir, Simone de. <u>Brigitte Bardot and the Lolita</u>
       <u>Syndrome.</u> New York: Arno Press, 1960.
            Brigitte Bardot, sex kitten, as discussed by
       Simone de Beauvoir, philosopher. French ambivalence
       toward Bardot, the new version of eternal woman who's
       driven vamp, girlfriend type of filmstar off the screen.
       Delight and disapproval of Bardot. A "penetrating and
       benign" examination of the Bardot myth.

166   "Bedtime Stories. " <u>Films and Filming</u> 16, 5(February,
       1970):31.
            Interview with Jacqueline Susann, former actress
       turned novelist. Thoughts on her books and films.

167   Behlmer, Rudy. "Clara Bow. " <u>Films in Review</u> 14, 8
       (October, 1963):451-65.
            A filmography and career sketch of the early
       actress.

168   Belfrage, Cedric. "Psyching the Hollywood Blonde. "
       <u>Motion Picture Classic</u> 31, 5(July, 1930):51.
            (See entry under "Images. ")

169   Bell, Arthur. "Crashing Trash with Holly Woodlawn. "
       <u>Village Voice</u> 15, 50(December 10, 1970):1, 14.
            Interview with "actress. "

170   Bell, Mary Hayley. What Shall We Do Tomorrow?
      New York: Lippincott, 1969.
      Reminiscences of Mills family.

171   Bellumari, C., ed. "Le donne del Cinema contro
      questo cinema. " Bianco E Nero (Rome) 33, 1-2
      (January-February, 1972):1-112. Special Issue.
      (See listing under "Film-makers. ")

172   Bengis, Ingrid. "Monroe According to Mailer: One
      Legend Feeds on Another. " Ms. 11, 4(October,
      1974):44.
      Review of Mailer's biography of Marilyn Monroe.

173   Bennett, Joan. The Bennett Playbill. New York:
      Holt, Rinehart and Winston, 1970.

174   Bergen, Polly. Polly's Principles. New York: Bantam
      Books, 1975.
      Polly tells "truth" about show business, the beauty
      trap and herself.

175   "Bette Davis. " Films and Filming 2, 8(May, 1956):
      11-13.
      A filmography.

176   "Betty Furness. " Films in Review 18, 9(November,
      1967):581.
      A filmography.

177   Billard, Ginette. "Philipe, the Actor, May End His
      Career--But Darrieux Seeks New Horizons. " Films
      and Filming 2, 1(October, 1955):10-11.
      On Danielle Darrieux, French actress in films
      since 1931.

178   "Billie Burke. " Films in Review 21, 10(December,
      1970):648-49.
      A filmography of the actress.

179   "Billie Dove. " Films in Review 19, 1(January, 1968):64.
      A filmography of leading lady of the 20's who
      could not adapt to new talkies.

180   Billquist, Fritiof. Garbo: A Biography. New York:
      Putnam, 1960.
      Translated from Swedish. Written by friend and
      fellow-actor.

181   "Biscuits and Beatitude à la Marguerite Clark." Thea-
      tre 29(June, 1919):387.

182   Blaisdell, George F. "Clara Kimball Young, Artist."
      Moving Picture World 22(October 3, 1914):41-2.

183   Blake, Ivan. "Pauline Starke Destroys an Illusion."
      Cinema Art 5(April, 1926):22, 47.
      Biographical notes with D. W. Griffith.

184   Bodeen, Dewitt. "Alice Brady." Films in Review 17,9
      (November, 1966):555-73.
      A filmography and career of the actress.

185   _____. "Anita Stewart." Films in Review 19,3
      (March, 1968):145-61.
      A filmography and career of the actress.

186   _____. "Bebe Daniels." Films in Review 15,7
      (August-September, 1964):413-30.
      A career sketch of leading lady of silent screen.

187   _____. "Betty Compson." Films in Review 17,7
      (August-September, 1966):396-418.
      A filmography and career of leading lady of the
      20's, in Christie comedies from 1915.

188   _____. "Blanche Sweet." Films in Review 16,9
      (November, 1965):549-70.
      A filmography and career of the actress.

189   _____. "Constance Talmadge." Films in Review
      18,10(December, 1967):613, 630.
      A filmography and career of the actress.

190   _____. "Dolores Del Rio." Films in Review 18,5
      (May, 1967):266-83.
      A filmography and career sketch of popular Mex-
      ican actress of the 20's and 30's.

191   _____. "Dorothy Gish." Films in Review 19,7
      (August-September, 1968):393-414.
      A filmography and career sketch of the actress.

192   _____. "Eleanor Boardman: On the Screen She
      Displayed Intelligence as Well as Beauty." Films
      in Review 24,10(December, 1973):593-608.
      A filmography. The career of actress Eleanor

Boardman, including an account of a recent meeting with her.

193 _____. "Elsie Ferguson." Films in Review 15, 9 (November, 1964):551-63.
A filmography and career sketch of leading lady of silent melodramas about upper classes. Popular from 1918 to 1927, then retired.

194 _____. "A Fan's Notes: Memories of Garbo." Focus on Film 15(Summer, 1973):19-30.
Recollections of Greta Garbo's films and life.

195 _____. "Florence Bates." Films in Review 17, 10 (December, 1966):641-54.
A filmography and career sketch of the character actress (1888-1954), adept at playing friendly or monstrous matrons. A former lawyer, she was persuaded by Hitchcock to play the role of a snobbish matron in "Rebecca" (1940) and remained in demand for a decade.

196 _____. "Gloria Swanson." Films in Review 16, 4 (April, 1965):193-216.
A filmography and career of the actress.

197 _____. "Jeanette MacDonald." Films in Review 16, 3(March, 1965):129-144.
A filmography and career of the actress.

198 _____. "John Barrymore and Dolores Costello." Focus on Film 12(Winter, 1972):17-37.
Retraces the careers of John Barrymore and his wife, gentle silent screen actress, Dolores Costello. Includes a filmography.

199 _____. "Lockwood and Allison." Films in Review 22, 5(May, 1971):275-98.
A filmography. Discusses careers of May Allison, early screen actress, and Harold Lockwood.

200 _____. "Marguerite Clark." Films in Review 15, 10 (December, 1964):611-25.
A filmography and career sketch of silent screen actress, one of Mary Pickford's rivals for innocent and waif-like roles.

201 _____. "May McAvoy." Films in Review 19, 8

(October, 1968):482-98.
A filmography and career of the actress.

202 _____. "Nazimova." Films in Review 23, 10 (December, 1972):577-604.
Bio-filmographical information on Alla Nazimova.

203 _____. "Pauline Frederick." Films in Review 16, 2
(February, 1965):69-90.
A filmography and career of the American silent
screen's leading lady.

204 _____. "Theda Bara." Films in Review 19, 5(May,
1968):266.
A filmography and career sketch of the actress.

205 Bogle, Donald. Toms, Coons, Mulattoes, Mammies
and Bucks. New York: Viking Press, 1973.
Notes on Hattie MacDaniel, Butterfly McQueen,
Dorothy Dandridge.

206 Booth, Clare. "The Great Garbo." Vanity Fair 37
(February, 1932):63, 87.

207 Bowden, J. E. A. "Eve Arden." Films in Review
24, 1(January, 1973):58-59.
Bio-filmographic information on Eve Arden, ac-
tress-comedienne.

208 Bowers, R. "Legendary Ladies of the Movies." Films
in Review 24, 6(June-July, 1973):321-29.
Report on recent public appearances by Joan Crawford, Bette Davis, Myrna Loy, and Sylvia Sidney, including their answers to questions from an audience of
fans.

209 Bowers, R. L. "Joan Blondell." Films in Review 23,
4(April, 1972):193-211.
Bio-filmographic information on Joan Blondell.

210 Bowers, Ronald. "Agnes Moorehead." Films in Review
17, 5(May, 1966):293-303.
A filmography and career of the actress.

211 _____. "Hepburn Since '57." Films in Review 21, 7
(August-September, 1970):423-25.
A filmography of Katherine Hepburn.

24   Women and Film

212   _____. "Ingrid Bergman." Films in Review 19, 2
           (February, 1968):71-88.
           A filmography and career of the actress.

213   _____. "Joan Crawford's Latest Decade." Films
           in Review 17, 6(June-July, 1966):366-68.
           A career sketch of the actress.

214   _____. "Loretta Young." Films in Review 20, 4
           (April, 1969):193-217.
           A filmography and career of the actress.

215   _____. "Lucille Ball." Films in Review 22, 6(June-
           July, 1971):321-42.
           A filmography and career of the actress-comedi-
           enne.

216   _____. "Marlene Dietrich: '54-'70." Films in
           Review 22, 1(January, 1971):17-22.
           A filmography.

217   _____. "Ruby Keeler." Films in Review 22, 7(Aug-
           ust-September, 1971):405-14.
           A filmography and career of the actress.

218   _____. "Vivien Leigh." Films in Review 16, 7(Aug-
           ust-September, 1965):403-18.
           A filmography and career sketch of the actress.

219   Bozinova, I. "Doroteja Tonceva." Kinoizkustvo (Sofia)
           27, 4(April, 1972):36-45.
           Article on the film career of the Bulgarian ac-
           tress, Doroteja Tonceva.

220   Brady, Alice. "Movies and Mummers." Drama 14
           (November, 1923):46-7.
           Discussion of motion pictures by stage and screen
           star.

221   Braucourt, G. "Le Charme discret de la Bourgeoisie."
           Ecran (Paris) 9(November, 1972):62-64.
           A film review of "The Discreet Charm of the Bour-
           geoisie" and an interview with its star, Stephane Audran.

222   Braun, Eric. "A Code of Behaviour." Films and
           Filming 16, 7(April, 1970):24-30 and 16, 8(May, 1970):
           22-26 and 16, 9(June, 1970):108-12.

English actresses who established themselves in
Hollywood, including Deborah Kerr.

223 _____ . "Diana Dors: On Her Own Terms. " Films
and Filming 19, 5(February, 1973):22-28.
An assessment of her career and acting from her
teenage years to her latest films.

224 _____ . "Doing What Comes Naturally. " Films and
Filming 17, 1(October, 1970):27-32 and 17, 2(Novem-
ber, 1970):38-42.
A filmography and career of Mae West.

225 _____ . "Forty Years a Queen. " Films and Filming
11, 8(May, 1965):7-14.
Career of Joan Crawford.

226 _____ . "Myrna Loy on Comedy. " Films and Filming 14, 6(March, 1968):9-11.
Interview.

227 _____ . "The Indestructibles. " Films and Filming
19, 12(September, 1973):34-40.
First part of a series of articles on the changing
patterns of stardom on the British screen. Emphasis
is placed on the careers of Margaret Lockwood and
Chili Bouchier, character actresses.

228 "Brigitte Helm. " Films in Review 19, 4(April, 1968):
254-55.
A German actress of the 20's.

229 Brinson, Peter. "The Great Come-Back. " Films and
Filming 1, 3(December, 1954):4-5.
The career of Judy Garland.

230 Britt, Simon. "Audrey Hepburn. " Films and Filming
10, 6(March, 1964):9-12.
A career sketch of the actress.

231 Bronner, Edwin. "Luise Rainer. " Films in Review
6, 8(October, 1955):390-93.
The career of the popular stage actress in 30's
and later in films.

232 Brooks, Louise. "Gish and Garbo: The Executive
War on Stars. " Sight and Sound 28, 1(Winter,

1958-59):12-17+

233 _____. "On Location with Billy Wellman." Film
Culture 53-54-55(Spring, 1972):145-61.
Actress Louise Brooks describes the filming of
"Beggars of Life" (1928). Contains bio-filmographic
information on Louise Brooks and William Wellman.

234 _____. "On Location with Billy Wellman." Focus
on Film 12(Winter, 1972):51-56.
A reprint of article published in London Magazine.

235 Brown, Mrs. Catherine Estelle (Hayes). Letters to
Mary. with Foreword by Charles MacArthur. New
York: Random House, 1940.
Biography of Helen Hayes, written by her mother,
in the form of letters to Helen Hayes' daughter, Mary
MacArthur.

236 Brown, Curtis F. Ingrid Bergman. New York: Pyramid Publications, 1973.

237 Broz, J. "Nonkonformismus Jane Fondové." Film a
Doba (Prague) 19, 10(October, 1973):525-27.
The acting and opinions of Jane Fonda.

238 Brundidge, Harry T. Twinkle, Twinkle Movie Star!
New York: E. P. Dutton, 1930.

239 Bruno, Michael. Venus in Hollywood: the Continental
Enchantress from Garbo to Loren. New York: Lyle
Stuart, 1970.
(See entry under "Images.")

240 Buckley, Michael. "Shelley Winters." Films in Review
21, 3(March, 1970):146-60.
A filmography and career of the actress.

241 Bühler, W. -E. "Mae Marsh." Filmkritik (Munich)
16, 1(January, 1972):29-30.
A bio-filmography of the actress. Part of a bio-
filmographic dictionary of performers and stunt people
who acted in John Ford's films.

242 Burke, Billie. With Powder on My Nose. (With Cameron Shipp.) New York: Coward McCann, 1959.
Mrs. Florenz Ziegfeld, Jr. A rather rattle-

brained account of how to be a woman. Also wrote
With a Feather on My Nose, an autobiography, 1949.

243 Burke, P. E. "Fame Came Too Soon to Miss Julie."
      Films and Filming 3,10(July, 1957):10.
      A career sketch of Anita Björk.

244 Burton, Hal. Acting in the Sixties. London: British
      Broadcasting Corp., 1970.
      Based on a series of programmes originally shown
      on BBC. Discusses Vanessa Redgrave, Maggie Smith,
      Dorothy Tutin.

245 Busby, M. "Enchantresses on the Screen." Photoplay
      37(March, 1930):36-7, 131.

246 Cahn, William. The Laugh Makers: A Pictorial His-
      tory of American Comedians. New York: Putnam,
      1957.
      Includes comediennes Judy Holiday, Lucille Ball,
      Marie Dressler, Polly Moran. A history of comedy,
      primarily radio and television comics.

247 Calendo, J. "Dietrich and the Devil." Inter/View 26
      (October, 1972):26-30, Part I; 27(November, 1972):
      23, 45, Part II.
      The screen personality of Marlene Dietrich as
      created by Von Sternberg. It is suggested that Mick
      Jagger carries on in the Dietrich tradition.

248 _____ . "Geri Miller: My Naughty Naughty Ways as
      Told to John Calendo." Inter/View 32(May, 1973):
      33, 41.
      On her life and opinions.

249 _____ . "The Legend of Kim Novak." Inter/View
      22(June, 1972):9-13, 53.
      Kim Novak's career and a comparison with other
      stars.

250 _____ . "Merle Oberon Is Not a Hindu." Inter/View
      34(July, 1973):30-31, 43.
      Merle Oberon reviews her past career and des-
      cribes her new film "Interval."

251 _____ . "New Hollywood: A Short History." Inter/
      View 30(March, 1973):15-18.

The forces which have shaped the new Hollywood: promiscuity, drugs and radical opinions, as seen by some stars including Dyan Cannon, Mia Farrow, Sharon Tate, Jane Fonda, Raquel Welch, Peter Fonda.

252 _____. "Susannah York." Inter/View 29(January, 1973):36-37.
Short interview with Susannah York about some of the films she has made.

253 _____. "The Twentieth Century Foxe." Inter/View 28(December, 1972):10-12, 41.
Cyrinda Foxe talks about herself, the things and people she likes and dislikes and her plans for the future.

254 "Cara Williams." Films in Review 19, 10(December, 1968):663-64.
A filmography.

255 Card, Louise. "The Intense Isolation of Louise Brooks." Sight and Sound 27, 5(Summer, 1958):240-44.
The private life of Louise Brooks, leading lady of the 20's who has remained an attractive enigma.

256 Carey, G. "Film Favorites." Film Comment 7, 4 (Winter, 1971-72):70-72.
Analysis of the film "Happiness" with emphasis on the performance of actress Laurette Taylor.

257 Carey, Gary. "The Lady and the Director: Bette Davis and William Wyler." Film Comment 6, 3(Fall, 1970):18-24.
Discusses three films William Wyler directed with Bette Davis: "Jezebel," 1938; "The Letter," 1940; "The Little Foxes," 1941. Also discusses their disagreement over the interpretation of her role in "Little Foxes" and their subsequent failure to make any more films together.

258 Carlyle, John. "Joan Fontaine." Films in Review 14, 3(March, 1963):146-59.
A filmography and career of British-born American leading lady, sister of Olivia de Havilland.

259 Carnell, R. "Barbra Streisand's Animal Crackers."

Lumière (Canberra) 29(November, 1973):20-21.
Discusses Streisand's roles in "What's Up, Doc?"
and "The Owl and the Pussycat" in terms of the animal imagery employed.

260　"Carole Landis. " Films in Review 16, 5(May, 1965):
323-25.
A career sketch.

261　"A Carole Landis Index. " Films in Review 16, 6(June-
July, 1965):397-99.
A filmography of the actress.

262　Carpozi, George, Jr. The Brigitte Bardot Story. New
York: Belmont Books, 1961.
Paperback.

263　　　　. Marilyn Monroe--Her Own Story. New York:
Universal Publishing & Distributing Corp. , 1973.

264　Carr, Chauncy. "Janet Gaynor. " Films in Review 10,
8(October, 1959):470-78, 500.
A filmography and career of the actress.

265　　　　. "Ruth Chatterton. " Films in Review 13, 1
(January, 1962):7-17.
A filmography and career sketch of actress popular in the 20's and 30's. After stage success, she
later had success as a novelist.

266　Carr, Harry C. "How Griffith Picks His Leading Women. " Photoplay 15(December, 1918):24-5.
An interview with D. W. Griffith.

267　Carr, Larry. Four Fabulous Faces. New Rochelle:
Arlington House, 1971.
(Swanson, Garbo, Crawford, Dietrich)

268　Carson, L. M. K. "It's Here! Hollywood's Ninth
Era. " Esquire 83(February, 1975):67.
(See entry under "Film-makers. ")

269　Carstairs, John Paddy. Movie Merry-go-round. London: Newnes, 1937.
Includes "Stars, " and "Average Day in the Life
of a Star. "

270   Castle, Irene.   Castles in the Air.   Garden City,
      N. Y. :   Doubleday, 1958.
         By Irene Castle, dancer, as told to Bob and Wan-
      da Duncan.   Of Irene and Vernon Castle, dance team.

271   Cernev, G.   "Aktrisata i zritelite. "   Kinoizkustvo
      (Sofia) 28, 5(May,   1973):26-32.
         The career of the Bulgarian actress, Nevena
      Kokanova.

272   _____ .   "Predi 'Tjutjun. '"   Kinoizkustvo (Sofia) 28, 1
      (January,   1973):36-44.
         A survey of the lyrical heroines created by Bul-
      garian actress, Nevena Kokanova, between 1957 and
      1961.

273   Chase, D.   "Charlotte. "   Inter /View   29(January,   1973):
      29-30.
         Donald Chase examines Charlotte Rampling's film
      acting career, especially in "Rotten to the Core, "
      "Georgy Girl, "   "The Damned. "

274   Christian, Linda.   Linda, My Own Story.   New York:
      Crown Publishers, 1962.
         Autobiography of actress and wife of Tyrone
      Power.

275   "The Cinema in Retrospect. "   Close-Up (London)
      3(November,   1928):16-25 and (December,   1928):31-41.
         Mary Pickford in the early stages.

276   "Claire Dodd. "   Films in Review 18, 5(May,   1967):319.
         A filmography of the actress.

277   "Clara Kimball Young. "   Films in Review 12, 8(October,
      1961):505-06.
         A filmography of her Vitagraph one-reelers.

278   "Close-up on Yvette Mimieux. "   Cinema 1, 2(1963):12-16.
         Her "heroine" image.

279   Clurman, Harold.   On Directing.   (An American Film
      Institute Book.)   New York: Macmillan and Sons,
      1972.
         Directors and performers discuss the relationship
      between their arts.   Includes statements by Leslie Caron
      and Ingrid Thulin.

280 Cohen, S. "Marilyn Chambers 99-44/100% Pure. "
     Inter/View 36(September, 1973):8-9.
     Marilyn Chambers, the star of the film "Behind
     the Green Door," talks about her attitude towards sex
     and pornography.

281 Colaciello, R. "At Home with Monique van Vooren. "
     Inter/View 21(May, 1972):42-43.
     Actress Monique van Vooren is interviewed about
     her personal life.

282 _____ . "At Home with Ultra Violet. " Inter/View
     23(July, 1972):17, 44.
     Ultra Violet discusses her new lifestyle and her
     plans for a film,"The Last Supper. "

283 _____ . "Lady D'Arbanville Talks and Talks and
     Talks to Robert Colaciello. " Inter/View 31(April,
     1973):8, 43.
     Actress Patti D'Arbanville sketches a short por-
     trait of her life.

284 _____ and G. O'Brien. "Interview with Marisa Ber-
     enson. " Inter/View 20(March, 1972):6-7.

285 Cole, Clayton. "I Was Not Found on a Soda Fountain
     Stool. " Films and Filming 2, 8(May, 1956):6.
     Interview, career sketch of Bette Davis.

286 Collins, William S. "Lois Wilson. " Films in Review
     24, 1(January, 1973):18-35.
     Excellent biographical article on the first Miss
     America of 1915, Miss Alabama, Lois Wilson. Twenty-
     year screen career, left for Broadway in 1937, return-
     ed. A filmography.

287 Comingore, Dorothy. "Dorothy Comingore Finds the
     Committee Cute. " Film Culture 50-51(Fall-Winter,
     1970):65-67.
     The testimony of Dorothy Comingore, actress who
     made few films but will always be remembered as the
     second Mrs. Kane, before the House Committee on Un-
     American Activities.

288 Comsa, D. "Cei trei oameni furiosi: Fonda-tatal,
     Fonda-fiica, Fonda-fiul. " Cinema (Bucharest) 11, 5
     (May, 1973):32.

Activities of the Fonda family in politics.

289   Condon, Frank. "Come Up and Meet Mae West."
      Collier's 93(June 16, 1934):26, 42.

290   Connor, Edward. "The Serial Lovers." Films in Re-
      view 6, 7(August-September, 1955):328-32.
      The Pathé serials starring Allene Ray and Walter
      Miller.

291   "Constance Moore." Films in Review 18, 10(December,
      1966):663-64.
      A filmography.

292   "Conversation with Lillian Gish." Sight and Sound 27, 3
      (Winter, 1957-58)128-30.

293   Conway, Michael, et al. The Films of Greta Garbo.
      Introduction by Parker Tyler. New York: Crown
      Publishers, 1963.

294   _____ and Mark Ricci, eds. The Films of Jean
      Harlow. New York: Bonanza Books, 1965.

295   _____. The Films of Marilyn Monroe. New York:
      Citadel Press, 1964.

296   Cook, P. "The Sound Track." Films in Review 24, 9
      (November, 1973):557-59.
      Evaluation of a new record album, "Classic Film
      Scores for Bette Davis."

297   Cooper, Gladys. Gladys Cooper, by Gladys Cooper.
      London: Hutchinson and Co., Ltd., 1931.
      Actress's correspondence, reminiscences.

298   Cooper, Miriam and Bonnie Herndon. Dark Lady of
      the Silents. New York: Bobbs-Merrill, 1973.
      Miriam Cooper's life in early Hollywood.

299   Corliss, Richard. "Leni Riefenstahl: A Bibliography."
      Film Heritage 5, 1(Fall, 1969):27.
      Biography and extensive bibliography of books,
      articles on her and filmography of the films in which
      she appeared and directed.

300   Cottrell, E. "Les aventures de Zouzou." Inter/View

27(November, 1972):21, 43-44.
An interview. Zouzou talks about her acting and singing careers in general and her part in "L'Amour, l'après-midi."

301   Cottrell, John. Julie Andrews: The Story of a Star. London: Barker, 1969.

302   Coulson, Alan. "Anna Neagle." Films in Review 18,3 (March, 1967):149-62.
A filmography and career of the actress.

303   Courtney, Marguerite (Taylor). Laurette. Introduction by Samuel Hopkins Adams. New York: Rinehart, 1955.
A biography of actress Laurette Taylor, 1884-1946.

304   Cowie, Peter. "Katherine Hepburn." Films and Filming 9,9(June, 1963):21-23.
A career sketch.

305   Craig, Edith and Christopher St. John. Ellen Terry's Memoirs. London: Gallancy, 1933; New York: G. P. Putnam's Sons, 1932.
An autobiography written in 1906-1907, in which the British theatre actress describes her interest in the cinema as a spectator.

306   Crawford, Joan. My Way of Life. New York: Simon and Schuster, 1971.

307   _____. "They Made Me a Myth." Sight and Sound 21,4(April-June, 1952):162-64.
Career notes.

308   _____ with Jane Kisner Ardmore. A Portrait of Joan. Garden City, N. Y.: Doubleday and Co., Inc., 1962.

309   Crichton, Kyle. "Bad, But Very Good." Collier's 94(November 17, 1934):18, 50-51.
About Bette Davis.

310   Crinello, K. "The Second Mrs. Kane: Dorothy Comingore." Focus on Film 9(Spring, 1972):31-34.
Retraces the life and career of the actress best remembered in her role as the second Mrs. Kane.

311   Croce, Arlene. The Fred Astaire and Ginger Rogers
         Book. New York: Bridge and Lazard, Dutton, 1972.

312   Cutrone, R. and V. Fremont. "Tamara Is Cleopatra. "
         Inter/View 35(August, 1973):14-15.
               Tamara Dobson, star of "Cleopatra Jones, " talks
         about her part in the film.

313   Dandridge, Dorothy and Earl Conrad. Everything and
         Nothing: the D. D. Tragedy. New York: Abelard-
         Schuman, 1970.
               The tragic biography of D. D. --who died at age of
         42. She had cautioned him that an autobiography of her
         life would hold back the march of Black womanhood.

314   Daniels, Bebe. "Reminiscences: Hollywood Yesterday. "
         Californian 1(May, 1946):36.

315   Daniels, Bebe Virginia. Life with the Lyons: the
         Autobiography of Bebe Daniels and Ben Lyon. Lon-
         don: Odhams Press, 1953.
               Actress' reminiscences.

316   Davidson, Carol. "'Letter to Jane'--A Critique. "
         Women and Film 1, 3-4(1973):52.
               (See entry under "Images. ")

317   Davies, Wallace. "Truth About Pearl White. " Films
         in Review 10, 9(November, 1959):537-48.
               Her career.

318   Davis, Bette. The Lonely Life: An Autobiography.
         New York: G. P. Putnam's Sons, 1962.

319   Davis, Henry. "Clara Kimball Young. " Films in Re-
         view 12, 7(August-September, 1961):419-25.
               A filmography and career of the actress.

320   Deans, Mickey and Ann Pinchot. Weep No More My
         Lady. New York: Hawthorne Books, Inc. , 1972.
               Judy Garland.

321   De Carl, Lennard. "Alexis Smith. " Films in Review
         21, 6(June-July, 1970):355-67.
               A filmography and career of the actress.

322   Dee, Ruby. Contemporary Black Leaders. Edited by

Elton C. Fox. New York: Dodd, 1970.

323 _____ . "The Tattered Queens: Some Reflections
on the Negro Actress." Negro Digest 15(April,
1966):32-36.

324 De Havilland, Olivia. Every Frenchman Has One.
New York: Random House, 1962.

325 De Laborderie, Renaud. Brigitte Bardot ... Spotlights
in Words and Pictures. Manchester: Collection:
"Great Ones Series No. 1, " 1964.

326 _____ . Sophia Loren ... Spotlights in Words and
Pictures. Manchester: Collection: "Great Ones
Series, No. 2, " 1964.

327 Dent, Alan. Vivien Leigh: A Bouquet. London:
Hamilton, 1969.
A biography of the actress includes a special
chapter devoted to screen and a special Appendix on
screen appearances.

328 Denton, Clive. "On Film. " Take One 1, 6(1967):30.
Reviews. Includes notes on the career of actress
Mary Morris.

329 Devillers, M. "Marlène plus belle que sa légende. "
Ecran (Paris) 19(November, 1973):18.
Account of Marlene Dietrich's concert tour in
Paris.

330 Dexter, Grant. Life Stories of the Stars. London:
Star Screen Club, n. d.
Includes Rita Hayworth, Betty Grable, Greer
Garson.

331 "Diana Sands. " Film Comment 1, 4(1963):28-29.
Discussion of film "An Affair of the Skin"; includes information on Sands' career.

332 Dickens, Homer. "Carole Lombard. " Films in Review
12, 2(February, 1961):70-86.
Filmography and career sketch of actress.

333 _____ . The Films of Katherine Hepburn. New York:
The Citadel Press, 1970.

334 _____. The Films of Marlene Dietrich. New York:
The Citadel Press, 1968.

335 _____. "Ginger Rogers." Films in Review 17, 3
(March, 1966):129-55.
A filmography and career sketch of the actress.

336 _____. "Maria Montez." Films in Review 14, 1
(January, 1963):59-61.
A filmography and career sketch of the actress.

337 "Diegnes fala de Moreau e 'Joana'." Filme Cultura
(Rio de Janeiro) 7, 23(January-February, 1973):19-20.
An interview. Carlos Diegnes talks about his
film "Joana, a francesa" starring Jeanne Moreau.

338 Dietrich, Marlene. "La Belle Dame sans merci."
Saturday Review (London) 152(August 15, 1931):209-
10.

339 _____. Marlene Dietrich's ABC. Garden City,
N.Y.: Doubleday, 1962.

340 "A Director's Spell." Films and Filming 8, 9(June,
1962):11-12.
An interview with Simone Signoret. Talks of directors with whom she had worked.

341 Djentemirov, M. "Era un film cu Greta Garbo."
Cinema (Bucharest) 10, 6(June, 1972):40-41.
On Garbo's continuing fascination for cinema
audiences.

342 "Dodd and Bari." Films in Review 21, 8(October,
1970):516-17.
A filmography of Lynn Bari, famous for her roles
as the "other woman," and Claire Dodd.

343 Doherty, Edward Joseph. The Rain Girl, the Tragic
Story of Jeanne Eagels. Philadelphia: Macrae
Smith Co., 1930.
Jeanne Eagels, 1890-1929.

344 Dooley, R. B. "Jane Wyatt." Films in Review 23, 1
(January, 1972):28-40.
Bio-filmographic information on Jane Wyatt.

345 Dorr, John. "The Movies of Mr. Griffith and Carol
     Dempster." Cinema 7, 1(Fall, 1971):23-34.
     Discusses films of Dempster (leading lady of si-
     lent screen) with Griffith.

346 Downing, Robert. "Ethel Barrymore, 1879-1957."
     Films in Review 10, 7(August-September, 1959):385-
     89.
     Career of the actress.

347 _____. "Helen Hayes' Golden Jubilee." Films in
     Review 7, 2(February, 1956):62-66.
     A filmography and career sketch of the actress.

348 Doyle, Neil. "Jennifer Jones." Films in Review 13,
     7(August-September, 1962):390-400.
     A filmography and career sketch of the actress.

349 _____. "Olivia De Havilland." Films in Review
     13, 2(February, 1962):71-85.
     A filmography and career sketch of the actress.

350 Dressler, Marie. The Life Story of an Ugly Duckling.
     New York: R. M. McBride, 1924.
     "... autobiographical fragment in seven parts."

351 _____. My Own Story. As told to Mildred Harring-
     ton. Boston: Little, Brown, 1934. Reprinted by
     Blue Ribbon Books, Inc., 1936.
     Includes anecdotal glimpses of many other female
     stars.

352 Dunbar, Janet. Flora Robson. London: Geo. G.
     Harry, 1960.
     A biography of the English actress with emphasis
     on her stage career, though films are mentioned.

353 Dundy, Elaine. "On Interviewing a Star." Village
     Voice 11, 29(May 5, 1966):25-26.
     Discusses Vivien Leigh's career.

354 Dunham, Harold. "Bessie Love." Films in Review
     10, 2(February, 1959):86-99.
     A filmography and career sketch of the actress.

355 _____. "Florence Vidor." Films in Review 21, 1
     (January, 1970):21-39.

A filmography of silent screen actress.

356 _____ . "Mae Marsh. " <u>Films in Review</u> 9, 6(June-
    July, 1958):306-21.
    A filmography and career sketch of the actress.

357 Durgnat, Raymond.   "B. B. " <u>Films and Filming</u> 9, 4
    (January, 1963):16-18.
    Brigitte Bardot as a sex symbol.

358 _____ . "Mth Marilyn Monroe. " <u>Film Comment</u>
    10, 2(March-April, 1974):23.
    The myth of Marilyn Monroe.

359 _____ and J. Kobal. <u>Greta Garbo</u>. New York:
    Dutton/Vista, 1965.

360 "Duse in the Movies. " <u>Literary Digest</u> 54(June 2,
    1917):1702-3.
    Eleanora Duse, actress, Italian tragedienne.

361 "Edna May Oliver. " <u>Films in Review</u> 13, 1(January,
    1962):57-59.
    A filmography of American character actress.

362 Edwards, Leo.   "The Incomparable Mary. " <u>Feature
    Movie Magazine</u> (Chicago) 4(October 10, 1915):8-9.
    About Mary Pickford.

363 Ehrenstein, David. "Anna Karina. " <u>Film Culture</u> 48-
    49(Winter-Spring, 1970):52-53.
    Karina in Godard's films.

364 "Ella Raines. " <u>Films in Review</u> 18, 1(January, 1967):
    62-63.
    A filmography of the popular actress of the 40's.

365 Elley, D. "Beata Tyszkiewicz. " <u>Focus on Film</u> 16
    (Autumn, 1973):13.
        A bio-filmography. Details of the career of the
    Polish actress, Beata Tyszkiewicz.

366 _____ . "Experiences: an Interview with Susannah
    York. " <u>Focus on Film</u> 9(Spring, 1972):25-30.
        Susannah York talks about her experiences in
    working for the cinema.

367 _____. "Valentina Cortese." Focus on Film 14
        (Spring, 1973):11.
        A bio-filmography of the actress.

368 _____. "Wistfulness and Dry Hankies: Susannah
        York." Focus on Film 10(Summer, 1972):42-50.
        A filmography. Study of Susannah York's career
        and acting performances.

369 Ellis, Shirley. The Negro in American Film. New
        York: U. S. Information Service, 1957.

370 Elwood, Muriel. Pauline Frederick, On and Off the
        Stage. Chicago: A. Kroch, 1940.

371 [No entry]

372 Essays on Cinema. Arno Reprint Series, 1973.
        Reprints of selections of articles published be-
        tween 1928-34 in Hound and Horn, an influential maga-
        zine of that era. Eclectic variety of subjects, includ-
        ing one on "Garbo.

373 Essoe, Gabe. "Elizabeth Taylor." Films in Review
        21, 7(August-September, 1970):393-410.

374 "Esther Ralston." Films and Filming 20, 10(December,
        1969):647-48.
        A filmography of the 20's and 30's leading lady.

375 "An Ethel Barrymore Index." Films in Review 14, 6
        (June-July, 1963):357-60.
        A filmography of the actress.

376 Euvrard, M. "Geneviève Bujold, 'Le rôle d'acteur
        malheureusement ....'" Cinéma Québec (Montreal)
        2, 6-7(March-April, 1973):11-14.
        An interview. Geneviève Bujold talks about being
        an actress and about making her latest film, "Kamour-
        aska. "

377 Evans, Dale. No Two Ways About It. Westwood, N. J. :
        Fleming Revell, 1963.

378 Evans, Peter. Bardot: Eternal Sex Goddess. New
        York: Drake Publishers, Inc. , 1973.

Gossip about private life of Brigitte Bardot.
"Tidbits are essential to understanding of Bardot's career and to whole fabric of the women's lib movement. "

379   "Excerpts from the Transcript of Godard--Gorin's 'Letter to Jane. '" Women and Film 1, 3-4(1973):45.
An abridged transcript of the soundtrack to the
film "Letter to Jane" (Fonda) produced by Jean-Luc
Godard and Jean-Pierre Gorin.

380   Eyles, A. "Felicia Farr. " Focus on Film 9(Spring,
1972):7.
A bio-filmography.

381   _____. "Geraldine Page. " Focus on Film 14(Spring,
1973):13-14.
A bio-filmography.

382   _____. "Julie Christie. " Focus on Film 16(Autumn,
1973):9-10.
A bio-filmography of the actress.

383   _____. "Juliet Mills. " Focus on Film 15(Summer,
1973):16.
A bio-filmography of the English actress.

384   "Faith and the Fighting Spirit. " Theatre 29(April,
1919):249.
An interview about Katherine MacDonald, star of
DeMille's "Squaw Man. "

385   Fajardo, R. "Gina Says. " Inter/View 33(June, 1973):
17-18.
Gina Lollobrigida gives her opinions on herself,
life, etc.

386   Fallaci, Oriana. The Egotists. Chicago: Regnery,
Co. , 1968.
Includes interviews with Ingrid Bergman, Geraldine Chaplin, Magnani, Moreau. Bad, movie-magazine
approach.

387   Farmer, Frances. Will There Really Be a Morning?
New York: G. P. Putnam's Sons, 1972.
An unglamorous autobiography of Frances Farmer,
former movie, radio and Broadway star of the 30's, an
alcoholic inmate of insane asylum.

388   "Fay Tincher--an Ingenuish Vampire. "   Theatre 29(June,
       1919):389.

389   Feiden, R.   "Interview with Nicholas and Alexandra,
       a. k. a.   Janet Suzman and Michael Jayston. "
       Inter/View 20(March, 1972):31.
       A brief discussion of the film, "Nicholas and Alex-
       andra, " and acting in general.

390   Feinstein, Herbert.   "Lana, Marlene, Greta, et al. :
       the Defense Rests. "   Film Quarterly 12, 1(Fall,
       1958):30-35.
       Films in which women testify on the witness
       stand.

391   Fenin, George.   "MM. "   Films and Filming 9, 4(Janu-
       ary, 1963):23-24.
       Marilyn Monroe as a sex symbol.

392   Fernandez Cuenca, Carlos.   Greta Garbo.   San Sebas-
       tian, X Festival International del Cine, Sección de
       Actividades Culturales, 1962.   71 pp.
       Includes bibliography.

393   "Filmex Announces Extraordinary Success of Second
       Exposition. "   American Cinematographer 54, 1(Janu-
       ary, 1973):61.
       Eleven-day non-competitive event included a spe-
       cial tribute to Myrna Loy.

394   Fiskin, Jeffrey.   "An Interview with Marlo Thomas. "
       Cinema 5, 4(1969):8-10.

395   Fleet, Simon.   "Garbo: The Lost Star. "   Films and
       Filming 3, 3(December, 1956):14.

396   Flinn, Tom.   "Joe, Where Are You?"   The Velvet
       Light Trap 6(Fall, 1972):3.
       Article on the Von Sternberg-Dietrich relationship.

397   Flynn, Errol.   "Women of Hollywood and their Attitude
       toward Men. "   Photoplay 51(September, 1937) 29-35,
       95.

398   Ford, Charles.   "Sara Bernhardt. "   Films in Review
       5, 10 (December, 1954):515-18.

Discusses films in which the great stage actress appeared.

399   Fox, J. "Maureen O'Hara: The Fighting Lady. "
      Films and Filming 19, 3(December, 1972):32-40.
      Describes the actress' charm and beauty and her portrayal of forceful feminine characters.

400   "Frances Farmer. " Films in Review 21, 10(December, 1970):655-56.
      On the actress.

401   "Frances Robinson. " Films in Review 22, 10(December, 1971):657.
      A filmography of supporting actress.

402   Frank, Gerold. Judy. [Garland]. New York: Harper and Row, 1975.
      A biography. Frank also did: Beloved Infidel with Sheilah Graham, Too Much Too Soon (Diana Barrymore); I'll Cry Tomorrow (Lillian Roth);

403   Franklin, Joe and Laurie Palmer. The Marilyn Monroe Story. New York: R. Field Co. ; Greenberg, trade distributors, 1953.

404   Frewin, Leslie. Dietrich: the Story of a Star. New York: Stein and Day, 1967. Previous edition, 1955, titled Blond Venus.

405   Funke, Lewis and John E. Booth, editors. Actors Talk About Acting. New York: Avon, 1961.
      Helen Hayes, Vivien Leigh, Shelley Winters, Lynn Fontanne, Maureen Stapleton, Katherine Cornell, Anne Bancroft.

406   Gabor, Zsa Zsa and Gerold Frank. Zsa Zsa Gabor: My Story. Cleveland: World Publishing Co. , 1960.
      "My story written for me by Gerold Frank. "

407   Gaither, Gant. Princess of Monaco: the Story of Grace Kelly. New York: Holt, 1957.

408   Gambetti, Giacomo. Marilyn Monroe. Roma: Collana di cinema "Lo schermo, " 1964.

409   Garbo, Greta. "What the Public Wants. " Saturday

Review (London) 151(June 13, 1931):857.

410 Gardiner, H. C. In All Conscience. Plainview, N. Y. :
     Books for Libraries, Inc., n. d. [Reprint of 1959
     edition.]
     Includes essay "Bardot and the Admen," pp. 221-
     22.

411 Gebhart, Myrtle. "The Real Ruth Roland. " Picture
     Play Magazine (December, 1926).

412 Geltzer, Geo. "Ruth Roland. " Films in Review
     11, 9(November, 1960):539.

413 "Geneviève. " Take One 2, 11(May-June, 1970):14-18.
     The career of actress Geneviève Bujold.

414 George, Manfred. "Hildegarde Neff. " Films in Review
     6, 9(November, 1955):445-48.
     Her career.

415 _____ . Marlene Dietrich; eine Eroberung der Welt
     in sechs Monaten. Berlin: Häger, 1931.
     24 pp., illustrated, portrait.

416 _____ . "Marlene Dietrich's Beginning. " Films in
     Review 3, 2(February, 1952):77-80.
     Her early career.

417 Georgiev, L. "Ija Savina. " Kinoizkustvo (Sofia) 28, 5
     (May, 1973):56-63.
     The career of Soviet actress, Ija Savina.

418 Germanova, I. and A. Saskova. "Ja za rezissera-
     edinomyz-Lennika. " Iskusstvo Kino (Moscow) 10
     (October, 1972):69-71.
     An interview with the Soviet actress, Alla Demi-
     dova, who talks about her new roles.

419 _____ . "Novaja rol-novaja tema. " Iskusstvo Kino
     (Moscow) 10(October, 1972):71-72.
     The Soviet actress, Tat'Jana Konjuhova, talks
     about her new roles.

420 "Gertrude Michael. " Films in Review 16, 5(May, 1965):
     326-27.
     A filmography of supporting actress.

421 Gibson, Helen. "In Very Early Days. " Films in Re-
     view 19, 1(January, 1968):28-34.
       An autobiographical sketch by a leading lady of
     the silent screen; former stunt girl and wife of cowboy
     actor, Hoot Gibson.

422 Gill, Brendan. Tallulah. New York: Holt, Rinehart
     and Winston, 1972.
       Mostly a pictorial history of Miss Bankhead's
     career.

423 Gillette, D. C. "Hollywood Image-wreckers. " Journal
     of the Producers Guild of America (Los Angeles) 15,
     2(June, 1973):3-6, 17.
       (See entry under "Images. ")

424 Gilliatt, Penelope. "The Most Amicable Combatants. "
     New Yorker 48, 31(September 23, 1972):64-71.
       Museum of Modern Art's Tracy-Hepburn retro-
     spective.

425 _____. Unholy Fools; Wits, Comics, Disturbers of
     the Peace: Film and Theatre. New York: Viking
     Press, 1973.
       Elaine May, Beatrice Lillie are mentioned.

426 Gilling, T. "Safety Zone. " Sight and Sound 16, 3(Sum-
     er, 1972):140-41.
       Angela Lansbury talks about her film career and
     working in Hollywood.

427 Gingold, Hermione. Sirens Should Be Seen and Not
     Heard. Philadelphia: Lippincott, 1963.

428 Girls Who Do Stag Movies. Los Angeles, California:
     Holloway House Publishing Co. , n. d.
       No author; paperback, but American Cinematogra-
     pher book reviewer claims "surprisingly articulate views
     of problems peculiar to these films reveal unsuspected
     professionalism and a grasp of the socio-ethical issues
     involved. "

429 Gish, Lillian. Dorothy and Lillian Gish. New York:
     Scribner, 1973.
       A biography/autobiography of the Gish sisters.
     Like a big photo album.

430 _____ . Lillian Gish; the Movies, Mr. Griffith, and
Me. Englewood Cliffs, N. J. : Prentice-Hall, 1969.
An autobiography of the actress.

431 _____ . "Silence Was Our Virtue. " Films and Filming 4, 3(December, 1957):9.
Discusses her silent career.

432 Gordon, Ruth. Myself Among Others. New York:
Atheneum, 1971.
A "kind of" autobiography of the screenwriter and
Academy Award supporting actress (1968, "Rosemary's
Baby").

433 Gornand, A. "Evelyne Dress, actrice ... " Image et
Son (Paris) 266(December, 1972):53-56.
The French actress, Evelyne Dress, discusses
her roles, particularly her part in "Beau Masque. "

434 Gorney, J. "Betty Grable, 1916-1973. " Films in Review 24, 7(August-September, 1973):385-401.
Bio-filmographic information on Betty Grable.

435 "Govorjat laureaty festivalja. " Iskusstvo Kino (Moscow)
7(July, 1973):17.
The Soviet actress, Ljudmila Savel'Eva, replies
to a questionnaire at the Moscow Film Festival.

436 Gow, Gordon. "Cool It. " Films and Filming 17, 5
(February, 1971):18-22.
An interview with Lee Remick. A filmography.

437 _____ . "Mary. " Films and Filming 20, 3(December,
1973):58-61.
A preview of a revival of the work of Mary Pickford.

438 _____ . "A Star at Dawn. " Films and Filming 17, 8
(May, 1971):61.
Carrie Snodgrass' career. Refers to "Diary of a
Mad Housewife" (scripted by Eleanor Perry).

439 "Grace Kelly. " Films in Review 13, 4(April, 1962):
245-46.
A filmography.

440 Granlund, Nils Thor, with Sid Feder and Ralph Han-

cock. Blondes, Brunettes, and Bullets. New York:
McKay, 1957.

441   Gress, Elsa. "Die Asta: a Personal Impression. "
Sight and Sound 42,4(Autumn, 1973):209.
Friend's personal recollections of the late famous
Danish silent screen star, Asta Nielsen.

442   [No entry]

443   Griffith, Richard. Marlene Dietrich: Image and Legend. New York: Museum of Modern Art Film Library, 1963.

444   Guiles, Fred Lawrence. Marion Davies: A Biography.
New York: McGraw-Hill, 1972. Includes bibliography.
Biography of William Randolph Hearst's mistress,
a comedienne and mime and quite popular actress.

445   _____. Norma Jean: the Life of Marilyn Monroe.
New York: McGraw-Hill Book Co. , 1969.

446   Guy, Rory. "Every Young Man's Capsule Guide to the
Pin-Up. " Cinema (Los Angeles) 5, 2(n. d.):2-9.
Mostly illustrations.

447   _____. "The Year of the Steigers. " Cinema 3, 2
(March, 1966):19-21, 31-32.
An interview with actress Claire Bloom, actor-
husband Rod Steiger, and sketch of their careers.

448   Hagen, Ray. "Claire Trevor. " Films in Review 14,9
(November, 1963):541-52.
A filmography, career sketch.

449   _____. "Jane Russell. " Films in Review 14,4
(April, 1963):226-35.
A filmography and career sketch.

450   _____. "Lauren Bacall. " Films in Review 15,4
(April, 1963):217-29).
A filmography and career of the actress.

451   _____. "Mercedes McCambridge. " Films in Review 16,5(May, 1965):292-300.
A filmography and career of the actress.

452   Hale, Louise Clossner.   "The New Stage Fright: Talking Pictures. "   Harper's 161(September, 1930):417-
24.

453   Hall, Gladys.   "Samuel Goldwyn Chooses Women Train-
ed to Please Men. "   Motion Picture Magazine 36
(October, 1928):50-51, 106.

454   Hamblett, Charles.   Who Killed Marilyn Monroe?   or
Cage to Catch Our Dreams.   London: L. Frewin,
1966.

455   Hanna, David.   Ava, A Portrait of a Star.   New York:
G. P. Putnam's Sons, 1960.
Ava Gardner.

456   Hardwick, L. H.   "Type Casting: Negro Stereotype on
the Screen. "   Hollywood Quarterly 1:2(January,
1946):234-6.

457   Harriman, Mary Chase.   "Sweetheart. "   New Yorker
10(April 7, 1934):29-33.
About Mary Pickford.

458   Harris, Eleanor.   The Real Story of Lucille Ball.
New York: Farrar, Straus and Young, 1954.

459   Harvey, Stephen.   Joan Crawford.   New York: Pyramid
Publications, 1974.
One of the "Pyramid Illustrated History of the
Movies" series.

460   Haskell, Molly.   "Sources, Themes, Actors, Actresses
for Truffaut's Films. "   Village Voice 15, 16(April
16, 1970):57, 61, 63.
Refers to "Mississippi Mermaid. "

461   Havoc, June.   Early Havoc.   New York: Simon and
Schuster, 1959.
The autobiography of the child vaudeville star who
went on to Broadway and to become a movie star, but
covers up to only the 14th year of her life.

462   Hay, R. C.   "Doctor Ginger Rogers. "   Inter/View 26
(October, 1972):21-24.
Ginger Rogers on her career in films.

463   _____. "Gary Merrill, Maine Man. " Inter/View
           38(November, 1973):20-21.
           An interview. Actor Gary Merrill talks about his
       present work and his ex-wife, Bette Davis.

464   _____. "Lena!" Inter/View 29(January, 1973):20-
           25.
           Lena Horne talks about her singing career in gen-
       eral, and about her parts in "Stormy Weather" and
       "Cabin in the Sky. "

465   _____. "Sincerely, Bette Davis. " Inter/View 28
           (December, 1972):14-18.
           An interview with Bette Davis.

466   Hayes, Helen (with Lewis Funke). A Gift of Joy. New
           York: M. Evans, distributor; Philadelphia, Lippin-
           cott, 1965.

467   _____ and Sanford Dody. On Reflection. New York:
           Crest Books, 1969.
           An autobiography.

468   Head, June. Star Gazing. London: Peter Davies,
           1931.
           Discusses the growth of the star system and pre-
       dicts its decline. Talks of Mary Pickford and Pola
       Negri.

469   "Helen Winston: Obituary. " New York Times (Aug-
           ust 26, 1972):28.
           Actress and producer.

470   Hicks, Schuyler. "A Lady to Remember. " Cinema 1,
           5(August-September, 1963):12-13.
           Career of actress, Edna May Oliver.

471   Higham, Charles. "Kate and Spencer: the Story Be-
           hind the Legend. " McCall's CII, 6(March, 1975):94.
           Excerpts from Kate: the Life of Katherine Hep-
       burn. W. W. Norton and Co. , Inc. , published in 1975.

472   Hill, Derek. "A Window on Dors. " Films and Film-
           ing 1, 7(April, 1955):10.
           Career of Diana Dors, British actress, blonde
       bombshell since the 40's.

473 Hinxman, M. "Bette." <u>Sight and Sound</u> 41, 1(Winter,
     1971-72):17-18.
         Interview with Bette Davis on the set of "Madame
     Sin" and her reminiscences about her Hollywood career.

474 Hirschfeld, Bert. <u>Diana.</u> New York: Domino Pocket
     Books, 1963.
         About Hollywood "goddesses. "

475 Hobson, Valerie. "The Actress: An Independent
     Speaks. " <u>Sight and Sound</u> (Summer, 1951):22.
         Making a living as an actress/actor for indepen-
     dent productions.

476 Holloway, Ron. "We Are Playing with Reality. " <u>Film
     Journal</u> 1, 1(Spring, 1971):5.
         A conversation with Vilgot Sjöman and Lena
     Nyman. Director Sjöman and his leading actress,
     Nyman, discuss his films "I Am Curious Yellow" and
     "I Am Curious Blue. " A student of Bergman, Sjöman
     allows his actors great freedom during the creation of
     his films. He uses no script and performers must rely
     on themselves, on their abilities and experience.

477 "Hollywood's New Black Beauties. " <u>Sepia</u> 22(March,
     1973):37-44.
         Lola Falana, Brenda Sykes, Cicely Tyson, Diana
     Ross, Mae Mercer, Kathy Imrie, Paula Kelly, Rosa-
     lind Cash, Vonetta McGee, Freda Payne, Diana Sands,
     Lisa Moore, Denise Nicholas, Judy Pace, Margaret
     Ware. New images of Black women.

478 Hood, Edward. "Edie Sedgwick. " <u>Film Culture</u> 45
     (Summer, 1967):34.
         Marilyn Monroe and Sedgwick compared.

479 Hornblett, Charles. <u>The Hollywood Cage.</u> New York:
     Hart Publishing Co.; London: L. Frewin, 1969.
         Interviews with some stars. Discusses the price
     of stardom and images, such as whores, femme fatales.
     Scandal-sheet type reporting.

480 Horne, Lena. <u>Lena.</u> Garden City, N.Y.: Doubleday,
     1965.

481 Horton, Luci. "Battle Among the Beauties: Black
     Actresses Vie for Top Movie Roles. " <u>Ebony</u> 29

(November, 1973):144-45.
Pam Grier, Vonetta McGee, Gloria Hendry,
Tamara Dobson.

482   Houston, Penelope.   "After the Strike. " Sight and
       Sound 29, 3(Summer, 1960):108-12.
       The strikes of the Screen Actors Guild and the
       Writers Guild of America.

483   Hoyt, Edwin P.   Marilyn: the Tragic Venus.   Radnor,
       Pa: Chilton Book Co. , 1973.   New edition.

484   Hrbas, J.   "Portréty. "   Film a Doba (Prague) 18, 7
       (July, 1972):337.
       Portrait of the Czech actress, Marie Rosulkova.

485   _____. "Portréty. "   Film a Doba (Prague) 18, 11
       (November, 1972):561.
       Portrait of the Czech actress, Jirina Svorcová.

486   _____. "Portréty. "   Film a Doba (Prague) 18, 12
       (December, 1972):617.
       Portrait of the Czech actress, Nelly Gaierová.

487   _____. "Portréty. "   Film a Doba (Prague) 19, 1
       (January, 1973):1-3.
       Portrait of the Czech actress, Marta Vancurová.

488   _____. "Portréty. "   Film a Doba (Prague) 19, 2
       (February, 1973):57.
       Portrait of the Czech actress, Jirina Petrovická.

489   _____. "Portréty. "   Film a Doba (Prague) 19, 3
       (March, 1973):113.
       Portrait of the Czech actress, Antonie Hegerliková.

490   _____. "Portréty. "   Film a Doba (Prague) 19, 4
       (April, 1973):169-70.
       Portrait of the Czech actress, Helga Cocková.

491   _____. "Portréty. "   Film a Doba (Prague) 19, 5
       (May, 1973):225-27.
       Portrait of the Czech actress, Jirina Sejbalova.

492   _____. "Portréty. "   Film a Doba (Prague) 19, 6
       (June, 1973):281-83.
       Portrait of the Czech actress, Jarmila Smejkalová.

493 _____ . "Portréty. " Film a Doba (Prague) 19, 8
      (August, 1973):393-95.
      Brief portrait of the Czech actress, Jitka Zeleno-
      horská.

494 _____ . "Portréty. " Film a Doba (Prague) 19, 10
      (October, 1973):506-07.
      Portrait of the Czech actress, Alena Procházková.

495 _____ . "Portréty. " Film a Doba (Prague) 19, 11
      (November, 1973):561-63.
      Portrait of the Czech actress, Jane Andresiková.

496 Hudson, Richard M. and Raymond Lee. Gloria Swan-
      son. New York: A. S. Barnes and Co. , 1970.
      A biography. Many reminiscences by other fa-
      mous people. Many quotes from her.

497 Huff, Theodore. "The Career of Greta Garbo. " Films
      in Review 2, 10(December, 1951):1-17.
      A filmography.

498 Hughes, Elinor. Famous Stars of Filmdom (women.)
      Boston: L. C. Page, 1931.
      Poor.

499 Hume, Rod. "She Saw the Vision--and Became a Star. "
      Films and Filming 2, 9(June, 1956):15.
      A filmography and career of Jennifer Jones.

500 "Ill-Used Actresses. " Films in Review 14, 10(Decem-
      ber, 1963):638.
      A filmography of Beverly Garland.

501 "Ingrid Thulin in G'wich Village. " Village Voice 4, 45
      (September 2, 1959):7-8.

502 "Is Hollywood Afraid to Star a Sexy Actress?" Sepia
      18(June, 1969):10-15.

503 "Isabel Dawn: Obituary. " New York Times (June 30,
      1966):39.
      Actress and screenwriter.

504 Jacobs, Jack. "Margaret Sullavan. " Films in Review
      11, 4(April, 1960):193-207.
      A filmography and career of 30's and 40's actress.

505   . "Norma Shearer. " Films in Review 11, 7
(August-September, 1960):390-405.
A filmography and career of the actress.

506   James, Howard. "Elke Sommer: Celluloid Pagan. "
Cinema 1, 3(1963):24-25.
Her sex-appeal.

507   "Jan Sterling and Ruth Roman. " Films in Review 20, 7
(August-September, 1969):455-456.
Filmographies of the actresses.

508   "Jane Powell. " Films in Review 20, 6(June-July, 1969):
392.
A filmography.

509   "Jane Wyman. " Films in Review 18, 5(May, 1967):312-
13.
A filmography.

510   "Janis Paige. " Films in Review 17, 1(January, 1966):
61-62.
A filmography and career of the actress.

511   Janowska, Alina. "Truth Behind a Mask. " Films and
Filming 8, 2(November, 1961):10, 41.
The Polish actress discusses her career; the dif-
ferences in acting for stage, screen and TV.

512   "Jean Peters. " Films in Review 15, 3(March, 1964):
183-84.
A filmography.

513   "Jeanne Crain. " Films in Review 17, 5(May, 1966):327.
A filmography of the actress.

514   Jeanne Moreau. Paris: Collection "Vedettes du Cinéma, " 1964.

515   "Joan Greenwood. " Sight and Sound 25, 4(Spring, 1956):
191.
A filmography and career sketch of the British
leading lady of the 40's.

516   "Joan Leslie. " Films in Review 15, 5(May, 1964):319.
A filmography of the actress.

517   Jones, Charles Reed. Breaking Into the Movies. New
          York: Unicorn Press, 1927.
          Advice on "how to be a movie star."

518   Jones, Siriol Hugh. "Personal Appearances." Sight
          and Sound 26, 2(Autumn, 1956):92-93.
          Joan Crawford and Marilyn Monroe: their person-
      al appearances in London.

519   "Judy Garland: Star Quality." Sight and Sound 20, 2
          (June, 1951):53.

520   "June Duprez." Films in Review 19, 2(February, 1968):
          128.
          A filmography of the British leading lady.

521   Kanin, Garson. Tracy and Hepburn: An Intimate Mem-
          oir. New York: The Viking Press, 1971.

522   Karpinski, M. "Maja Komorowska-Tyszkiewicz." Kino
          (Warsaw) 7, 3(March, 1972):12-15.
          An analysis of the performance of the Polish ac-
      tress, Maja Komorowska-Tyszkiewicz.

523   Katkov, Norman. The Fabulous Fanny: the Story of
          Fanny Brice. New York: Knopf, 1953.
          A biography of the stage and film star.

524   Katz, Marjorie. Grace Kelly. New York: Coward-
          McCann, 1970.

525   Kempton, Sally. "Viva of the Visions." Village Voice
          13, 19(February 22, 1968):1, 51.
          Career of avant-garde actress, Viva.

526   Keown, Eric. Margaret Rutherford. (Theatre World
          Monograph No. 7.) London: Rockliff, 1956.
          Emphasis on her stage career.

527   Kierhan, Thomas. Jane. New York: G. P. Putnam's
          Sons, 1974.
          "Intimate biography" of Jane Fonda.

528   Kincaid, Jamaica. "Pam Grier, the Mocha Mogul of
          Hollywood." Ms 4, 2(August, 1975):49.
          Article on Black actress Grier.

529   Kirkland, S.   "Susan Tyrrell, the Lady from 'Fat City. '"
       Inter/View 26(October, 1972):18-20, 52.
              An interview.   Susan Tyrrell talks about her life,
       career and her feelings about acting.

530   Kiss/Koller and A. Ibrányi-Kiss.   "'Kamouraska':
       Geneviève Bujold. "   Cinema Canada (Toronto) 7(April-
       May, 1973):42-45.
              An interview.   Geneviève Bujold talks about her
       stage and screen career with special reference to "Kam-
       ouraska. "

531   Kivu, D.   "Anna Magnani. "   Cinema (Bucharest) 11, 10
       (October, 1973):45.
              Obituary.

532   Kleiser, P. B.   "Willow Springs: Gespräch mit Magda-
       lena Montezuma und Werner Schroeter. "   Filmkritik
       (Munich) 17, 9(September, 1973):408-15.
              An interview.   Remarks by Magdalena Montezuma
       and Werner Schroeter about "Willow Springs. "

533   Klumph, Inez and Helen.   Screen Acting, Its Require-
       ments and Rewards.   New York: Falk Publishing
       Co. , 1922.
              Written with assistance and advice of Lillian and
       Dorothy Gish, Colleen Moore and others.

534   Knight, Arthur.   "Marlene Dietrich. "   Films in Review
       5, 10(December, 1954):497-514.
              A filmography and career sketch of the actress.

535   Knowles, Eleanor.   Films of Jeanette MacDonald and
       Nelson Eddy.   New York: A. S.   Barnes and Co. ,
       1974.

536   Knox, Donald.   The Magic Factory: How MGM Made
       "An American in Paris. "   New York: Praeger Pub-
       lishers, 1973.
              This interesting account of a classic in movie mus-
       icals is constructed from recollections by the major con-
       tributors to the film.   Included are statements by ac-
       tresses Leslie Caron and Nina Foch, editor Adrienne
       Fazan, script-timer Honore (Nora) Janney, literary con-
       sultant Lilly Messinger, dress unit designer Mary Ann
       Nyberg, costume designer Irene Sharoff, and publicist
       Emily Torchia.

537   Kobal, John.   Marlene Dietrich.   New York: E. P.
       Dutton and Co. , 1968.

538   _____.   "The Time, the Place and the Girl: Rita
       Hayworth. "   Focus on Film 10(Summer, 1972):15-29.
       A filmographical study of the actress-personality and
       the qualities that contributed to making her a star, fol-
       lowed by a close analysis of her career.

539   Koch, M.   "Interview with Russ Meyer and Edy Will-
       iams. "   Inter/View 19(February, 1972):22-23.
       An interview.   Russ Meyer and Edy Williams talk
       about Meyer's films.

540   _____.   "Joan Blondell: the Great Golddigger Still
       Digging Hollywood. "   Inter/View 24(August, 1972):
       24-29.
       Joan Blondell talks about her career in the past
       and at present.

541   Koller, G. C.   "The True Nature of Micheline Lanctôt. "
       Cinema Canada 10-11(October-January, 1973-74):26-
       27, 73-74.
       A portrait of the Québécoise star of Gilles Carle's
       "La vraie nature de Bernadette" and other films.

542   Kuz'mina, Elena.   "Pisu, kak mogu, o tom, cto pomn-
       ju. "   Iskusstvo Kino (Moscow) 6(June, 1973):88-97.
       The Soviet actress Elena Kuz'mina talks about
       her career.

543   Kyrou, Ado.   Norma Jean Baker dite Marilyn Monroe.
       Paris: E. P. Denoël, 1972.
       A short French pictorial history of Marilyn Mon-
       roe's career.

544   Laclos, Michel.   Jeanne Moreau.   Paris: Collection
       "Vedettes du cinéma, " 1964.

545   Laing, E. E.   Greta Garbo: the Story of a Specialist.
       London: J. Gifford, 1946.

546   Lajeunesse, J.   "Entretien avec Françoise Lebrun. "
       Image et Son (Paris) 273(June, 1973):99-102.
       An interview.   Actress Françoise Lebrun talks
       about the film "La maman et la putain" and her part
       in it.

547   Lake, Veronica and Donald Bains. Veronica: the Auto-
       biography of Veronica Lake. New York: Citadel,
       1971.

548   Lamarr, Hedy. Ecstasy and Me: My Life as a Wo-
       man. New York: Macfadden-Bartell, 1966.

549   Lambert, Gavin. "Portrait of an Actress." Sight and
       Sound 21, 1(August-September, 1951):12-19.
       On Bette Davis.

550   Lanchester, Elsa. Charles Laughton and I. New York:
       Harcourt, Brace, 1938.
           Describes stage and film career of Laughton and
       Lanchester. Dated. Seems to be mostly about Laugh-
       ton.

551   Landis, Jessie Royce. You Won't Be So Pretty (But
       You'll Know More). London: W. H. Allen, 1954.
       The actress's memoirs.

552   Lane, John Francis. "Claudia Cardinale." Films and
       Filming 9, 4(January, 1963):19-21.
       Italian actress Claudia Cardinale as a sex symbol.

553   _____. "Neopolitan Gold." Films and Filming 3, 7
       (April, 1957):9-14.
       Discusses career of Sophia Loren.

554   Ledóchowski, A. "Latarnia w salonie." Kino (Warsaw)
       8, 12(December, 1973):20-24.
           An analysis of the performance of the principal
       female role in the film "Zazdrość i medycyna" played
       by actress Ewa Krzyżewska.

555   Lee, Raymond. The Films of Mary Pickford. New
       York: A. S. Barnes and Co., 1970.

556   Lejeune, Caroline. Cinema. London: Alexander
       Maclehose and Co., 1931.
           A film critic analyzes her art. Articles on Mary
       Pickford and Nazimova.

557   "Letter to an Unknown Woman, Namely, Jack Smithby
       Ondine." Film Culture 45(Summer, 1967):21.
       The New York Maria Montez cult.

558   Lewis, Arthur H.   It Was Fun While It Lasted.   New
       York: Trident Press, 1973.
           Interviews with people who helped make movies,
       including directors, producers, cameramen; but the only
       women are actresses--Mae West and Zsa Zsa Gabor are
       included.

559   Lewis, G.   "Gloria Jean Tells in Her Own Words What
       It Was Like to Be a Star at Twelve. "   Films in Re-
       view 24,9(November, 1973):513-22.
           A filmography and interview.   Gloria Jean talks
       about her career as a child star and describes her life
       in recent years.

560   _____.   "Vilma Banky. "   Films in Review 24, 2(Feb-
       ruary, 1973):123.
           A letter.   Brief bio-filmographic information on
       Vilma Banky.

561   Lewis, J. H.   "A Magnetic Thespian. "   American He-
       brew 125(June 14, 1929):163.
           About Sophie Tucker.

562   "Lilian Harvey. "   Films in Review 18,9(November,
       1967):587-88.
           A filmography of the British leading lady who in
       the 30's became a star of German films

563   Lindberg, I.   "Øjeblikke med Asta. "   Kosmorama
       (Copenhagen) 18,110(September, 1972):244-45.
           A young Danish film critic's impressions of Asta
       Nielsen, the Danish actress famous for her screen por-
       trayal of Hamlet.

564   Lindsay, Karen.   "Elegy for Jayne Mansfield, July
       1967, " in Sisterhood Is Powerful, edited by Robin
       Morgan.   New York: Vintage Books, 1970.
           A poem, p. 496.

565   Lindsay, Michael.   "An Interview with Jeanne Moreau. "
       Cinema 5, 3(1969):14-17.
           Her career.

566   "Liv Ullmann. "   Focus on Film 14(Spring, 1973):6-7.
           A bio-filmography of the Swedish actress.

567   Lockwood, Margaret.   Lucky Star, the Autobiography

of Margaret Lockwood. London: Odhams Press,
1955.

568   London, Julie. "The Two Faces of Ferrer." Films
         and Filming 4,9(June, 1958):12.
              The actress discusses working with José Ferrer
      on "The Great Man."

569   Löthwall, L.-O. "Knef och krig." Chaplin (Stockholm)
         14,8(1972):295.
              An interview with Hildegarde Neff; discusses her
      autobiography.

570   "Louise Fazenda." Films in Review 13,7(August-Sep-
         tember, 1962):444-46.
              Sketch of leading lady of Mack Sennett era.

571   Love, Bessie. "On Working Behind the Camera."
         Films and Filming 8,10(July, 1962):16, 44.
              Learning to be a script girl after being a well-
      known actress.

572   Luft, Herbert. "Asta Nielsen." Films in Review 7,1
         (January, 1956):19-26.
              Her career.

573   _____. "Greer Garson." Films in Review 12,3
         (March, 1961):152-64.
              A filmography and career of actress.

574   Lyndina, E. "Prostota pravdy." Iskusstvo Kino (Mos-
         cow) 5(May, 1973):60-74.
              A portrait of the Soviet actress, Nadezda Fedoso-
      va.

575   Lyons, D. "Mary Woronov: No Sugar This Cookie."
         Inter/View 32(May, 1973):31.
              Interview. Mary Woronov on her acting career,
      especially her role in "Sugar Cookies."

576   "Mable Normand, Key to Many Laughs in Keystone Com-
         edies." Moving Picture World 21(July 11, 1914):
         230.

577   Macavei, O. "Beata." Cinema (Bucharest) 10,4(April,
         1972):45.
              A filmography and interview. The Polish actress,

Beata Tyszkiewicz, discusses the concept of the "star."

578   McBride, Mary Margaret. The Life Story of Constance
       Bennett. New York: Star Library Publications, Inc.,
       1932.

579   McCallum, John. That Kelly Family. New York: A.
       S. Barnes and Co., 1957.
            The biography of Grace Kelly's family told by an
       old family friend.

580   McClelland, Douglas. "The Brooklyn Bernhardt."
       Films and Filming 11, 6(March, 1965):11-15.
            On Susan Hayward.

581   _____. "Eleanor Parker." Films in Review 13, 3
       (March, 1962):135-48.
            A filmography and career sketch of the actress.

582   _____. "Jeanne Crain." Films in Review 20, 6(June-
       July, 1969):357-67.
            A filmography and career sketch of the actress.

583   _____. "Susan Hayward." Films in Review 13, 5
       (May, 1962):266-76.
            Her career and filmography.

584   _____. Susan Hayward: the Divine Bitch. New
       York: Pinnacle Books, 1973.
            The first book devoted to the Irish redhead from
       Brooklyn.

585   McClure, Michael. "In Defense of Jayne Mansfield,"
       in Film Culture Reader, edited by P. Adams Sitney.
       New York: Praeger, 1970, p. 160.

586   McCreadie, Marsha. The American Movie Goddess.
       New York: Wiley, 1973.
            A collection of photos, essays, song lyrics, illus-
       trations and other materials from the 30's, 40's and
       50's. Images (as embodied in major female movie
       stars) were demanded by, foisted on, or evolved for
       the American public: Greta Garbo, Rita Hayworth,
       Marilyn Monroe.

587   MacDonald, Margaret I. "Clara Kimball Young Dis-
       cusses Picture Art." Moving Picture World 33(July

21, 1917):461.

588   McKenney, J. D. "Walt Disney, Showman and Educator,
      Remembers Daisy. " CTA 51(December, 1955):4
      On Daisy Duck.

589   MacLaine, Shirley. Don't Fall off the Mountain. New
      York: W. W. Norton, 1970.
      Her autobiography in a very easy, candid style.

590   _____. You Can Get There from Here. New York:
      W. W. Norton, 1975.

591   McVay, Douglas. "The Goddesses. " Films and Film-
      ing 11, 11(August, 1965):5-9.
      Movie goddesses: Harlow, Louise Brooks, Garbo,
      Dietrich. Continued in 11, 12(September, 1965):13-18.

592   _____. "Judy Garland. " Films and Filming 8, 1
      (October, 1961):10-11.
      A filmography.

593   _____. "The Lady Has Talent: Suzanne Pleshette. "
      Focus on Film 3(May-August, 1970):53-59.

594   Madden, James. "Irene Dunne. " Films in Review 20,
      10(December, 1969):605-20.
      A filmography and career sketch of the actress.

595   "Madge Bellamy. " Films in Review 21, 4(April, 1970):
      256.
      A filmography of the actress.

596   "Mae Marsh Since '32. " Films in Review 10, 3(March,
      1959):190-91.
      A filmography.

597   "Mae Murray: the Star Who Danced to Fame. " Theatre
      29(June, 1919):395.

598   Mailer, Norman. Marilyn: a Biography. New York:
      Grosset and Dunlap, Inc. , 1973.

599   Makin, William J. "Greta Garbo, " in Private Lives of
      the Film Stars. London: C. Arthur Pearson, Ltd.,
      1935.

600   "Making the Mighty Three-in-One into Logan's Family. "
       Films and Filming 7,10(July, 1961):7-8.
       An interview with Leslie Caron. Sketch of her
       career and her current work in "Fanny. "

601   Mallery, David. "Von Sternberg and Dietrich. " AFFS
       Newsletter (November, 1964):14-15.
       Dietrich with and without Sternberg.

602   Malonga, Gerard. "Let's Be Serious--A Profile of
       Baby Jane Holzer. " Film Culture 45(Summer, 1967):
       35-36.

603   Manoiu, A. "Mitul Marilyn si prabusirea 'visului Amer-
       ican. "' Cinema (Bucharest) 11,10(October, 1973):36-
       39.
       Portrait of Marilyn Monroe as a sex symbol. The
       myth has survived her death.

604   Mansfield, Jayne. "How I Pushed My Way into Movies. "
       Films and Filming 7,8(May, 1961):11.

605   and Mickey Hargitay. Jayne Mansfield's Wild,
       Wild World. Los Angeles: Holloway House, 1963.

606   Marcarelles, Louis. "Albert Finney and Mary Ure Talk
       About Acting. " Sight and Sound 30,2(Spring, 1961):
       56-61, 102.
       An interview.

607   Margueritte, Yves. Brigitte Bardot. Paris: Pauvert,
       1963.
       13 pp. illustrated.

608   "Mari Blanchard. " Films in Review 21,7(August-Sep-
       tember, 1970):446.
       A filmography and career of the actress.

609   Marill, A. H. "Jean Simmons. " Films in Review 23,
       2(February, 1972):71-88.
       Bio-filmographic information on Jean Simmons.

610   Marinacci, Barbara. Leading Ladies: A Gallery of
       Famous Actresses. Toronto/London: Alvin Redman,
       1961.

611   Marmorstein, Robert. "A Winter Memory of Valerie

Solanis. " Village Voice 13, 35(June 13, 1968):9-10.
An interview with Valerie Solanis. She talks of
her film and ideological activities.

612 Marowitz, Charles. "For Marilyn Monroe. " Village
Voice 7, 43(August 16, 1962):4-5.
In memoriam.

613 Marsh, Mae. Screen Acting. Los Angeles, Calif. :
Photostar Publishing Co. , 1921.

614 "Marsha Hunt. " Films in Review 14, 8(October, 1963):
511.
A filmography of American leading lady who began
her career in films in the mid-30's.

615 Martin, Thornton. Will Acting Spoil Marilyn Monroe?
Garden City, N. Y. : Doubleday, 1956.

616 Martineau, B. "Thoughts About the Objectification of
Women. " Take One 3, 2(February, 1972):15-18.
(See listing under "Images. ")

617 "Mary Boland. " Films in Review 16, 7(August-September, 1965):453.
A filmography of the stage tragedienne who in mid-
dle age settled in Hollywood and played innumerable flut-
tery matrons.

618 Mason, Geo. "Katherine the Great. " Films and Filming 2, 11(August, 1956):7.
Career notes on Katherine Hepburn.

619 Mead, Taylor. "Harlow. " Film Culture 40(1966):67.

620 Mekas, Jonas. "Marilyn Monroe. " Village Voice 7,
42(August 9, 1962):6.
In memoriam.

621 Mellen, Joan. Marilyn Monroe. New York: Galahad
Books, 1973.
A biography.

622 _____. Marilyn Monroe. New York: Pyramid Publications, 1973.

623 _____. Voices from the Japanese Cinema. New

York: Liveright, 1975.
Japan--its cinema and images of its women. Feu-
dal, authoritarian attitudes toward women--movement
away from this by new film-makers. Statement by
Sachiko Hidari--acclaimed actress and wife of Susumu
Han.

624   . "What Mae West Really Meant Was ... "
       Ms 1, 5(November, 1972):46.
       Discusses the paradoxes of Mae West, the image
of a free woman, a rarity in the 30's and even now.
She was a sex object, yet was self-sufficient.

625 Mercouri, Melina. I Was Born Greek. Garden City,
       N.Y.: Doubleday and Co., Inc., 1971.
       A biography.

626 Miller, Loren. "Uncle Tom in Hollywood. " in The
       Negro in American History: Black Americans, 1928-
       1968. Vol. I. Ed. by Mortimer J. Adler, et al.
       Chicago: Encyclopaedia Britannica Ed. Corp., 1969.

627 Milne, Tom. "Davies. " Sight and Sound 37, 4(Autumn,
       1968):200-01.
       On Marion Davies, William Randolph Hearst's
protégée.

628 "Misguided Genius. " Newsweek 84(September 16, 1974):
       91.
       Portrait of Leni Reifenstahl, German actress and
motion picture director.

629 "Miss Barbara Tennant. " Moving Picture World 12
       (June 22, 1912):1121.

630 "Miss Lottie Briscoe. " Moving Picture World 20(June
       20, 1914):1671.

631 "An MM Bibliography. " Films in Review 20, 10(Decem-
       ber, 1969):640.
       On Marilyn Monroe.

632 "Mona Freeman and Diana Lynn. " Films in Review 19,
       1(January, 1968):63-64.
       A filmography of two leading stars of the 40's.

633 Montesonti, Fausto. Greta Garbo. Roma: Collana di

cinema "Lo schermo, Vol. I," 1963.

634   Moore, Colleen. Silent Star. Garden City, N.Y.:
         Doubleday, 1968.
            An autobiography of the screen star.

635   Moore, Grace. You're Only Human Once. Garden
         City, N.Y.: Doubleday, 1944.
            An autobiography. From opera star to glamorous
      motion picture personality--short, meteoric career.

636   Moorehead, Agnes. "Article." Sight and Sound 25, 2
         (Autumn, 1955):84.
            The actress discusses her career.

637   Moravia, Alberto. Claudia Cardinale. (Series: "Oggi
         nel mondo," No. 9) Milano: Lerici, 1963.

638   Morella, Joe and Edward Z. Epstein. Judy: the Films
         and Career of Judy Garland. New York: Citadel,
         1969.

639   _____. Lana Turner. New York: Citadel, 1971.

640   Moret, H. "Rome, ville en deuil." Ecran (Paris) 19
         (November, 1973):19-20.
            A filmography. Obituary of the actress, Anna
      Magnani.

641   Morley, Sheridan. "Life and Living." Films and Film-
         ing 16,4(January, 1970):12-15.
            An interview with Lillian Gish: thoughts on her
      career.

642   Moro, F. "Sarita Montiel." Films in Review 24,5(May,
         1973):313-14.
            A letter and filmography on the actress.

643   Moshier, W. Franklyn. "Alice Faye." Films in Re-
         view 12,8(October, 1961):474-83.
            A filmography and career of leading lady singer of
      the 30's and 40's.

644   _____. "Marjorie Main." Films in Review 17,2
         (February, 1966):96-108.
            A filmography and career sketch of the actress.

645   Most, Mary. "Une Créature du Cinéma." Cinema 5,
      1(1969):10-12.
         A career sketch of Catherine Deneuve.

646   Murray, Eunice with Rose Shade. Marilyn: the Last
      Months. New York: Pyramid Books, 1975.

647   Najdenova, V. "Nevena Kokanova." Iskusstvo Kino
      (Moscow) 10(October, 1973):140-49.
         An assessment of the career of Bulgarian actress,
      Nevena Kokanova.

648   "Nancy Carroll Index." Films in Review 15, 5(May,
      1964):287-91.
         A filmography of stage, screen actress.

649   "Natalia Bondarčuk y 'Solaris.'" Cine Cubano (Havana)
      78-80(1973):40-43.
         An interview. Natalija Bondarčuk, actress in the
      Soviet film, "Soljaris," speaks about the film.

650   Nathan, George Jean. The Sex Appeal Fiction. New
      York: Knopf, 1935.
         Minimizes sex appeal as ingredient for stardom.

651   Naumburg, Nancy, ed. We Make the Movies. Norton,
      1937.
         Includes "the actress plays her part," Bette
      Davis. (Also see Cutting the Film, listed under "Film-
      makers.")

652   Neal, Patricia. "What Kazan Did for Me." Films and
      Filming 4, 1(October, 1957):9, 31.
         Actress discusses Elia Kazan as a director, and
      the film "A Face in the Crowd."

653   Negri, Pola. Memoirs of a Star. Garden City, N. Y. :
      Doubleday, 1970.
         The autobiography of the Polish siren of silent
      screen.

654   Nemcek, Paul. The Films of Nancy Carroll. New
      York: Lyle Stuart, 1969.

655   _____. Nancy Carroll: A Charmer's Almanac.
      New York: Lyle Stuart, 1970.

656   Newquist, Roy. A Special Kind of Magic. New York:
        Rand McNally and Co. , 1967.
            A series of interviews with the director and stars
        of the film, "Guess Who's Coming to Dinner?" Includes
        Katherine Hepburn and Katherine Houghton.

657   Nielsen, Asta. Die schweigende Muse. Rostock:
        Hinstorff Verlag, 1961.
            Memoirs of the silent screen star.

658   Niver, Kemp. Mary Pickford: Comedienne. Edited
        by Bebe Bergsten. Los Angeles: Historical Films,
        1970.

659   Noa, Wolfgang. Marlene Dietrich. Berlin: Henschel-
        verlag, 1966.

660   Noble, Peter. Bette Davis, a Biography. London:
        Skelton Robinson, 1948.

661   _____ . The Negro in Films. New York: Arno
        Press, 1970.
            Includes Lena Horne, Ethel Waters, Butterfly
        McQueen, Katherine Dunham, Hattie McDaniel.

662   Noë, Yvon. Clara Bow. Paris: Nouvelle librairie
        française, 1932.
            Subtitle: avec une notice de Yvon Noë et vingt-
        sept photographes hors-texte. 47-page pamphlet.

663   Nogueira, Rui. "I Am Not Going to Write My Mem-
        oirs. " Sight and Sound 38, 2(Spring, 1969):58-62,
        109.
            An interview with Gloria Swanson.

664   _____ . "Psycho, Rosie and a Touch of Orson. "
        Sight and Sound 39, 2(Spring, 1970):66-70.
            An interview with Janet Leigh. This candid talk
        includes her views on the actor and the part, Von Stern-
        berg, Orson Welles, Hitchcock, Fosse, Frankenheimer.

665   Nolan, Jack Edmund. "Films on TV. " Films in Re-
        view 24, 4(April, 1973):221-23, 227.
            Compares Hildegard Knef's career, as told in her
        autobiography, to facts as revealed by her films shown
        on television, with additional biographical-filmographic
        information.

666 _____. "Vera Miles. " Films in Review 24, 5(May,
       1973):281.
       A biographical sketch of the actress and an im-
       pressive filmography.

667 Nordberg, Carl-Eric. "Greta Garbo's Secret. " Film
       Comment 6, 2(Summer, 1970):26.
       One chapter from author's book on Garbo. Points
       out the fact that although she portrays many kinds of
       women in her films, they each have much in common,
       blend into the identical woman. Includes photos and
       filmography.

668 Nordstrom, Kristina. "Mae West in Venice. " Women
       and Film 1, 3-4(1973):93.
       Discussion of the 1973 Venice Film Festival,
       which included a retrospective on Mae West.

669 Nourissier, Francois. Brigitte Bardot. Bonn, 1963.

670 _____. Brigitte Bardot. Paris: B. Grasset, 1960.
       37 pp. illustrated booklet.

671 Oberon, G. "Lee Grant, No Complaints. " Inter /View
       24(August, 1972):20-21, 50.
       Lee Grant talks about her work and opinions.

672 "Obituary. " Screen World 17(1966):233.
       On Abby Berlin.

673 O'Brien, G. "Interview with Cloris Leachman. " Inter /
       View 19(February, 1972):16.
       The actress talks about her role in "The Last
       Picture Show. "

674 _____. "Interview with Cybill Shepherd. " Inter /
       View 19(February, 1972):14-15.
       Cybill Shepherd discusses her part in "The Last
       Picture Show, " her plans for the future, and her opin-
       ions of some other films.

675 An Old Timer. "Before They Were Stars: Lillian
       Gish, et al. " New York Dramatic Mirror 81(April
       3, 1920):642, 661.
       About Lillian Gish, actress and director. A
       series of articles including Alla Nazimova 81(March
       27, 1920):588, 609; Anita Stewart 81(April 24, 1920):

796, 817; and Norma Talmadge 81(April 17, 1920):
744, 765.

676 "Olga Petrova." Moving Picture World 22(December
12, 1914):1507.
The Russo-Polish actress who wrote her own
scripts and produced her own movies.

677 Oliva, L. "8/10." Film a Doba (Prague) 18(July,
1972):394.
Extract from an interview with Bette Davis origi-
nally published in L'Europeo, Milan.

678 Ongare, A. "Jane Fondová a Sobe." Film a Doba
(Prague) 19, 10(October, 1973):528-29.
An interview. Jane Fonda talks about film pro-
duction, life, politics, etc. Translated from Ciné-
Revue.

679 Orth, M. "How to Succeed: Fail, Lose, Die." Newsweek 83(March 4, 1974):50-51.
Examines and interviews new female stars Jacqueline Bissett, Ellen Burstyn, Karen Black, Marsha Mason, Cloris Leachman, Madeline Kahn, Susan Anspock.
Male roles outnumber women 12-1.

680 Ott, Frederick W. Films of Carole Lombard. Secaucus, N.J.: Citadel Press, 1972.

681 Ottolinghi, O. "Bette Davis. Un Monstru sacru."
Cinema (Bucharest) 10, 8(August, 1972):32-33.
An interview.

682 Pacheco, Joseph. "Claudette Colbert." Films in Review 21, 5(May, 1970):268-82.
A filmography and career sketch of the actress.

683 "The Pagan Bardot." Cinema 1, 1(1963):17-21.
Drawings of Brigitte Bardot.

684 Paine, Albert Bigelow. Life and Lillian Gish. New
York: Macmillan, 1932.

685 Palmborg, Rilla Page. The Private Life of Greta Garbo. New York: Doubleday, Doran, 1931.

686 Parish, James Robert. The Fox Girls. New Rochelle,
N.Y.: Arlington House, 1971.

687 _____ . Good Dames. South Brunswick, N. J. : A.
S. Barnes and Co. , 1974.
Includes chapters on Eve Arden, Agnes Moore-
head, Angela Lansbury, Thelma Ritter, Eileen Heckart.
Biographical data and photos of each, plus filmographies.

688 _____ . Liza. New York: Pocket Books, 1975.
An unauthorized biography of Liza Minnelli.

689 _____ . The Paramount Pretties. New York: Castle
Books, 1972.
About Paramount actresses: Swanson, Bow, Col-
bert, Lombard, Dietrich, Miriam Hopkins, Sylvia Sid-
ney, Mae West, Dorothy Lamour, Paulette Goddard.
With photos and complete filmographies.

690 _____ . The RKO Girls. New Rochelle, N. Y. : Arlington House Publishers, 1974.

691 _____ . The Slapstick Queens. Edited by T. Allan
Taylor. South Brunswick: A. S. Barnes and Co. ,
1973.
American comedy actresses. Biographies, photos
and filmographies of Marjorie Main, Martha Raye, Joan
Davis, Judy Canova, Phyllis Diller.

692 _____ and Gene Ringgold. "Dorothy McGuire. "
Films in Review 15, 8(October, 1964):466-79.
A filmography and career sketch of the actress.

693 _____ , _____ . "Kay Francis. " Films in Review
15, 2(February, 1964):63-85.
A filmography and career of lady-like star of women's films in the 30's.

694 Parsons, Louella O. Jean Harlow's Life Story. New
York: Dell Publishing Co. , 1937. Re-issued Dunel-
len, N. J. : Dell Publishing Co. , 1964.
Harlow, 1911-1937.

695 Pascal, John. The Jean Harlow Story. New York:
Popular Library, 1964.

696 Passek, J. -L. "Hommage. Mae West. Sex Transit
gloria mundi. " Cinéma (Paris) 181(November, 1973):
20-21.
Rapid survey of the career of Mae West.

697   "The Passing of Beulah: Will Hattie McDaniel's Death
       Mark the End of a Long Era of 'Kitchen Comedy'
       Roles for Negroes on Radio and Screen?" Our World
       8(February, 1953):12-15.

698   Patrichi, Gina. "A Convinge cu sufletul." Cinema
       (Bucharest) 10, 3(March, 1972):49.
            The Rumanian actress, Gina Patrichi, speaks of
       her film roles.

699   "Patricia Ellis." Films in Review 21, 6(June-July,
       1970):388-89.
            A filmography of leading lady of the 30's.

700   "Patricia Morison." Films in Review 19, 6(June-July,
       1968):391-92.
            A filmography and career sketch of the actress.

701   "Patricia Neal." Films in Review 15, 3(March, 1964):
       180.
            A filmography.

702   Payton, Barbara. I Am Not Ashamed. Los Angeles:
       Holloway House, 1963.
       Paperback.

703   "Peggy Dow." Films in Review 15, 8(October, 1964):
       517-18.
            A filmography of leading lady who before retiring
       to marry made a strong impression in several films of
       the early 50's.

704   Pérez, M. "Judy Garland." Positif (Paris) 144-45
       (November-December, 1972):54-66.
            Study of the career of Judy Garland.

705   Peterson, M. "At the Deli with Liza Minnelli." Inter/
       View 21(May, 1972):16-17.
            Liza Minnelli discusses her career, with emphasis
       on "Cabaret."

706   "Petula Clark." Films in Review 20, 10(December,
       1969):647.
            A filmography of the British child actress who
       later became a successful singer.

707   "Phyllis Kirk." Films in Review 15, 1(January, 1964):

61-62.
A filmography.

708 "Phyllis Thaxter. " Films in Review 14, 4(April, 1963):
254-55.

709 Pickard, R. "Celeste Holm. " Films in Review 24, 10
(December, 1973):633-35.
A filmography and letter. Information on Celeste
Holm's career as an actress.

710 Pickford, Mary. The Demi-Widow. Indianapolis: The
Bobbs-Merrill Co. , 1935.

711 _____ . ... My Rendezvous with Life. New York:
H. C. Kinsey and Co. , Inc. , 1935.
About her faith. 37 pp.

712 _____ . Sunshine and Shadow. Foreword by Cecil
B. de Mille. New York: Doubleday and Co. , 1955.
An autobiography--talks about many of her films.

713 _____ . Why Not Look Beyond. London: Methuen,
1936.
39 pp. On "Immortality. "

714 _____ . Why Not Try God? New York: H. C. Kinsey and Co. , 1934.
35 pp.

715 "Picture Personalities: Miss Florence E. Turner, the
Vitagraph Girl. " Moving Picture World 7(July 23,
1910):187-8.

716 Pile, S. , J. Moran and P. T. Close. "Getting Intimate
with Edy Williams. " Inter /View 34(July, 1973):16-
18.
An interview. Edy Williams talks about her career and the films of her husband, Russ Meyer.

717 Pinto, Alfonso. "Lilian Harvey. " Films in Review 21,
8(October, 1970):478-90.
A filmography and career of the British actress
who became a star of German films in the 30's.

718 Platt, Frank Cheney. Great Stars of Hollywood's Gold-
en Age. New York: New American Library, 1966.

Includes "Garbo, the Mystery of Hollywood," by
A. R. St. Johns; "Why Jean Harlow Died," by M.
Doherty; and "Carole Lombard," by A. R. St. Johns.

719   Postal, Bernard. "The Reward of Courage." Ameri-
      can Hebrew 129(September 11, 1931):330, 354.
      A biographical sketch of Sylvia Sidney.

720   Preston, Catherine Craig. "The Movies and I." Films
      in Review 8,7(August-September, 1957):334-37.
      Reminiscences about her and her husband, Robert
      Preston's, careers.

721   Puig, Manuel. Betrayed by Rita Hayworth. Translated
      by Suzanne Jill Levine. New York: Dutton, 1971.

722   Puzo, L. "Marie Wilson." Films in Review 24, 2
      (February, 1973):125.
      Letter and filmography.   Brief bio-filmographic
      information on Marie Wilson.

723   Quasimodo, Salvatore. Anita Ekberg. Milano: Lerici,
      1965.

724   Quirk, Lawrence J. "Bette Davis." Films in Review
      6,10(December, 1955):481-99.
      A filmography and career sketch of the actress.

725   _____. The Films of Ingrid Bergman. New York:
      The Citadel Press, 1970.

726   _____. The Films of Joan Crawford. New York:
      The Citadel Press, 1970.

727   _____. "Joan Crawford." Films in Review 7,10
      (December, 1956):481-501.
      A filmography and career sketch of the actress.

728   Raborn, G. "Lana Turner." Films in Review 23, 8
      (October, 1972):465-81.
      Bio-filmographic information on Lana Turner.

729   Remond, A. "Entretien-portrait: Monica Vitti, 'Je
      suis une créature d'Antonioni....'" Cinéma (Paris)
      181(November, 1973):12-14.
      An interview.   Monica Vitti discusses her career.

730   Reynolds, Debbie and Bob Thomas. If I Knew Then. New York: B. Geis Associates, 1962.

731   Rheinhardt, Emil A. The Life of Eleanora Duse. London: Martin Secker, 1920.

732   Rice, Susan. "Some Women's Films." Take One 3, 2 (February, 1972):30-31.
"T. R. Boskin" (Herbert Ross); "L'Opéra Mouffe" (Agnes Varda); "It Only Happens to Others" (Nadine Trintignant).

733   Richards, Dick. Ginger: Salute to a Star. Brighton, England: Clifton Books, 1969.
Ginger Rogers. (Not recommended--Rehrauer.)

734   Ringgold, Gene. "Ann Harding." Films in Review 23, 3(March, 1972):129-53.
Bio-filmographic information.

735   _____. "Audrey Hepburn." Films in Review 22, 10 (December, 1971):585-605.
A filmography and career sketch of the actress.

736   _____. "Barbara Stanwyck." Films in Review 14, 10(December, 1963):577-602.
A filmography and career sketch of the actress.

737   _____. "Constance Bennett." Films in Review 16, 8(October, 1965):472-95.
A filmography and career sketch of the stage and screen actress and film producer.

738   _____. The Films of Bette Davis. New York: Bonanza Books, 1966.
A filmography of Miss Davis' films with photos, synopses of plot and critical reviews.

739   _____. "Myrna Loy." Films in Review 14, 2(February, 1963):69-92.
A filmography and career sketch of the actress.

740   _____. "Rosalind Russell." Films in Review 21, 10 (December, 1970):585-610.
A filmography and career sketch of the actress.

741   Robinson, David. "The Players' Witness. Notes on

Some Early Acting Performances Preserved in the
National Film Archive. " Sight and Sound 29, 3(Summer, 1960):148-51. Illustrated.

742 _____. "20's Show People. " Sight and Sound 37, 4
(Autumn, 1968):198-202.
The 20's girls: Marion Davies, Gloria Swanson.

743 Robyns, Gwen. Light of a Star: the Career of Vivien
Leigh. New York: A. S. Barnes and Co. , 1970.

744 Rollins, Charlemae Hill. Famous Negro Entertainers
of Stage, Screen and Television. New York: Dodd,
Mead and Company, 1967.
Contains biographies of Lena Horne and Eartha
Kitt.

745 Roman, Robert. "Linda Darnell. " Films in Review
17, 8(October, 1966):473-86.
A career sketch of the actress.

746 _____. "Marilyn Monroe. " Films in Review 13, 8
(October, 1962):449-68.
A filmography and career sketch of the actress.

747 _____. "Marta Toren. " Films in Review 10, 7(August-September, 1959):445-46.
Career of the Swedish actress.

748 _____. "Thelma Ritter. " Films in Review 20, 9
(November, 1969):549-60.
A filmography and career sketch of the actress.

749 Ronan, M. "Silver Screen Blues; Lack of Good Roles
for Actresses. " Senior Scholastic 102(May 14, 1973):
30-1.

750 Roper, Michell. "Mannerisms--In the Grand Manner. "
Films and Filming 1, 12(September, 1955):7.
The career of Bette Davis.

751 _____. "They Called Her a Dresden Shepherdess. "
Films and Filming 1, 11(August, 1955):5.
The career of Vivien Leigh.

752 Rosemon, Ethel. "An Extra Girl's Part in World-War
Picture. " Motion Picture Classic 7(September, 1918):
39-42, 72.

753 Rosten, Norman. Marilyn: An Untold Story. New
          York: New American Library, 1973.
       Poet's tender homage to a lost friend, Marilyn
     Monroe.

754 Rosterman, Robert. "Judy Garland. " Films in Review
          13, 4(April, 1962):206-19.
       A filmography and career sketch of the actress.

755 Roth, Lillian. I'll Cry Tomorrow. New York: Frede-
          rick Fell, Inc. , Publishers, 1951.
       The autobiography of the child star, promising
     movie star and alcoholic.

756 Rutherford, Dame Margaret. Margaret Rutherford: An
          Autobiography. As told to Gwen Robyns. London:
          W. H. Allen, 1972.
       An autobiography as told to Gwen Robyns including
     a section on her film work from 1936-1953, and Holly-
     wood, and her academy award for "The VIP's" in 1963.

757 S. , J. B. "American Players in England. " Moving
          Picture World 21(July 18, 1914):441.

758 Samuels, Charles. Judy. New York, 1965.
       A biography of Judy Garland.

759 Sarris, Andrew. "Acting Aweigh! " Film Culture 38
          (Fall, 1965):47-61.
       What constitutes the best screen acting, ten best
     actresses/actors (1915-1928), five best annual perform-
     ances (1929-1946)--actresses, actors, supporting and
     character players.

760 _____ . "Garbo's Charisma. " Village Voice 9, 36
          (June 25, 1964):10.

761 _____ . "Ginger Rogers/Fred Astaire Musicals. "
          Village Voice 9, 29(May 7, 1964):17.

762 _____ . The Primal Screen. New York: Simon and
          Schuster, 1973.
       "Judy Garland" on p. 269 is mostly a review of
     Mel Torme's book The Other Side of the Rainbow.
     "The Musical: The Fred and Ginger Show, " p. 75, is
     mostly about the genre but also about Astaire/Rogers'
     musicals currently being played.

763 Sayler, Oliver M. <u>Revolt in the Arts.</u> New York:
     Brentano, 1930.
     On Ruth Chatterton.

764 Schoondergang, H. J. <u>B. B. lacht, Brigitte huilt.</u>
     (Series: "Humanitas-boijes, No. 41; Idolen en sym-
     bolen, 18. ") Tielt/Den Haag: 1962.

765 Scott, A. "Madeline Kahn, Boom Boom Girl. " <u>Inter/
     View</u> 39(December, 1973):12-13.
     Madeline Kahn talks about her acting career, es-
     pecially her roles in "Paper Moon, " "What's Up Doc, "
     and "Black Bart. "

766 "The Screen Answers Back. " <u>Films and Filming</u> 8, 8
     (May, 1962):11-18, 44-45.
     (See entry under "Critics. ")

767 Sears, Gwen. "Elsie Ferguson, America's Own Ac-
     tress. " <u>Theatre</u> 29(May, 1919):298, 302.

768 "Secret of a Movie Maid. " <u>Ebony</u> 5(November, 1949):
     52-56.
     On Lillian Moseley and Black women stereotyped
     to maid roles.

769 "Sharon Tate's Films. " <u>Films in Review</u> 20, 8(October,
     1969):516.

770 "She Said Yes to 'Dr. No. '" <u>Cinema</u> 1, 4(June-July,
     1963):21-25.
     About actress Ursula Andress' decision to play in
     first James Bond movie.

771 Shearer, Norma. "I'm Tame as a Lion. " <u>American
     Magazine</u> 20(July, 1935):58-9, 120-4.
     Autobiographical sketch.

772 Sheehan, Marion Turner, ed. <u>Spiritual Woman.</u> N. Y. :
     Harper, 1955.
     Includes articles on "Woman in Entertainment, "
     by L. Gish.

773 Sheldon, E. L. "Fabulous Fortunes Made by Beautiful
     Women in Moving Pictures. " <u>Delineator</u> 88(March,
     1916):5-6, 49.

774   Shields, Jonathan. "Gene Tierney." Films in Review
      22,9(November, 1971):541-554.

775   Shipman, David. "The All-Conquering Governess."
      Films and Filming 12, 11(August, 1966):16-20.
      A career sketch of actress Julie Andrews.

776   _____. "Doris Day." Films and Filming 8, 11(Aug-
      ust, 1962):14-16, 55.
      A career sketch.

777   _____. "What Ever Happened to Bette Davis?"
      Films and Filming 9, 7(April, 1963):8-9
      A career sketch of Bette Davis.

778   Shulman, Irving. Harlow: An Intimate Biography. New
      York: Bernard Geis Associates, 1964.
          Bibliographer Rehrauer calls book "defamation of
      character." Suggests you try The Films of Jean Harlow
      by Conway (see entry 294).

779   "Signe Hasso." Films in Review 18,9(November, 1967):
      589-91.
          A filmography and career sketch of the Swedish
      actress popular in America in the 40's.

780   Silver, Charles. Marlene Dietrich. New York: Pyra-
      mid Publications, 1974.

781   Strbu, E. "Gina Patrichi." Cinema (Bucharest) 10, 8
      (August, 1972):36-37.
          An interview. The Rumanian actress discusses
      the role and position of film actresses.

782   _____. "Ioana Bulca." Cinema (Bucharest) 10, 1
      (January, 1972):48-49.
          An interview, filmography, with Rumanian actress,
      Ioana Bulca.

783   _____. "Margareta Pogonat." Cinema (Bucharest)
      10, 6(June, 1972):8-9.
          An interview and filmography. Margareta Pogonat
      talks about her work as an actress in the theatre and
      the cinema.

784   Sirkin, E. "Film Favorites." Film Comment 7, 4
      (Winter, 1971-72):66-69.

Analysis of the film "Alice Adams" with emphasis
on the performance of Katherine Hepburn.

785   Sjolander, Ture. Garbo. New York: Harper and Row,
1971.

786   Slatzer, Robert F. The Life and Curious Death of Marilyn Monroe. New York: Two Continents Publishing
Group, Inc. , 1974.

787   Slide, Anthony. "The Colleen Bawn. " Vision (Spring,
1967).
On serial queens.

788   _____. The Griffith Actresses. South Brunswick:
N. J. : A. S. Barnes and Co. , 1973.
Talks of the actresses who worked with D. W.
Griffith: Blanche Sweet, Mary Pickford, Dorothy Gish,
Lillian Gish, Mae Marsh, Miriam Cooper, Clarine Sey-
mour, Carol Dempster, Betty Jewel, Riza Royce, Lupe
Velez.

789   _____. "The Kalem Serial Queens. " The Silent
Picture (Winter, 1968).
On actresses in Kalem serial productions.

790   Smith, Ella. Starring Miss Barbara Stanwyck. New
York: Crown Publishers, Inc. , 1974.

791   Smith, Helena Huntington. "Ugly Duckling. " New
Yorker 4(January 18, 1930):24-7.
Gloria Swanson.

792   Smith, Jack. "The Memoirs of Maria Montez. " Film
Culture 31(1963-64):3.

793   _____. "The Perfect Filmic Oppositeness of Maria
Montez. " Film Culture 27(1962-63):28.

794   Smith, Kate. Living in a Great Big Way. Blue Rib-
bon Books, 1938.
(See "On to Hollywood, " p. 119-33.)

795   "Society of the Spectacle. An Interview with Brigitte
Bardot. " Cineaste 4, 4(Spring, 1971):18, 35.
Why Brigitte Bardot joined the May, 1968 revolu-
tionary struggle.

796   Solovej, Elena. "Kuda iscezajut talanty?" <u>Iskusstvo</u>
        <u>Kino</u> (Moscow) 7(July, 1973):97-101.
        A young actress, Elena Solovej, describes the
        problems she has encountered in her career.

797   Sonbert, Warren. "Vivian." <u>Film Culture</u> 45(Summer,
        1967):33.
        Reminiscences about Vivian, underground film
        star who was the subject of Bruce Connor's film,
        "Vivian," and Andy Meyer's "Match Girl."

798   "Sophia Loren." <u>Films in Review</u> 13, 10(December,
        1962):633-36.
        A filmography.

799   "Sophia Loren: Earth Mother." <u>Cinema</u> 2, 1(February-
        March, 1964):20-25.
        A picture essay.

800   Spears, Jack. "Colleen Moore." <u>Films in Review</u> 14,
        7(August-September, 1963):403-24.
        A filmography and career sketch of the actress.

801   _____. "Mary Pickford's Directors." <u>Films in Re-
        view</u> 17, 2(February, 1966):71-95.

802   _____. "Norma Talmadge." <u>Films in Review</u> 17, 1
        (January, 1967):16.

803   Springer, John. "Beulah Bondi." <u>Films in Review</u> 14,
        5(May, 1963):282-91.
        A filmography and career sketch of the actress.

804   _____. The Fondas: the <u>Films and Careers of
        Henry, Jane and Peter Fonda.</u> New York: Citadel,
        1970.

805   _____. "Nancy Carroll." <u>Films in Review</u> 7, 4
        (April, 1956):157-63.
        A career sketch of the actress.

806   _____. "Sylvia Sidney." <u>Films in Review</u> 17, 1(Jan-
        uary, 1966):6-16.
        A filmography and career sketch.

807   _____, A. Bresson and M. Moran. "Jean Arthur,
        Great Star as Great Lady." <u>Inter/View</u> 22(June,

1972):22-24.
    Jean Arthur's reminiscences about some of her films.

808   Stainton, Walter. "Irene Castle." Films in Review 13, 6(June-July, 1962):347-55.
    A filmography and career of the dancing and dramatic star.

809   _____. "Pearl White in Ithaca." Films in Review 2, 5(May, 1951):19-25.
    Wharton studio in Ithaca, New York, where "Perils of Pauline" was filmed.

810   Stanbrook, Alan. "The Star They Couldn't Photograph." Films and Filming 9, 5(February, 1963):10-14.
    The career of Jeanne Moreau.

811   Stanke, Don. "Martha Hyer." Films in Review 22, 4 (April, 1971):196-210.
    A filmography and career of leading lady in many routine films of the 50's.

812   _____. "Rita Hayworth." Films in Review 23, 9 (November, 1972):527-51.
    Bio-filmographic information.

813   Steele, Joseph Henry. Ingrid Bergman, an Intimate Portrait. New York: D. McKay Co., 1959.

814   Steiger, Brad. Judy Garland. New York: Ace Publishing Corp., 1969.

815   Stein, Jeanne. "Aline MacMahon." Films in Review 16, 10(December, 1965):616-32.
    A filmography and career of the actress of the 30's.

816   _____. "Fay Bainter." Films in Review 16, 1(January, 1965):27-38.
    A filmography and career sketch of the actress.

817   Sternberg, Josef von. "Acting in Film and Theatre." Film Culture 1, 5-6(Winter, 1955):1-4, 27-29.
    Motion picture actors function not as artists but as stars. Refers to Marlene Dietrich.

818   Stevens, Ashton.   "Mabel Taliaferro Talks About Pic-
         tures. " Moving Picture World 10(December 23,
         1911):971-2.

819   Stuart, A.   "Assurance. " Films and Filming 19, 9(June,
         1973):28-29.
              A filmography.   An assessment of actress Linda
      Hayden's career.

820   Suchianu, D. I.   "Ingrid Bergman ... si dulcea ei ser-
         iozitate. " Cinema (Bucharest) 11, 4(April, 1973):44-
         45.
              Analysis of the roles played by Ingrid Bergman.

821   _____ .   "Katherine Hepburn: actrita completa. "
         Cinema (Bucharest) 11, 7(July, 1973):29-31.
              The career in films of actress Katherine Hepburn.

822   _____ .   "Mesageru romantismului actori. " Cinema
         (Bucharest) 11, 2(February, 1973):27-31, 34-38, 40-
         41, 43.
              Brief portraits of famous romantic actors and
      actresses.

823   _____ .   "Un personaj al epocii sale. " Cinema (Bu-
      charest) 11, 8(August, 1973):32-35.
              An account of the life and career of Marlene
      Dietrich.

824   "Sue Lyon: Modern American Gothic. " Cinema 2, 2
         (July, 1964):24-28.
              Picture essay.   ("Lolita. ")

825   Sullavan, Margaret.   "The Making of a Movie Star. "
         American Magazine 117(May, 1934):50-1, 112.

826   Summers, M.   "Butterfly McQueen Was One of 'The
         Women, ' Too. " Filmograph 3, 4(1973):7-8.

827   _____ .   "Rosalind Russell in 'The Women. '" Filmo-
         graph 3, 3(1973):44.

828   Summers, Murray.   "Mae Busch. " Films in Review
         7, 3(March, 1956):141-42.
              A career sketch of the actress.

829   "Susan St. James. " Cinema 4, 2(Summer, 1968):10-11.
              A picture essay.

830   Sweet, Blanche. "Keep Your Public Guessing. " Motion
         Picture Director (Hollywood, Calif.) 2(August, 1926):
         21-3.

831   Talmadge, (Mrs.) Margaret L. The Talmadge Sisters.
         Philadelphia: Lippincott, 1924.

832   Talmey, Allene. Doug and Mary and Others. New
         York: Macy-Masius, 1927.
              Includes Lillian Gish, Gilda Gray, Gloria Swanson.

833   Taylor, Elizabeth. Elizabeth Taylor: An Informal Me-
         moir. New York: Harper and Row, 1965.

834   Taylor, John Russell. "Swanson. " Sight and Sound 37,
         4(Autumn, 1968):201-02.
              On Gloria Swanson.

835   Temple, Shirley and editors of Look. My Young Life.
         Garden City, N. Y. : Garden City Publishing Co. ,
         1945.

836   "Thelma Todd. " Films in Review 21, 2(February, 1969):
         128.
              A filmography.

837   Thon, K. "Jane Fonda i Oslo. " Font (Oslo) 7, 1(1973):
         11-14.
              An interview. From Jane Fonda's press confer-
         ence in Oslo concerning the war in Viet Nam.

838   Thorpe, Edward. "Katie Could Do It. " Films and
         Filming 1, 9(June, 1955):5.
              Career notes on Katherine Hepburn.

839   "Tinker Bell, Mary Poppins, Cold Cash. " Newsweek
         66(July 12, 1965):74.
              Disney characters are popular and profitable.

840   Toppin, Edgar A. The Biographical History of Blacks
         in America Since 1528. New York: McKay, 1971.
              Based on a series of weekly articles in the Chris-
         tian Science Monitor, March 6-June 12, 1969. Includes
         Diahann Carroll and Ethel Waters.

841   Tormé, Mel. The Other Side of the Rainbow with Judy
         Garland on the Dawn Patrol. New York: William

Morrow and Co. , Inc. , 1970.

842   Tournês, A. "Laura Betti. " Jeune Cinéma (Paris) 71
      (June, 1973):29-32.
          An interview with the actress, Laura Betti, who
      talks about her work and her attitudes toward the cine-
      ma.

843   Tozzi, Romano. "Katherine Hepburn. " Films in Re-
      view 8, 10(December, 1957):481-502.
          A filmography and career notes.

844   _____. "Lillian Gish. " Films in Review 13, 10(Dec-
      ember, 1962):577-602.
          A filmography and career sketch of the actress.

845   _____. "Simone Signoret. " Films in Review 11, 5
      (May, 1960):310-12.
          Her career.

846   "The Tragic Mask of Bardolatry. " Cinema 1, 2(1963):
      27-29.
          Discusses the career of Brigitte Bardot.

847   Trebay, G. "Don Murray. " Inter /View 37(October,
      1973):20-21.
          An interview. Don Murray discusses his acting
      career, especially his relationship with Marilyn Monroe
      in "Bus Stop. "

848   Tully, Jim. "Anna Q. Nilsson. " Vanity Fair 27(Sep-
      tember, 1926):71, 118.

849   _____. "Greta Garbo. " Vanity Fair 30(June, 1928):
      66-67.

850   _____. "Pola Negri. " Vanity Fair 26(August, 1926):
      55, 92.

851   _____. "Zasu Pitts. " Vanity Fair 30(August, 1928):
      62, 88.

852   Tunney, Kieran. Tallulah--Darling of the Gods. New
      York: E. P. Dutton and Co. , Inc. , 1973.
          A biography. Tallulah appeared in 17 films.

853   Turton, T. P. "Mary Beth Hughes. " Films in Review

22, 8(October, 1971):485-97.
A filmography and career of the 40's second feature actress.

854   Tuska, Jon. Films of Mae West. Secaucus, N. J.:
      Citadel Press, 1973.

855   "The Two Faces of Shirley." Films and Filming 8, 5
      (February, 1962):11-12, 47.
      An interview with Shirley MacLaine. A discussion on films she's been in.

856   Tynan, Kenneth. "The Abundant Miss Bergman."
      Films and Filming 5, 3(December, 1958):9-10.
      On Ingrid Bergman.

857   _____. "Garbo." Sight and Sound 23, 4(April-June,
      1954):187-90.
      A career sketch of Garbo.

858   Uselton, Roi. "Barbara La Marr." Films in Review
      15, 6(June-July, 1964):352-62.
      A filmography and career sketch of the actress.

859   _____. "Death by Airplane." Films in Review 7, 5
      (May, 1956):210-14.
      Actors and actresses killed in plane crashes.

860   _____. "Death by Suicide." Films in Review 8, 4
      (April, 1957):156-66.
      Actors and actresses who committed suicide.

861   _____. "Renee Adorée." Films in Review 19, 6
      (June-July, 1968):345-57.
      A biography and filmography of the French actress who appeared in many American silent films and who was also a circus performer.

862   Vallance, T. "Liza Minnelli." Focus on Film 10(Summer, 1972):7.
      Bio-filmography.

863   "Veda Ann Borg." Films in Review 16, 3(March, 1965):
      188-90.
      A filmography of the American character actress who played the archetypal hard-boiled blond in a hundred second features.

864 Vermilye, Jerry. Bette Davis. New York: Pyramid
     Publications, 1973.

865 _____. "Jean Arthur. " Films in Review 17, 6(June-
     July, 1966):329-46.
        The career and filmography of the actress.

866 Vincent, Mal. "Ava Gardner. " Films in Review 16, 6
     June-July, 1965):343-57.
        A filmography and career sketch.

867 Vinson, James, ed. Contemporary Dramatist. New
     York: St. Martin's, 1973.
        A bibliography on Elaine May, actress and direc-
     tor, given on pp. 519-20.

868 Viotti, Sergio. "Britain's Hepburn. " Films and Film-
     ing 1, 2(November, 1954):7.
        A career sketch of Audrey Hepburn.

869 "Virginia Gilmore. " Films in Review 22, 1(January,
     1971):48-49.
        A filmography and career of the leading lady of
     the 40's who appeared in many routine films.

870 Viva. Superstar. New York: Putnam, 1970.
        A novel by the screen actress.

871 Voluntaru, Maria. "Mi-am facut datoria. " Cinema
     (Bucharest) 11, 8(August, 1973):48-49.
        Rumanian actress, Maria Voluntaru, describes
     her attitudes to her work.

872 Wagenknecht, Edward Charles. Lillian Gish, An Inter-
     pretation. Seattle: University of Washington Book
     Store, 1972.

873 _____. Seven Daughters of the Theatre. Norman:
     University of Oklahoma Press, 1964.
        Marilyn Monroe is mentioned.

874 _____, ed. Marilyn Monroe: A Composite View.
     Philadelphia: Chilton Book Co. , 1969.
        A biography of Marilyn Monroe in three parts:
     1) Interviews with Marilyn Monroe, 2) Memories of
     Marilyn Monroe, 3) Reflections on Marilyn Monroe.
     All by different authors.

875   Walker, Alexander. Stardom: the Hollywood Phenomen-
        on. New York: Stein and Day, 1970.
            A history of the development of the stars. Atten-
        tion is given to Gish, Garbo, Negri, Davis and Craw-
        ford.

876   Ward, M. "Pat Loud. " Film Comment 9, 6(November-
        December, 1973):21-23.
            (See entry under "Images. ")

877   Warhol, A. and J. Kobal. "Gloria! Miss Swanson in
        excelsis. " Inter/View 25(September, 1972):23-29.
            An interview. Gloria Swanson talks about her ca-
        reer.

878   _____ and R. Colaciello. "Sylvia Miles in Holly-
        wood. " Inter/View 27(November, 1972):16-17.
            Sylvia Miles talks about her part in "Heat. "

879   "Waste. " Films in Review 13, 2(February, 1962):125-
        26.
            A filmography of Viveca Lindfors and Betty Gar-
        rett.

880   Waterbury, Ruth. Elizabeth Taylor. New York: Apple-
        ton Century, 1964.
            A biography.

881   Waters, Ethel. To Me It's Wonderful. New York:
        Harper, 1972.
            An autobiography.

882   Weintraub, Joseph, ed. The Wit and Wisdom of Mae
        West. New York: G. P. Putnam's Sons, 1967.

883   "Wells-Bishop. " Films in Review 21, 8(October, 1970):
        516.
            A filmography of the American leading lady of rou-
        tine films who used Julie Bishop and Jacqueline Wells
        as her screen names.

884   Weltman, Manuel and Raymond Lee. Pearl White, the
        Peerless Fearless Girl. New York: A. S. Barnes
        and Co. , 1969.

885   West, Mae. Goodness Had Nothing to Do with It. 2nd
        ed. New York: Macfadden-Bartell, 1970.

886 "What Is a Star?" Films and Filming 11, 12(September,
     1965):5-7.
          An interview with Bette Davis. Her acting pref-
     erences.

887 White, Pearl. Just Me. New York: George H. Dor-
     an, 1919.

888 Whitehall, Richard. "Anna Magnani. " Films and
     Filming 7, 10(July, 1961):15-17.
          Her films and career.

889 _____. "The Blue Angel. " Films and Filming 9, 1
     (October, 1962):19-23.
          The career of Marlene Dietrich.

890 _____. "D. D. " Films and Filming 9, 4(January,
     1963):21-22.
          Diana Dors as a sex symbol.

891 _____. "Danielle Darrieux. " Films and Filming 8,
     3(December, 1961):12-13, 43, 45.
          A filmography and career sketch of French ac-
     tress.

892 _____. "The Face of the Vampire. " Cinema (Los
     Angeles) 3, 3(July, 1966):11-15.
          On "vamps, " emphasizing Pola Negri.

893 _____. "The Flapper. " Cinema (Los Angeles) 3, 4
     (December, 1966):18-22.
          On Colleen Moore, Clara Bow and others.

894 _____. "Greta Garbo. " Films and Filming 9, 12
     (September, 1963):42-48.

895 Wikarska, Carol. "An Interview with Tra Giang at the
     Moscow Film Festival. " Women and Film 1, 5-6
     (1974):45.
          An interview with the Vietnamese actress.

896 Wild, Roland. Greta Garbo. (Popular Lives Series.)
     London: Rich and Cowan, 1933.

897 Wilson, Benjamin. "Brief Biographies of Popular Play-
     ers: Flora Finch. " Motion Picture Magazine 9
     (April, 1915):112.

898   Windeler, Robert. Julie Andrews: A Biography. New
       York: G. P. Putnam's Sons, 1970.

899   _____. Sweetheart: the Story of Mary Pickford.
       London and New York: W. H. Allen, 1973.
             No one else has written a biography on her. Mary
       Pickford wrote three books: Sunshine and Shadow, My
       Rendezvous with Life, and Why Not Try God? Now a
       recluse, she took to bed in 1965. She was the first
       movie star, "America's Sweetheart." Her fortune of
       $50,000,000 represents the single largest amount of
       money amassed by a woman by virtue of her own labors.
       She was in 200 silent films and four talkies before re-
       tiring in 1932 at her peak because fans couldn't accept
       her without curls and talking in a high-pitched voice.
       As an actress she was under-rated in her day, and as
       an actress and comedienne she is still under-rated.

900   Winge, John. "Asta Nielsen." Sight and Sound 19, 2
       (April, 1950):58-59.
             In appreciation to Danish actress.

901   "Women Capture Screen Honors for 1933." Literary
       Digest 116(November 4, 1933):42.

902   Wood, Peggy. Actors--and People: Both Sides of the
       Footlights. N.Y. & London: Appleton, 1930.

903   _____. How Young You Look: Memoirs of a Mid-
       dle-sized Actress. New York & Toronto: Farrar
       and Rinehart, Inc., 1941.

904   Woodbury, Joan. "Show Biz." Take One 2, 11(May-
       June, 1970):32-34.
             Pay for extras. Refers to her own experiences.

905   Wright, Jacqueline. The Life and Loves of Lana Tur-
       ner. New York: Wisdom House, 1961.

906   Young, Christopher. "Judith Anderson." Films in Re-
       view 21,4(April, 1970):193-96.
             A filmography and career synopsis of the actress.

907   _____. "June Allyson." Films in Review 19,9(Nov-
       ember, 1968):537-47.
             A filmography and career of "cute" Hollywood
       leading lady.

908   Young, Clara Kimball. "Clara Kimball Young Discus-
        ses Reelism Versus Realism. " Theatre 27(February,
        1918):125.

909   Young, Loretta. The Things I Had to Learn. Indiana-
        polis: Bobbs-Merrill, 1961.

910   Yurman, C. "Mae West Talks About the Gay Boys. "
        Gay 24(July 20, 1970):3.

911   Yvonne. "The Importance of Cicely Tyson. " Ms 3, 2
        (August, 1974):45.
            (See entry under "Images. ")

912   Zarov, M. "Ja voshiscalsja ee talantom. " Iskusstvo
        Kino (Moscow) 9(September, 1973):130-31.
            Obituary of Alla Tarasova.

913   "Zasu Pitts. " Films in Review 14, 7(August-September,
        1963):441-42.
            A filmography.

914   Zetterling, Mai. "Some Notes on Acting. " Sight and
        Sound 21, 2(November-December, 1951):83, 96.
            The Swedish actress gives her views on overcom-
        ing breaks in continuity. (She began directing films in
        1960.)

915   Zierold, Norman. Garbo. New York: Popular Libra-
        ry, 1969.

916   Zolotow, Maurice. Marilyn Monroe. New York: Har-
        court, Brace and Co. , 1960.

917   _____ . Stagestruck: the Romance of Alfred Lunt
        and Lynn Fontanne. London: Heinemann, 1965.
            The stage actress and actor who appeared in a
        few films.

918   Zukor, Adolph. The Public Is Never Wrong. New
        York: G. P. Putnam's Sons, 1953.

Chapter 2

WOMEN FILM-MAKERS

A. Reference and Historical Works

919 Aaronson, Charles S., ed. International Motion Picture
     Almanac, N.Y.: Quigley Publishing Co., 1929.

920 Academy of Motion Picture Arts and Sciences and Writ-
     ers Guild of America, West. Who Wrote the Movie
     and What Else Did He Write? (1936-69). Los An-
     geles: The Academy, 1970.
          If you browse through the whole book, you can
     find what she wrote. 2000 writers are alphabetically
     listed with credits. Includes a film index and an awards
     index.

921 Alicoate, Charles A., ed. The Film Daily Yearbook,
     1929-1968. New York: Film Daily, Inc.

922 Annuario del Cinema Italiano, 1966-1967. Rome: Fer-
     rau, Conedizioni.

923 Balshofer, Fred and Arthur C. Miller. One Reel a
     Week. Berkeley and Los Angeles: University of
     California Press, 1967.
          (See entry under "Actresses.")

924 Barsom, Richard Meron. Nonfiction Film. New York:
     Dutton, 1973.
          A critical history of documentary film. Among
     the women mentioned are: Leni Riefenstahl, Charlotte
     Zwerin, Frances Flaherty, Mary Fields, Ruby Grier-
     son.

925 Baxter, John. Hollywood in the Sixties. New York:
     A. S. Barnes and Co., 1972.

926   _____ . Hollywood in the Thirties. New York: A.
           S. Barnes and Co. , 1968.

927   Bibliography of Articles on Women and Film. British
           Film Institute, 81 Dean Street, London W1, England.
           Includes, also, a set of essays on the image of
       women in film.

928   Billings, Pat and Allen Eyles. Hollywood Today. New
           York: A. S. Barnes and Co. , 1971.

929   Blum, Daniel. Daniel Blum's Screen World. 1949-66,
           Vol. 1-17.
           Lists films released each year with stills and
       credits.

930   _____ . A Pictorial History of the Silent Screen.
           New York: Putnam, 1953.

931   Boussinot, Roger, ed. L'Encyclopédie du cinéma.
           Paris: Bordas, 1967.
           A history of French cinema.

932   Brownlow, Kevin. The Parade's Gone By. New York:
           Knopf, 1968.

933   Burton, Jack. The Blue Book of Hollywood Musicals.
           Watkins Glen, N. Y. : Century House, 1953.
           Year-by-year account of Hollywood musicals,
       1927-1952. Lists songs and singers. Indexed by mo-
       vie, so have to scan whole book to find women's cred-
       its.

934   Dawson, Bonnie and Cynthia Montilla. Women and
           Film. Albany, N. Y. : State Department of Educa-
           tion, 1973.

935   Dickinson, Thorold and Catherine de la Roche, eds.
           Soviet Cinema. London: Falcon Press, 1948.

936   Enser, A. G. S. Filmed Books and Plays: A List of
           Books and Plays from Which Films Have Been Made,
           1928-1967. London: Deutsch, 1968.
           Author and title index. Again, to glean out those
       books or plays written by women that have been filmed,
       it is necessary to go through the whole author index,
       but the browsing is interesting for there are many fe-

male entries. Includes a film bibliography. Some wo-
men mentioned are: Clare Booth, Pearl Buck, Taylor
Caldwell, Harper Lee, Agatha Christie, Rona Jaffe,
Lillian Hellman, Katherine Anne Porter.

937   Fielding, Raymond. A Technological History of Motion
         Pictures and Television. Berkeley: University of
         California Press, 1967.
              An anthology; articles from 1920-1963 from Jour-
         nal of the Society of Motion Picture and Television En-
         gineers.

938   Ford, Charles. Femmes cinéastes, ou Le Triomphe
         de la Volunté. Paris: Denöel/Gonthier, 1972.

939   Fordin, Hugh. The World of Entertainment. Garden
         City, N.Y.: Doubleday and Co., Inc., 1975.
              Description and discussion of Hollywood's greatest
         musicals and musical stars.

940   Gedlud, Carolyn. "Defining Women's Films." Univer-
         sity of California Extension Media Center Supplement
         42, 21(September 16, 1974):16-20.

941   Gow, Gordon. Hollywood in the Fifties. New York:
         A. S. Barnes and Co., 1971.

942   Graham, Peter John. A Dictionary of the Cinema.
         London: Zwemmer and New York: A. S. Barnes
         and Co., 1968.

943   Griffith, Linda (Arvidson) (Mrs. D. W.). When Movies
         Were Young. New York: Dover Publications, 1969.
         (See entry under "Actresses.")

944   Griffith, Richard. The Talkies. New York: Dover
         Publications, 1971.
         (See entry under "Actresses.")

945   Halliwell, Leslie. The Filmgoer's Companion. New
         York: Hill and Wang, 1974.
              A collection of facts about films and people who
         make them; in dictionary format.

946   Hardy, Forsyth. Scandinavian Film. London: Falcon
         Press, 1952.

947   Hibben, Nina.   Eastern Europe.   New York: A. S.
       Barnes and Co., 1969.
       A history of Eastern European cinema.

948   Higham, Charles.   The Art of the American Film,
       1900-1971.   New York: Doubleday, 1974.
       A history arranged as a series of directorial bio-
       graphies.

949   _____ and Joel Greenberg.   Hollywood in the Forties.
       New York: A. S. Barnes and Co., 1968.

950   Humphrey, Eleanore.   "The Creative Woman in Motion
       Picture Production. "   Unpublished Master's thesis.
       Los Angeles: University of Southern California, Au-
       gust, 1970.

951   International Motion Picture Almanac, 1933-1972.   New
       York: Quigley Publications.

952   Jacobs, Lewis.   The Documentary Tradition.   New
       York: Hopkinson and Blake, 1971.

953   _____.   The Emergence of Film Art.   New York:
       Hopkinson and Blake, 1969.

954   _____.   The Rise of American Film.   New York:
       Teachers College Press, 1969.

955   Kanin, Garson.   Hollywood: Stars and Starlets, Ty-
       coons and Flesh-Peddlers, Moviemakers and Money-
       makers, Frauds and Geniuses, Hopefuls and Has-
       Beens, Great Lovers and Sex Symbols.   New York:
       Viking Press, Inc., 1974.

956   Kleinhans, Chuck.   "Seeing Through Cinema Verité. "
       Jump Cut.   2(July-August, 1974):14.
       (See listing under "Images. ")

957   Knight, Arthur.   The Liveliest Art.   New York and
       Toronto: The New American Library, 1957.

958   Limbacher, James L.   Film Music: From Violins to
       Video.   Metuchen, N. J.:   Scarecrow Press, 1974.
       Part I--52 articles by experts--composers, schol-
       ars, critics.   Part II--all films by title with name of
       composer and year of release.   Cross-indexed list of
       composers' names and their films.

959 "List of Consciousness Raising Films," in Sisterhood
     Is Powerful. Edited by Robin Morgan. New York:
     Vintage Books, 1970, p. 582+.

960 Lyons, Timothy J. The Silent Partner: The History
     of the American Film Manufacturing Co., 1910-1921.
     New York: Arno Press, 1974.

961 McCarthy, Todd and Charles Flynn. Kings of the B's.
     New York: E. P. Dutton and Co., Inc., 1975.
         An anthology of film history and criticism of B-
     movies. Lesser-known directors and their B (and C-
     Z) rated films discussed. Filmographies of 325 direc-
     tors including: Dorothy Arzner, Ida Lupino, Stephanie
     Rothman. Article by Linda May Strown, film writer
     for many magazines and associate producer of Academy
     Award documentary, "Hillstrom Chronicle." Article
     on "The Phantom Lady in 'film noir.'"

962 McCarty, Clifford, ed. Film Composers in America: A
     Checklist of their Work. Hollywood: Oxford Press,
     1953.
         Lists 165 composers alphabetically, and their film
     compositions in chronological fashion from latest to ear-
     liest. (Only 400 copies printed, but highly recommended
     by Rehrauer.) Film music has plural authorship of many
     scores. Almost half the picture composers are "un-
     known" or "anonymous." Limited.

963 _____. Published Screenplays: A Checklist. Kent
     State University Press, 1971.
         Screenplays are listed alphabetically and screen-
     writers credited. If one knows the name of the screen-
     writer, can look up her work. There is an index in
     the back by name, so one can find all published screen-
     plays of an individual screenwriter.

964 Manvell, Roger and Heinrich Fraenkel. The German
     Cinema. New York: Praeger Publishers, 1971.
         The authors' historic account of German film in-
     cluding a discussion of the Nazi's use of Leni Riefen-
     stahl's "Triumph of the Will" as propaganda.

965 Mekas, Jonas. Movie Journal: The Rise of a New
     American Cinema, 1959-1971. New York: Collier
     Books, 1972.

A history of avant-garde film in U. S. Mostly
from his writings for the Village Voice.

966   Michael, Paul. The Academy Awards: A Pictorial
      History. New York: Crown Publishers, 1968.

967   _____. The American Movies Reference Book: the
      Sound Era. Englewood Cliffs, N. J. : Prentice-Hall,
      1969.
         Six sections: History, Players, Films (including
      credits), Directors, Producers, the Academy Awards.
      Individual names listed under each section.

968   The New York Times Film Reviews 1913-1968 and In-
      dex. 6 vols. New York: New York Times and Ar-
      no Press, 1970.

969   Noble, Peter, ed. The British Film and Television
      Yearbook, 1947-1968. London: British Yearbook.

970   Parish, James Robert and Michael R. Pitts. Film Di-
      rectors: A Guide to Their American Films. Me-
      tuchen, N. J. : The Scarecrow Press, Inc. , 1974.
         Alphabetical listing of directors and a listing of
      their films. Includes: Dorothy Arzner, Lois Weber,
      Ida Lupino, Frances Marion, Alice Guy-Blaché, Ida
      May Park.

971   Passek, J. -L, et al. "Dictionnaire des réalisateurs
      années 60. " Cinéma (Paris) 178-179(July-August,
      1973):48-118.
         Dictionary of filmographic details on American
      directors from 1960 to the present.

972   _____. Dictionnaire des réalisateurs des républiques
      d'U. R. S. S. " Cinéma (Paris) Part I, 176(May, 1973):
      90-103; Part II, 177(June, 1973):96-105.
         A filmographic dictionary of directors of the re-
      publics of the USSR.

973   Perilli, Patricia. Film Music Index. Hamden, Conn. :
      Shoe String Press, Inc. , 1974.

974   Pickard, R. A. E. Dictionary of 1000 Best Films.
      New York: Association Press, 1971.
         1000 films produced in U. S. and abroad since
      1903, listed by title; described briefly. Production

credits and leading players are given. Selective but
useful since it credits photography, art direction, music
and editing. It has no index, however.

975 Pickard, Roy. A Companion to the Movies. New York:
     Hippocrene Books, Inc. , 1972.
     (See entry under "Actresses. ")

976 Ramsey, Terry. A Million and One Nights. New York:
     Simon and Schuster, 1926. 2 vols.
     (See entry under "Actresses. ")

977 Renan, Sheldon. An Introduction to the American Un-
     derground Film. New York: E. P. Dutton and Co. ,
     1967.

978 Robinson, David. Hollywood in the Twenties. New
     York: A. S. Barnes and Co.
     Paragraphs on Frances Marion, Dorothy Arzner,
     Lillian Gish. (See entry under "Actresses. ")

979 Rosenberg, Bernard and Harry Silverstein, eds. The
     Real Tinsel. New York: The Macmillan Co. , 1970.
     (See entry under "Actresses. ")

980 Rosten, Leo C. Hollywood: the Movie Colony, the
     Movie Makers. New York: Harcourt, Brace, 1941.

981 Rotha, Paul and Richard Griffith. The Film Till Now:
     A Survey of World Cinema. 4th rev. ed. London:
     Spring Books, 1967.
     A fine history--scattered throughout are refer-
     ences to women.

982 Sadoul, Georges. The Cinema in Arab Countries.
     Beirut-London: Interarab Centre of Cinema and
     Television, 1966.

983 _____. Dictionary of Film Makers. Translated and
     edited by Peter Morris. Berkeley: University of
     California Press, 1972.
     Includes: organizers, directors, script writers,
     cinematographers, art directors, composers, producers,
     inventors. But does not include: actors, actresses,
     technicians, editors, sound engineers, camera opera-
     tors. If one has a specific name in mind, this will
     give a brief summary of her career. To look for wo-

men, one must browse through the whole book of 1,300 entries.

984   . Dictionary of Films. Berkeley: University of California Press, 1972.
An alphabetical listing of 1,200 films from various countries. Gives film credits including dates, director, screenwriter, assistant director, photographer, art director, editors, cast, producer. Must scan for females.

985   . The French Film. London: The Falcon Press, 1953.
A history of French cinema.

986   . Histoire générale du cinéma. Paris: Editions Denoel, 1946-. Vol. I.
A history of World Cinema. A comprehensive, scholarly and detailed history of the art of film.

987 Schickel, Richard. Movies; the History of an Art and an Institution. New York: Basic Books, 1964.
A bibliography.

988 Schuster, Mel. Motion Picture Directors: A Bibliography of Magazine and Periodical Articles, 1900-1972. Metuchen, N.J.: The Scarecrow Press, Inc., 1973.
Good reference especially for earlier women directors. Includes fan magazine as well as film journal articles.

989 Scott, Evelyn F. Hollywood: When Silents Were Golden. New York: McGraw Hill, 1972.
(See entry under "Actresses.")

990 Sennett, Ted. Lunatics and Lovers. New Rochelle, N.Y.: Arlington House, 1973.
Comedies. Chapter 2, "The Cinderella Syndrome"; Chapter 3, the relationships between "Wife, Husband, Friend, Secretary"; Chapter 4, "Poor Little Rich Girl"; Chapter 8, "Boss-Ladies and Other Liberated Types." Includes appendices on the players, directors and writers of these comedies. Many women actresses, no women directors, some screenwriters including Frances Goodrich, Gladys Lehman, Katheryn Scala, Lynn Starling, Virginia Van Upp. Includes a filmography of all films discussed in the book.

991   Slide, Anthony. Early American Cinema. (Internation-
      al Film Guide Series.) New York: A. S. Barnes
      and Co.; London: A. Zwemmer, Ltd., 1970.
      (See entry under "Actresses.")

992   Smith, Sharon. Women Who Make Movies. New York:
      Hopkinson and Blake, 1975.
           An excellent source for identifying women film-
      makers. Smith divides her book into three parts. The
      first gives an overview which traces the history of wo-
      men in cinema and groups them according to country.
      Part two identifies those new women film-makers who
      are making films outside of Hollywood. Part three is
      a directory which lists women film-makers throughout
      the U. S. Women film-makers identified in this book
      include producers, directors, writers, editors and even
      cinematographers. An invaluable resource. Discussion
      of their films. Interviews with Shirley Clarke, Barbara
      Loden, Faith Hubley.

993   Thomas, Lawrence. The MGM Years. New York:
      Columbia House; distributed by Arlington House, 1972.

994   Verdone, Mario. La Moda e il costume nil film: an-
      tologia. Rome: Bianco e Nero, 1950.

995   Wagner, Robert W., editor. "Special Issue: Women
      in Film." Journal of the University Film Associa-
      tion 26, 1-2(1974). Department of Photography and
      Cinema, 156 W. 19th Ave., Ohio State University,
      Columbus, Ohio 43210 $2.

996   Warren, Madeline. The Women Who Wrote the Movies.
      New York: Bobbs-Merrill, 1975 (expected publish-
      ing date).
           On women screenwriters.

997   Weaver, John T. Forty Years of Screen Credits, 1929-
      1969. Metuchen, N. J.: Scarecrow Press, 1970.
      2 vols.
      (See entry under "Actresses.")

998   _____. Twenty Years of Silents, 1908-1928. Me-
      tuchen, N. J.: Scarecrow Press, 1971.
      (See entry under "Actresses.")

999   Wheeler, Helen. Womanhood Media: Current Resources

About Women. Metuchen, N. J. : Scarecrow Press,
1972.
Contains a section on film resources.

1000 "Women in Film. " Film Quarterly 5, 1(Winter, 1971-
72) 65 pp. Special Issue.
Includes critical reviews and a list of films dealing with the subject of modern women.

1001 Women in Film: A Bibliography. Women in the Arts,
Albany Area NOW, Box 6064, Albany, N. Y. , 11568.
Lists a variety of films by and about women.

1002 "Women's Studies Films and Video Tape, " in Women:
A Select Bibliography. University of Michigan:
University Library, 1975.
This bibliography includes a list of all Women's
Studies films and video tapes available at the Audio-
Visual Center of the University of Michigan. Copies
of bibliography are available from: Library Extension
Service, 2360 Bonisteel Blvd. , University of Michigan,
Ann Arbor, Michigan 48105.

B. Catalogues

1003 Ahlum, Carol and Jacqueline M. Fralley, eds. Feminist Resources for Schools and Colleges: A Guide
to Curriculum Materials. The Feminist Press,
Box 334, Old Westbury, N. Y. 11568.
A 16-page annotated bibliography of books, pam-
phlets, slide shows, films and tapes.

1004 _____ . "Feminist Resources for Schools and Colleges: A Guide to Curricular Materials. "
A booklet listing feminist materials available
from: The Clearing House on Women's Studies, The
Feminist Press, SUNY/College at Old Westbury, Box
334, Old Westbury, N. Y. 11568.

1005 The American Film Institute Catalogue Feature Films
1921-1930. New York and London: R. R. Bowker,
1971.

1006 Art and Cinema. Visual Resources, Inc. , One Lin-
coln Plaza, New York, N. Y. 10023.

Triennial Publication lists visual resources,
$35/year.

1007   Artel, Linda, J. and Kathleen Weaver.   Film Pro-
       grammers' Guide to 16mm Rentals.   1972.   Reel
       Research, P.O. Box 6037, Albany, Ca.   94706.

1008   Bartlett, Freude.   Serious Business Catalog.   1609
       Jaynes St., Berkeley, Ca.   94703.   1974.
       Free catalog lists films distributed by Serious
       Business.

1009   Bowser, Eileen, ed.   Film Notes.   New York: Muse-
       um of Modern Art, 1969.
       "Chronological Annotated List of American Fic-
       tion Films Produced Between 1894-1950, Presently
       Distributed to Colleges and Universities by the Dept.
       of Film of New York, Museum of Modern Art." Notes
       for each film and indexes to film-makers and film
       titles.

1010   Canyon Cinema Catalog.   Industrial Center Bldg.,
       Room 220, Sausalito, Ca.   94965.
       Free catalog lists films available for distribution.

1011   Cinema Femina, 250 West 57th Street, New York, New
       York   10019.
       A referral service for film-makers and individuals
       who wish to program women's films.

1012   Dawson, Bonnie, ed.   Women's Films in Print.   San
       Francisco: Booklegger Press, 1975.
       An annotated guide to 800 films by women.   Only
       16mm films available for rent are listed.   Some 370
       film-makers and their works are included.   An excel-
       lent resource.

1013   Film-makers Cooperative Catalog.   175 Lexington
       Ave., New York, N.Y.   10016.
       Catalog lists films for distribution. $2 donation.

1014   Films by Women.   Canadian Film-makers' Distribu-
       tion Centre, 406 Jarvis St., Toronto, Ontario M4Y
       2G6.
       Free fifteen-page booklet lists films available
       for distribution by Canadian women film-makers.

1015   Freude. "Films by Women: A Suggested Program. "
        Canyon Cinema News 4/5(September/October, 1973):
        14.
             Filmographies.

1016   Grimstad, Kirsten and Susan Rennie. The New Wo-
        man's Survival Catalog. New York: Coward, Mc-
        Cann and Geoghegan; Berkeley Publishing Co.,
        1975.
             Included in the catalog is a section on "Women
        and Film. " Discusses New Day Films, a women's
        films distributor. Also lists some outstanding recent
        films by women with description and information on
        where they can be rented or bought. List includes:
        Amalie R. Rothschild, Liane Brandon, Joyce Chopra,
        Claudia Weill, Julia Reichert and James Klein, Jill
        Foreman Hultin, Faith and John Rubley, Jan Oxenberg,
        Harriet Kriegel, Jean Shaw, Judith Shaw Acuna, Marie
        Celine Canfield, Suzanne Armstrong, Jane Warren
        Brand, Barbara Brown, Nancy Greiner, Lorraine Mc-
        Connel, Ann Weiner, Helen Zaglen, Ariel Dougherty,
        Sheila Page, Louise Alaimo, Judy Smith, Ellen Sor-
        rin.

1017   Mendenhall, Janice. Films on the Women's Move-
        ment. Federal Women's Program Coordinator,
        General Services Admin. , Washington, D. C.
        20405.
             An annotated list of about 90 films, mostly
        shorts.

1018   Motion Pictures: Catalogue of Copyright Entries.
        1942-1969. Copyright Office: The Library of Con-
        gress.

1019   Museum of Modern Art Film Rental Catalog.   11 West
        53rd St. , New York, N. Y.   10019.
             Free catalog of films available for rental

1020   New Day Films Catalogue. P. O. Box 315, Franklin
        Lakes, N. J.   07417.
             Lists films available through this cooperative
        distributor.

1021   Newsreel Catalogue.   322 Seventh Ave. , New York,
        N. Y.   10001, or Antioch Union, Yellow Springs,
        Ohio.

Has available a number of films concerning women's movement.

1022   Whole Film Catalogue, Films, Inc.   1144 Wilmette, Wilmette, Ill.
          Includes number of films by and about women.

1023   Women and Film: A Resource Handbook.   The Project on the Status and Education of Women, Assoc. of American Colleges, 1818 R Street, N.W., Washington, D.C.   20009.
          Booklet tells how to plan a film festival, lists feature films pertinent to women's roles, complete listing of films, with descriptions and distributors, from the First New York Women's Film Festival.

1024   Women and Film--La Femme et la Film, 1896-1973. International Festival Program.   4 Maitland St. Toronto, Ontario, M4Y 1C5, Canada.
          An access catalog which lists distributors and films.

1025   Women Make Movies, Inc. Catalogue.   257 W. 19th St., New York, N.Y.   10011.
          Distributor's catalogue.

1026   Women Make Movies Poster-Catalog.   107 West 26th St., New York, N.Y.   10001.
          Free catalog.

1027   The Women's Film Co-Op Catalogue.   200 Main Street, Northhampton, Mass.   01060.
          Lists films by and about women which they and other companies distribute.

1028   Women's Films--A Critical Guide.   Bloomington, Ind.: Indiana University Audio-Visual Center, 1975.
          Reference guide to recent women's films.   Useful for women's studies.   Listing of films available for rental or purchase from University of Indiana and elsewhere.   Film notes by Carolyn Geduld.   Not comprehensive.

1029   Women's History Research Center, Inc.   Films by and/or About Women.   Berkeley: Women's History Research Center, Inc., 1972.

Subtitled: Directory of Film-makers, Films and Distributors. Internationally, Past and Present. Also lists magazines and organizations for women. 72 pp.

C. Specific Works

1030 "ACE Honors Members. " American Cinemeditor 23, 4 (Winter, 1973-74):14.
        Editor Rita Roland is honored. Brief biography and filmography included.

1031 "Agnes Varda. " Current Biography Yearbook 1970. (1971):424-6.
        A portrait of the director.

1032 "Agnes Varda, Biography. " Current Biography 31 (July, 1970):40-3.
        A portrait of the French motion picture director and screenwriter.

1033 Albert, Dora. "Writing for the Motion Picture Magazines. " Writer 51(July, 1938):211-15.

1034 Albertson, Lillian. Motion Picture Acting. New York: Funk and Wagnalls, 1947.
        Dramatics coach at Paramount and RKO Studios in the 30's and 40's--a text for acting. This actress, director and dramatics coach doesn't glamorize the work. Gives direct, simple, basic tips.

1035 Alden, Mary. "The Woman Making Up for the Screen. " Opportunities in the Motion Picture Industry. Los Angeles: Photoplay Research Society, 1922.
        (See entry under "Actresses. ")

1036 Alward, Jennifer. "Memoirs of a Censor. " Take One 4, 10(March-April, 1974):14.
        (See listing under "Critics. ")

1037 Amiel, M. "Nadine Trintignant. " Cinéma (Paris) 162(January, 1972):48-52.
        An interview and filmography. The directress, Nadine Trintignant, discusses her profession and her position as a woman.

1038   _____. "Nelly Kaplan." Cinéma (Paris) 162(January, 1972):53-58.
The director discusses her profession and her position as a woman.

1039   _____. "Nina Companeez." Cinéma (Paris) 162 (January, 1972):59-62.
The director, Nina Companeez, discusses her profession and her position as a woman.

1040   _____. "La politique des femmes (cinéastes)." Cinéma (Paris) 162(January, 1972):44-63.
Interview: Nadine Trintignant, Nelly Kaplan, and Nina Companeez who discuss their profession and their position as women. Includes a short notice on other women directors. Filmographies.

1041   Anderson, Madeline. "I Am Somebody." Film Library Quarterly 5, 1(Winter, 1971-72):39.
An interview with the director.

1042   Anderson, Sylvia. "Women on Women on Films." Take One 3, 2(November-December, 1970):10.
Director.

1043   "Anita Loos." Current Biography 35(February, 1974): 31-4.
A portrait of the screenwriter and author.

1044   "Anne Morrison Chapin: Obituary." New York Times (April 9, 1967):92.
Actress and screenwriter.

1045   Apon, A. and T. de Graaff. "Interview." Skrien (Amsterdam) 34-35(May-June, 1973):29-34.
Jean-Marie Straub and his wife, Danièle Huillet, discuss their work, particularly "Einleitung zu Arnold Schoenbergs Begleitmusik zu einer Lichtspielscene" and "Geschichtsunterricht."

1046   Archer, E. "Woman Director Makes the Scene." New York Times Magazine (August 26, 1962):46.
On Shirley Clarke.

1047   Armatage, K. "Joyce Wieland." Take One 3, 2(February, 1972):23-25.
A filmography and interview with Joyce Wieland, Canadian experimental film-maker.

1048 _____ . "Women in Film. " Take One 3, 11(May-
       June, 1972):45-48.

1049 _____ and Barbara Martineau. "Women in Film. "
       Take One 3, 8(November/December, 1971):35-38.
       Women's Film Event at Edinburgh Festival.

1050 Arnheim, Rudolf. "To Maya Deren, " in Film Culture
       Reader. P. Adams Sitney, ed. New York: Prae-
       ger Publishers, 1970, pp. 84-86.

1051 "Articles and Interview: Dorothy Arzner. " Cinema
       (USA) 34(Fall, 1974):2-20+.

1052 Ash, René L. The Motion Picture Film Editor. Me-
       tuchen, N. J. : Scarecrow Press, 1974.
       Lists and credits over 600 film editors.

1053 Auslender, Leland. "Distortion Techniques Used in
       Filming 'The Birth of Aphrodite. '" American Cin-
       ematographer. 52, 9(September, 1971):868.
       Film-maker refines techniques developed by his
       artist wife and wins "Best Experimental Film" award
       in Atlanta International Film Festival. The article is
       interesting for no camerawomen have been uncovered
       so far, and here we do have one woman's contribution
       to camera work.

1054 "Authors and Editors. " Publishers Weekly 197(May
       25, 1970):21-22.
       Edna O'Brien, Irish author and screen author.

1055 Aydelotte, W. "The Little Red Schoolhouse Becomes
       a Theatre. " Motion Picture 47, 2(March, 1934):34.
       Lois Weber and visual education in schools.

1056 "Background: Female Directors. " Film Series 2,
       No. 1(April, 1973):24. British Federation of Film
       Societies, 81 Dean Street, London W1V 6AA.
       Filmographies of women directors.

1057 Bailey, A. "Would Little Joan Littlewood Were Here!"
       Esquire 61(January, 1964):113.
       On Joan Littlewood, director.

1058 Ball, Eustace Hale. The Art of the Photoplay. N. Y. :
       G. W. Dillingham Co. , 1913.

1059 _____ . Photoplay Scenarios: How to Write and
Sell Them. N.Y.: Hearst International Library
Co., 1915.

1060 _____ . Traffic in Souls. N.Y.: G. W. Dilling-
ham Co., 1914.

1061 Barkhausen, Hans. "Footnote to the History of Riefenstahl's 'Olympia.'" Film Quarterly 28, 1(Fall,
1974):8.
Questions Riefenstahl's statement that the Nazi's
had no influence on Olympic games or production or
design of the Olympia films.

1062 Barsam, Richard Meran. "Leni Riefenstahl: Artifice
and Truth in a World Apart." Film Comment 9, 6
(November-December, 1973):32.
A biography and analysis of Leni Riefenstahl.

1063 Bataille, Gretchen. "Preliminary Investigations:
Early Suffrage Films." Women and Film 1, 3-4
(1973):42.
Analysis of six early suffragette films.

1064 Batten, Mary. "Actuality and Abstraction." Film
Comment 1, 2(Summer, 1962):55.
Discusses experimental film-maker Mary Ellen
Bute's biography and her electronically-composed films
which synchronize musical beats to patterns drawn by
a beam of light. Includes a portion of an interview
with her. (See Markopoulos' articles, entries, 1414-
15.)

1065 _____ . "Actuality and Abstraction; Interview."
Vision 1, 2(Summer, 1962):55
On Mary Ellen Bute.

1066 Beatty, J. "Assistant Directors and Their Importance." American Magazine 122(November, 1936):
46-7, 100-04.

1067 "Bedtime Stories." Films and Filming 16, 5(February,
1970):31.
An interview with Jacqueline Susann, former actress turned novelist. Thoughts on her books and
films.

1068   Beh, S. H.   "The Woman's Film. "   Film Quarterly
        25, 1(1971):48-49.

1069   "Behind the Lens. "   Time 99(March 20, 1972):92.
           A portrait of Carol Eastman, motion picture
        screenwriter; Elaine May, actress and director.

1070   Bellumari, C., ed.   "Le donne del cinema contro
           questo cinema. "   Bianco E Nero (Rome) 33, 1-2
           (January-February, 1972):1-112.   Special issue.
           Results of a questionnaire on the position of wo-
        men in the Italian film industry, including material
        from interviews with 15 women working in the fields
        of direction, script writing, acting, production and de-
        sign, etc.   Mentions: Ornella Abbagnato, Maria Gra-
        zia Baldanello, Isa Bartalini, Mara Blasetti, Suso
        Cecchi D'Amico, Luciana Corda, Marisa Crimi, Maria
        DeMatteis, Iaia Fiastri, Gabriella Genta, Ludovica
        Modugno, Maria Monti, Marina Piperno, Paola Pita-
        gora, Monica Vitti.

1071   Benesova, M.   "Entretiens ... avec Mme. Hermína
           Týrlová. "   APEC-Revue Belge du Cinéma (Brussels)
           1(1972):16-19.
           An interview with the Czech animation film-
        maker, Hermína Týrlová.

1072   Beranger, Clara.   Writing for the Screen (with story,
           picture treatment and shooting script).   Dubuque,
           Iowa: W. C. Brown Co., 1950.
           Author was screenwriter and director.

1073   Berg, Gretchen.   "Interview with Shirley Clarke. "
           Film Culture 44(1967):52.
           Clarke discusses her cine-dance films, a form
        of dance that can only take place on film.

1074   Berson, Arnold.   "The Truth About Leni. "   Films and
           Filming 11, 7(April, 1965):15-19.
           The career of Leni Riefenstahl; her place as an
        artist discussed.

1075   Bertsch, Marguerite.   How to Write for Moving Pic-
           tures.   New York: Geo. H. Doran Co., 1917.
           Author was director and editor for Vitagraph Co.
        and Famous Players Film Co.   Very detailed "How
        to" account.

1076   "Bessie Love on Working Behind the Camera. " Films
         and Filming 8, 10(July, 1962):16.

1077   Betancourt, Jeanne. "High School Women and Film:
         A Report from New York City. " Women and Film
         2(1972):56.
              High school film teacher and women's film expert
         reports on her students and the film curriculum she
         has developed which emphasizes women film-makers
         and images of women in film.

1078   _____ . "Report from New York: Women's Video
         Festival at 'The Kitchen. '" Women and Film 1, 3-
         4(1973):97.

1079   _____ . Women in Focus.   Dayton, Ohio: Pflaum
         Publishing, 1974.
              Lists films, film-makers, thematic index, pro-
         gram possibilities, distributors; 92 films about women
         and made primarily by women are listed. List of
         film-makers and their films.   Then a review of the
         film and a brief biographical sketch of the film-maker.
         The purpose of the book is to offer a program of
         films about real women in contrast to the stereotypes
         usually offered.   A guide for present and future film-
         makers.   A guide for purchasing new films.   The
         films offer a guide to understanding female sexuality
         and realistic and positive female models and expose
         the sexism in our culture.   Each review tells story
         of the work; assesses film critically, particularly from
         a feminist viewpoint; suggests what groups might be
         most interested in the film; and also suggests feminist
         readings related to each film.

1080   Betts, Ernest. Inside Pictures.   London: the Cres-
         set Press, 1960.
              (See entry under "Critics. ")

1081   "Biographical Note. " International Film 7(1970):137.
              On Márta Meszáros.

1082   "Biographical Sketch. " Time 28(October 12, 1936):32.
              On Dorothy Arzner.

1083   Birns, Tom.   "Report from the UCLA Film-Makers. "
         American Cinematographer 54, 4(April, 1973):434.
              Film students at UCLA talk about film-making.

Includes statement by Penelope Spheeris, stating her difficulties as female film-maker.

1084   Blaché, A. G. "Letter." Films in Review 15, 5(May, 1964):317.
       By A. G. Blaché, correcting mistake in article about her.

1085   Black, E. "Sketch." Overland 68(September, 1916): 198.
       On Lois Weber.

1086   "Bless Kristina Nordstrom." Show 2, 6(September, 1972):12.
       On Kristina Nordstrom.

1087   Bloch, Alice. "An Interview with Jan Oxenberg." Amazon Quarterly 2, 2(December, 1973):53-55.
       Film-maker interviewed.

1088   Bodeen, DeWitt. "Frances Marion." Films in Review 20, 2(February, 1969):71-91 and 20, 3(March, 1969):129-52.
       A filmography and career of the director and screenwriter.

1089   _____. "Nazimova." Films in Review 23, 10(December, 1972):577-604.
       (See listing under "Actresses.")

1090   Bonica, Joe, compiler. How Talkies Are Made. Hollywood: J. Bonica and Co., 1930.
       Includes "The Script Girl"; acting in talking pictures, Betty Compson.

1091   Boston, S. "Beware the 'Unisex' Deal." Film and Television Technician 39(March, 1973):9.
       On women's rights.

1092   Brakhage, Jane. "The Birth Film," in Film Culture Reader. P. Adams Sitney, editor. New York: Praeger Publishers, 1970.
       On p. 230, Jane Brakhage describes the film made by her husband, Stan, about the birth of their first child, and how at one point she herself filmed the event.

1093   Braucourt, G. "Les Cannibales et propos de Liliana
        Cavani. " Ecran (Paris) 6(June, 1972):68-69.
            Review of the film "I cannibali" and interview
        with Liliana Cavani in which she discusses the common
        themes of her three films: "Francesco de'Assisi, "
        "Galileo" and "I cannibali. "

1094   _____. "Faustine et le bel été. " Ecran (Paris)
        3(March, 1972):69-70.
            A review of the film "Faustine et le bel été, "
        combined with an interview with Nina Companeez,
        director.

1095   Braudy, Susan. "Bang! A Little Gift from Holly-
        wood. " Ms III, 7(January, 1975):34.
            Review of the film "Alice Doesn't Live Here Any
        More, " made primarily by women.

1096   _____. "The Woman Behind 'Nashville. '" Ms IV,
        1(July, 1975):22.
            On Joan Tewkesbury, screenwriter for "Nash-
        ville. "

1097   Breitrese, H. "Films of Shirley Clarke. " Film
        Quarterly 13, 4(Summer, 1960):57.
            The writer discusses the films and career of
        Shirley Clarke.

1098   Brien, A. "Joan Littlewood. " Vogue 144(September
        15, 1964):160.
            Joan Littlewood, director.

1099   _____. "Openings, London. " Theatre Arts 47
        (June, 1963):31.
            On Joan Littlewood, director.

1100   Brinnin, J. M. "The Flahertys: Pioneer Documen-
        tary Film Makers. " Harper's Bazaar 81(December,
        1947):146-47, 187+.

1101   "British Feature Directors. " Sight and Sound 27, 6
        (Autumn, 1958):303.
            A bio-filmography of a number of British direc-
        tors including Wendy Toye and Muriel Box.

1102   Buchanan, J. "I'll Keep on Persisting. " After Dark
        4, 8(December, 1971):26.
            On Karen Sperling.

1103   Burgess, E. Sevi. "Towards a Popular Feminist Cin-
       ema: An Interview with Lina Wertmuller." Wo-
       men and Film 1, 5-6(1974):6.
          An interview with the Italian director.

1104   Burrell, Walter. "Hollywood Stunt Girl." Ebony 27
       (December, 1971):147-48.
          On Peaches Jones.

1105   Bute, Mary Ellen (Director), "Abstronics." Films in
       Review 5-6(June-July, 1954):263.
          An experimental electronic film-maker (abstrac-
       tions plus electronics).

1106   Caillet, G. "Nicole Vedrès, cinéaste méticuleux, est
       une romancière échevelée." France Illustration
       388(March 21, 1953):398.
          A portrait of the French motion picture producer.

1107   Calhoun, Dorothy. "Do Women Rule the Movies?"
       Motion Picture Classic 27(August, 1928):30-31, 88.

1108   Callenbach, Ernest. "3 Reviews." Film Quarterly
       21, 2(Winter, 1967-68):52-55.
          Includes review of film "Phyllis + Terry" by
       Eugene and Carol Marner.

1109   Calvert, C. "Five Women Film-makers." Mademoi-
       selle 76(November, 1972):196.
          Portrait and illustration of: Madeline Anderson,
       motion picture director and producer; Julia Reichert,
       motion picture distributor; Amalie R. Rothschild, mo-
       tion picture distributor; Rosalind Schneider, producer;
       Claudia Weill, film-maker.

1110   Carey, Gary. "Written on the Screen: Anita Loos."
       Film Comment 6, 4(Winter, 1970-71):50.
          A biography of Anita Loos. Also within text
       Carey mentions a long list of female screenwriters
       who dominated the field in and around 1914 until the
       mid-1920's. Includes Clara Beranger, Agnes Chris-
       tine Johnson, Frances Marion, Olga Printzlan, Jose-
       phine Lovett, June Mathis (remembered for cutting
       "Greed" to shreds, primarily), Beulah Marie Dix,
       Jeanie MacPherson (C. B. De Mille's favorite), Bess
       Meredyth, Lenore J. Coffee. Plus complete filmo-
       graphy.

1111   Carlisle, Helen. "Actresses Who Are Today Successes
        in Other Lines of Studio Work. " Motion Picture
        Magazine 27(February, 1924):36-37, 86.

1112   "Carlos Alvarez signe preso. " Cine al Dia (Caracas)
        16(April, 1973):30.
        The imprisonment of Colombian film-makers,
        Carlos and Julia Alvarez.

1113   Carr, Catherine, ed. The Art of Photoplay Writing.
        Honnis Jordan Co. , 1914.
        Catherine Carr, scenario editor, North American
        Film Co.

1114   Carson, L. M. Kit. "Hollywood Hot List: Women
        Who Should Be Running the Show. " Ms III, 8(Feb-
        ruary, 1975):58.
        A sampling of women in film-making positions:
        Directors: Juleen Compton, Sarah Kernochan, Barbara
        Loden, Ida Lupino, Elaine May, Claudia Weill.
        Writers: Jay Presson Allen, Leigh Brackett, Joan
        Didion, Carole Eastman, Penelope Gilliatt, Joanna Lee,
        Gloria Katz, Gail Parent, Eleanor Perry, Judith Ros-
        coe, Renee Taylor, Joan Tewkesbury. Studio Execu-
        tives: Deanne Barkley, Andrea Eastman, Ronda
        Gomez-Quinones, Roselyn Heller, Nessa Hyams, Mon-
        ique James, Marcia Nassiter, Tina Nides, Judy Feif-
        fer, Helen Strauss. Independent Producers: Tamara
        Asseyev and Alex Rose, Lynne Littman, Audrey Maas,
        Julia Phillips, Joyce Selznick, Delores Taylor, Beverly
        Walker, Hannah Weinstein, Sandy Weintraub. Editors:
        Dede Allen, Verna Fields, Jill Godmilow, Tina Hirsch,
        Marcia Lucas, Marion Rothman. Casting: Barbara
        Miller, Geri Windsor/Linda Otto. Agents: Kay Brown,
        Arlene Donovan, Sue Mengers, Stevie Phillips, Marian
        Searchinger, Gloria Safier, Audrey Wood.

1115   _____. "It's Here! Hollywood's Ninth Era!" Es-
        quire 83, 2(February, 1975):65.
        Review of the various Hollywood "eras" describ-
        ing who and what dominated them. Details the latest,
        the "ninth era, " including sketches of producers (Julia
        and Mike Phillips), scriptwriters (Gloria Katz and
        Williard Huyck, Joan Tewkesbury) and star (Pamela
        Grier).

1116   Carter, A.   "The Muse of the Reel. "   Motion Picture
        21, 2(March, 1921):62.
        Interview with Lois Weber.

1117   "Catching Up with Ida Lupino. "   Modern Screen 66, 11
        (November, 1972):68.

1118   "Ce idei de film aveti?: Elisabeta Bostan. "   Cinema
        (Bucharest) X, 1(January, 1972):4.
        A group of Rumanian directors tell of their ideas
of film.

1119   Cetinjski, M.   "Zapeljane in Zapuscene. "   Ekran
        (Ljubljana) 10, 94-95(1972):154-57.
        Portraits of three Yugoslavian women documen-
tary film-makers: Mirjana Keser, Tatjana Suput,
Tatjana Zivanović.

1120   Chalmers, Helena.   The Art of Make-Up.   New York:
        Appleton and Co. , 1925.
        Author, instructor in make-up at American Aca-
demy of Dramatic Arts and Columbia University, gives
hints for make-up for stage, screen and social use.
Very general, not of much value but one of few books
that refers to screen make-up.   See Chapter XV, pp.
128-39, "Making-Up for Moving Pictures. "

1121   Charest, G. and A. Leroux.   "Elle est actrice, elle
        est femme, et pourtant ... elle tourne; elle s'ap-
        pelle Anna Karina. "   Cinéma Quebec (Montreal) 3,
        3(November-December, 1973):30-32.
        An interview. Anna Karina discusses the making
of her first film as director, "Vivre ensemble. "

1122   Child, Abigail.   "The Girls. "   Women and Film 1, 3-
        4(1973):73.
        A discussion of Mai Zetterling's film. In addi-
tion, there is a chronology of "Women in Sweden"
outlining significant feminine events.

1123   Childs, J.   "Penelope Gilliatt. "   Film Comment 8, 2
        (Summer, 1972):22-26.
        An interview with Gilliatt focusing on "Sunday
Bloody Sunday. "

1124   [No entry.]

1125   "Cineasti Femei. "   Cinema (Bucharest) 10, 8(August,
         1972):15-19.
                  Brief survey of women film-makers past and
         present.   Includes filmography.

1126   "Cinéma Vérité. "   Movie 8(April, 1963):12-15.
                  Characteristics, equipment, practitioners, etc.
         of cinéma vérité.   (Shirley Clarke is one.)

1127   Clark, Edith.   Designing Clothes for Movie Folk.
         Photoplay Research Society, Los Angeles.   Oppor-
         tunities in the Moving Picture Industry, Los An-
         geles: The Society, 1922.
                  Costume designer of the Christie Film Co. dis-
         cusses her craft.   Book 3, pp. 79-82.

1128   Clarke, S.   "The Cool World. "   Films and Filming
         10, 3(December, 1963):7.
                  On Shirley Clarke.

1129   Clemons, W.   "Loos Talk. "   Newsweek 84(Aug. 12,
         1974):77.
                  Portrait of Anita Loos.

1130   Cocteau, J.   "Four Letters by Jean Cocteau to Leni
         Riefenstahl. "   Film Culture 56-57(Spring, 1973):
         90-93.
                  A facsimile of letters from 1952 to 1960.   With
         English translation.

1131   Coffee, Lenore.   Storyline: Recollections of a Holly-
         wood Screenwriter.   London: Cassell, 1973.
                  Mostly about her personal life and friendships
         in Hollywood.

1132   Comden, Betty and Adolph Green.   Singin' in the Rain.
         New York: Viking Press, 1972.
                  Screenplay by Comden and Green.   Edited by
         Adrienne Fazan.   1952 release.

1133   Commire, Anne.   Something About the Author.   De-
         troit: Gale, 1971.
                  In Vol. 2, p. 88, portrait of Agnes Dazey, au-
         thor and screenwriter.

1134   Comsa, D.   "Personajul intre autenticitate si con-
         fectie. "   Cinema (Bucharest) 11, 4(April, 1973):26-
         29.

Analysis of the characters portrayed in Rumanian films in recent years. Director Iulian Mihu and directress Malvina Ursianu give their opinions.

1135 Confino, Barbara. "Interview: Agnes Varda." Saturday Review 55(August 12, 1972):35.
Comments on images of women. Also comments on being a woman director. "It is the image that is important, not so much who is making the film. However, if men are not ready to change the image of women, the women will have to make films to change it."

1136 "A Conversation--Shirley Clarke and Storm De Hirsch." Film Culture 46(1967):44.

1137 Cooper, K. "Kate Millett's 'Three Lives,'" Filmmakers' Newsletter 5, 3(January, 1972):28-33.
(See entry under "Images.")

1138 _____. "Shirley Clarke." Filmmakers' Newsletter 5, 8(June, 1972):34.
Director.

1139 Corliss, Richard, ed. The Hollywood Screenwriter. New York: Avon Books, 1972.
A paperback reprint of Film Comment articles. Mentions Anita Loos, Eleanor Perry, Penelope Gilliatt.

1140 _____. "The Hollywood Screenwriter." Film Comment 6, 4(Winter, 1970-71):4.

1141 _____. "Leni Riefenstahl: A Bibliography." Film Heritage 5, 1(Fall, 1969):27-36.
Books, articles, news stories, film in which she appeared. A filmography.

1142 Cornwell, Regina. "Maya Deren and Germaine Dulac: Activists of the Avant-garde." Film Library Quarterly 5, 1(Winter, 1971-72):29-38.

1143 _____. "'True Patriot Love': The Films of Joyce Wieland." Art Forum Vol. 10, No. 1.

1144 Cowie, P. "The Face of '63--Great Britain." Films and Filming 9, 5(February, 1963):19.
On Joan Littlewood, director.

1145   "Credits: Film Editor. " <u>Look</u> 34, 22(November 3,
            1970).
            Portrait of Dede Allen, editor.

1146   Cruikshank, H. 'Director Dorothy. " <u>Motion Picture</u>
            <u>Classic</u> 30, 1(September, 1929):33.
            A biographical sketch on Dorothy Arzner. Ir-
        ritated by emphasis on men all the time. She was
        an ambulance driver in the army who returned to a
        stenographer's job. She crashed in on Wm. C. de-
        Mille and got a job at the bottom--in the scenario de-
        partment, typing scripts. She became a script girl,
        film cutter, script writer, film editor, and finally got
        her first directing assignment, "Fashions for Women"
        with Esther Ralston. Box office success for both the
        star and the director (first staring role for Ralston).
        Description of her physically and emotionally. The
        fact she is female never aided nor hindered her chan-
        ces in her work. She assures us she will one day
        marry! A very positive last paragraph on Dorothy
        Arzner.

1147   Cussler, Margaret. <u>Not by a Long Shot: Adventures</u>
            <u>of a Documentary Film Producer</u>. New York: Ex-
            position, 1952.
            Personal memoir of female producer of documen-
        tary films.

1148   Daley, M. "Joan Didion. " <u>Publishers Weekly</u> 202
            (October 9, 1972):26-27.
            A portrait of the author and screenwriter.

1149   Dawson, Jan. "The Heartbreak Kid. " <u>Sight and</u>
            <u>Sound</u> 42, 3(Summer, 1973):176.
            A review of director Elaine May's second film.

1150   Day, Tilly. "Continuity. " <u>Films and Filming</u> 3, 12
            (September, (1957):36.
            Discusses the job of the script girl.

1151   de Acosta, Mercedes. <u>Here Lies the Heart</u>. New
            York: Reynal, 1960.
            A script writer's autobiography, includes her
        friendships with Garbo, Dietrich and others.

1152   Debrix, Jean. "Film Editing. " <u>Films in Review</u> 4,
            1(January, 1953):21-27.
            Editing: Dynamism and rhythm.

1153   De Hirsch, Storm and Shirley Clarke. "A Conversa-
        tion. " Film Culture 46(Autumn, 1967):44-54.
        On women as film-makers.

1154   Deleanu, V. S. "Letitia Popa: eu debutanta?" Cin-
        ema (Bucharest) 10, 10(October, 1972):38-39.
        An interview. The Rumanian director, Letitia
        Popa, discusses the films she has made for television.

1155   DeNeve, R. "Elinor Bunin; Another Opening, Another
        Show. " Print 26(January, 1972):42-44.
        A portrait of the artist and motion picture pro-
        ducer.

1156   Densham, Pen. "Life Times Nine. " American Cin-
        ematographer 55, 5(May, 1974):550.
        Director/cameraman writes of experience in
        working with nine young film-makers whose work "Life
        Times Nine" was eventually nominated for an Academy
        Award. Among those who contributed to the film were
        Kimmie Jensen (11), Celia Merkur (14), Melissa
        Franklin (14), Marilyn Becker (15). Nine young Can-
        adian film-makers. A collection of "commercials" on
        the subject of "Life. "

1157   Denton, F. "Lights! Camera! Quiet! Ready!
        Shoot!" Photoplay 13, 3(February, 1918):48.
        On Elsie Jane Wilson and Ida May Park.

1158   "Deren, Maya. " Film Culture 39(Winter, 1965):1-60.
        An entire issue devoted to her cine-dance films.
        (A bibliography on pp. 57-59.)

1159   Deren, Maya. An Anagram of Ideas on Art, Form and
        Film. Yonkers, N. Y.: Alicat Book Shop, 1946.

1160   _____ . "The Cleveland Lecture. " Film Culture
        29(1963):64.

1161   _____ . "Critic vs. Artist. " Village Voice 5, 38
        (July 14, 1960):10-11.
        The film-maker and critic discusses criticism.

1162   _____ . "Movie Journal. " Village Voice 5, 39(July
        29, 1960):6, 8 and 5, 44(August 25, 1960):6, 8 and
        6, 32(June 1, 1961):9, 17.
        Discusses directives to creativity.

1163   _____. "Notes, Essays, Letters." Film Culture
            39(Winter, 1964):1-86.
            A bibliography.

1164   _____. "On a Film in Progress and a Statement."
            Film Culture 22, 23(Summer, 1961):160-63.
            Philosophical and haiku aspects of her work.

1165   _____. "Reply to Farber's Article on Maya
            Deren." New Republic 115(November 11, 1946):
            630.

1166   _____. "Tempo and Tension," in The Movies as
            Medium. Lewis Jacobs, ed. New York: Farrar,
            Straus, and Giroux, 1970.
            The film-maker and theorist discusses film, pp.
            144-167.

1167   Diamonstein, Barbaralee. Open Secrets. New York:
            Viking, 1972.
            A portrait of Joan Didion, screenwriter, on pp.
            103-06.

1168   Didion, Joan. Play It As It Lays. New York: Far-
            rar, Straus and Giroux, 1970.
            Novel adapted to screen by author.

1169   _____. Slouching Toward Bethlehem. New York:
            Farrar, Straus and Giroux, 1968.

1170   Diehl, D. "A Portrait of Gloria Monty." Action 8, 1
            (January-February, 1973):20-22.
            An interview. Discusses Gloria Monty's career
            in directing daytime television.

1171   "The Directors and the Public; Symposium." Film
            Culture 1, 2(March-April, 1955):15.
            Questions asked of a group of directors including
            Ida Lupino: 1. What do you think of the public?;
            2. Can the majority of the public appreciate intellec-
            tual films?; 3. A particular category which appreci-
            ates your films?; 4. Concerned with critic's or pu-
            blic's opinion? Ida answers only two.

1172   "Distribution of Experimental and Independent Commer-
            cial Cinema." Village Voice (May 5, 1966):16, 31.
            A discussion: Jonas Mekas, L. Marcorelles and
            Shirley Clarke.

1173   Ditvoorst, Adriaan. "Biographical Note." Internation-
       al Film Guide 5(1968):118 and 8(1971):209.
          Female director.

1174   Dowd, N. "The Woman Director Through the Years."
       Special Issue. Action 8,4(July-August, 1973):15-18.
          Discusses some of the early women directors
       whose place in film history has been largely ignored.

1175   Dreyfus, C., ed. "Liliana Cavani: Interview." Ma-
       demoiselle 80(November, 1974):167+
          An interview with Liliana Cavani, Italian motion
       picture author and director.

1176   Drouzy, M. "Viva Varda." Kosmorama (Copenhagen)
       18,107(February, 1972):100-05.
          Directress Agnes Varda discusses themes and
       styles of her films from "La pointe courte" to "Lion's
       Love" and "Nausicaa."

1177   Dufour, F. "Marguerite Duras en toute liberté."
       Cinéma (Paris) 165(April, 1972):48-51.
          Marguerite Duras speaks of her political commit-
       ment, the content of her film "Jaune le Soleil" and the
       relationship between books and films.

1178   Duncan, Catherine. "As Others See Us." Sight and
       Sound 17,65(Spring, 1948):12-14.
          Her film about Australia made for the Australian
       N. F. B.

1179   [No entry.]

1180   "Edith Foster: Obituary." New York Times (May 10,
       1950):31.
          Educational film pioneer.

1181   Edwards, Anne. Hesitant Heart. New York: Random
       House, 1974.
          Fiction by screenwriter, Edwards.

1182   Edwards, N. "Women and Film Festival." Cinema
       Canada 9(August-September, 1973):14-18.
          Includes a report from some of the cities in
       Canada where the festival was sent on tour.

1183   Efros, Susan. "A Film Script." Canyon Cinemanews
       4/5(September/October, 1973):8.

(Sausalito, Calif.)

1184   Elek, Judit.   "Biographical Note. " International Film
        Guide 7(1970):136.
            Female director.

1185   Ellis, Robert.   "Ida Lupino Brings New Hope to Holly-
        wood. " Negro Digest 8(August, 1950):47-49.

1186   Emerson, John and Anita Loos.   Breaking into the
        Movies.   New York: The James A. McCann Co. ,
        1921.

1187   _____.   How to Write Photoplays.   New York: Mc-
        Cann, 1920.
            "Cutting the Picture, " pp. 79-82.

1188   Emmens, Carol.   "New Day Films: An Alternative in
        Distribution. " Women and Film 2, 7(1975):72.
            Six young, independent film-makers band together
        to form a feminist films distribution co-op: Julia
        Reichert, James Klein, Amalie Rothschild, Liane Bran-
        don, Joyce Chopra, Claudia Weill.

1189   Erens, Patricia.   "Interview with Jill Godmilow. "
        Women and Film 2, 7(1975):34.
            One of the directors of "Antonia: A Portrait of
        a Woman. "

1190   _____.   "Love and Anarchy. " Jump Cut 2(July-
        August, 1974):8.
            A review of Lina Wertmuller's film.

1191   _____.   "Making and Distributing 'Nana, Mom and
        Me. '" The Feminist Art Journal 4, 2(Summer,
        1975):12.
            A brief biographical sketch of the film-maker,
        Amalie Rothschild, and an analysis of her film.

1192   Erminy, P. , et al.   "Roto el tabú del cine espectacu-
        lar en Venezuela?" Cine al Dia (Caracas) 16(April,
        1973):24-30.
            An interview.   Mauricio Wallerstein and Abigail
        Rojas speak of their film "Cuando quiero llorar no
        lloro. "

1193   "The Expensive Arts: A Discussion of Film Distribu-

tion and Exhibition in U. S. " Film Quarterly 13, 4
(Summer, 1960):19-34.
A symposium: John Adams, Shirley Clarke,
Edward Harrison, Bill Kenly, Elodie Osborn, Amos
Vogel.

1194 Fabrikant, G. "Dede Allen: the Power Behind the
Screen. " Ms 2(February, 1974):34-36.
An interview with Allen, motion picture editor.

1195 Farber, M. "Maya Deren's Silent Films: Criticism. "
New Republic 115(October 28, 1946):555-56.

1196 Farrington, Mrs. Frank. "In the Costume Room. "
Moving Picture World 33(July 21, 1917):389-90.
Costume mistress of the Thanhouser studio des-
cribes her work.

1197 Fay, G. "London Panorama. " Theatre Arts 46(January, 1962):68.
On Joan Littlewood, director.

1198 "Feedback. " Take One 3, 4(March-April, 1971):4.
Letters and additional information on Take One
Vol. 3, No. 2, The Women's Issue.

1199 Feldman, J. and H. "Women Directors: Seem to Go
More Often Than They Come. " Films in Review
1, 8(November, 1950):9.
A condescending article which mentions Lois
Weber, June Mathis, Dorothy Arzner, Margarita Bas-
kaya, Vera Stroyevna, Olga Preobrashenskaia, Leni
Riefenstahl, Leontine Sagan, Germaine Dulac, Wanda
Jakubowska, Ida Lupino.

1200 La Femme and Le Film: Women and Film, Toronto
International Festival, 1973. 91 Charles Street
West, Toronto, Ontario M4Y 1R4, Canada.
Brochure with pictures and descriptions of all
films shown and directors and distribution information.

1201 Fenin, G. "The Face of '63--United States. " Films
and Filming 9, 6(March, 1963):55.
On Shirley Clarke.

1202 Ferguson, Lee. "Letter from NYC. " Take One 3, 2
(November-December, 1970):37.
Women's video collective in New York.

1203   Ferrari, A.   "Le second souffle du cinéma africain. "
        Téléciné (Paris) 176(January, 1973):2-9.
            An article and interview.   After a brief history
        of African cinema, the author reports on African films
        shown at the Dinard festival.   He then interviews
        Sarah Maldoror, who speaks of her film "Sambizanga. "

1204   Ferrini, F. and A. Rossi.   "Cinema/Psicana/isi/
        Politica. "   Bianco e Nero (Rome) 33,7-8(July-
        August, 1972):55-79.
            The relationship between psychoanalysis and po-
        litics in the films of directors Marguerite Duras and
        Philippe Gorrel.

1205   Field, Mary and F. Percy Smith.   Secrets of Nature.
        London: Faber and Faber, 1934.
        "Editing, " pp. 188-208.

1206   "Fifty Filmographies. "   Film Comment 6,4(Winter,
        1970-71):102.
            Includes filmographies of screenwriters Leigh
        Brackett, Betty Comden, Frances Goodrich and hus-
        band Albert Hackett, Frances Marion, Jane Murfin,
        Salka Viertal, Mae West.

1207   "Film Unions and the Low Budget Independent Film
        Production--An Exploratory Discussion. "   Film Cul-
        ture 22-23(Summer, 1961):134-50.
            A symposium: includes Shirley Clarke.

1208   "Filmex Announces Extraordinary Success of Second
        Exposition. "   American Cinematographer 54, 1(Jan-
        uary, 1973):61.
            Description of 2nd Los Angeles International Film
        Exposition, an 11-day noncompetitive event.   Mention
        is made of: Screenwriter Kay Kanin's participation in
        International Screenwriters Conference; Special tribute
        to Myrna Loy; Special short programs, including one
        on "Women and Film" followed by a panel discussion.

1209   "Filmmaking in Sweden. "   Interview 1-7(n. d.):24.
        On Susan Sontag.

1210   "Filmographies. "   Film Culture 29(1963):123.
        Including Maya Deren and Carmen D'Avino.

1211   "Filmography. "   International Film Guide 1(1964):165
        On Joy Batchelor.

1212   "Films by and about Women. " Film Library Quart-
        erly 5, 1(Winter, 1971-72):46-59.
            A series of brief reviews. (Also see entry under
        "Images. ")

1213   "The Films of Lotte Reiniger. " Film Culture 2, 3
        (1956):20.
            Subjects of her silhouette films.

1214   Flitterman, Sandy. "Heart of the Avant-Garde: Some
        Biographical Notes on Germaine Dulac. " Women
        and Film 1, 5-6(1974):58.
            Early independent progressive French film-maker
        Dulac is discussed.

1215   Flot, Y. "Breve rencontre avec Leni Riefenstahl. "
        Ecran (Paris) 9(November, 1972):28-30.
            An interview with Leni Riefenstahl at the Munich
        Olympics. She repeats her self-justification and denies
        Nazi affiliations.

1216   Ford, Charles. "Femmes Cinéastes. " Films in Re-
        view 24(January, 1973):49-50.
            Review of the book, Femme Cinéastes.

1217   _____ . "Femmes Cinéastes, ou le Triomphe de la
        Valonte. " Film Comment 9(May/June, 1973):69-71.
            Review of book.

1218   _____ . "The First Female Producer. " Films in
        Review 15, 3(March, 1964):141.
            Alice Guy-Blaché, director. As of this writing,
        91 years old. A secretary to Gaumont who bought
        Lumière's "gadget. " Made a dozen little films, later
        moved to New York and became producer of motion
        pictures.

1219   _____ . "Germaine Dulac. " Anthologie du Cinéma.
        31(January, 1968):6.

1220   Fowler, Marjorie. "On the Fine Art of Sharing ... "
        American Cinemeditor 25, 1(Spring, 1975):5.
            Some thoughts on the work relationship between
        the editor and director of a film, by a woman editor
        and member of the honorary editing society.

1221   "Frances Hubbard Flaherty: Obituary. " New York
        Times (June 24, 1972):34.

Film-maker and wife of Robert J. Flaherty.

1222   "Frances Marion: Obituary." New York Times (May
        14, 1973):34 and Newsweek 81(May 28, 1973):63 and
        Time 101(May 28, 1973):104.
            Portraits and obituaries of the screenwriter.

1223   Franz, William. The Screenwriter Looks at the
        Screenwriter. New York: Macmillan, 1972.
            Interviews. Gives a listing of writer's film cre-
        dits, then question and answer format. Includes
        screenwriter Kay Kanin, married to Michael Kanin,
        who is brother of Garson Kanin, another screenwriter.
        Interesting introduction to this only female represented
        in the book.

1224   "The Frost Bit." Newsweek 59(January 29, 1962):81
            On Shirley Clarke, director. Shirley Clarke di-
        recting Robert Frost in a feature-length documentary
        about himself.

1225   "Fun Palace." Drama Review 12(Spring, 1968):130.
            On Joan Littlewood, director.

1226   Galassini, G. "Sunday Bloody Sunday." Film Heri-
        tage 7, 4(Summer, 1972):29-31.
            Discussion of "Sunday Bloody Sunday" with par-
        ticular reference to Penelope Gilliatt's script.

1227   Gallub, Judith. "French Writers Turned Film
        Makers." Film Heritage 4, 2(Winter, 1968-69):19-
        25.
            French novelists and scriptwriters becoming di-
        rectors. Marguerite Duras, novelist, "Hiroshima Mon
        Amour. "

1228   Gance, Abel and Nelly Kaplan. "The Kingdom of the
        Earth." Film Culture 3, 5(December, 1957):10-13
        and 4, 1(January, 1958):14-16.
            Two film-makers discuss "polyvision. "

1229   Garson, Barbara. "Upfront with Lina Wertmuller. "
        Ms 3, 11(May, 1975):42.
            An interview with the Italian writer and director.

1230   Gassner, John. Best Film Plays, 1945. New York:
        Crown, 1946.

"A Tree Grows in Brooklyn," by Tess Slesinger and Frank Davis.

1231   and Dudley Nichols. eds. Twenty Best Film
        Plays. New York: Crown Publishers, 1943.
            Includes screen plays "Mrs. Miniver," 1943,
written by Claudia West et al.; "Rebecca," 1940, by
Robert Sherwood and Joan Harrison; "The Women,"
1939, by Anita Loos and Jane Murfin.

1232 Gauthier, G. "La femme dans le cinéma québécois. "
        Image et Son (Paris) 267(January, 1973):10-17.
            The place of the Quebec women in the work of
four film-makers: J. C. Labrecque, M. Lalonde, P.
Perrault, B. Gosselin.

1233 Geduld, Harry M. Authors on Film. Bloomington:
        Indiana University Press, 1972.
            Female view represented by V. Woolf; interview
by Margaret Reid with F. Scott Fitzgerald who discusses "flappers;" a tribute to Marlene Dietrich by
Ernest Hemingway.

1234 Geraghty, Sheila. "The Life of a Private Secretary
        in Filmland. " Cosmopolitan 104(February, 1938):
        46-47, 121-22.

1235 Gibson, Helen. "In Very Early Days. " Films in Re-
        view 19,1(January, 1968):28-34.
            (See listing under "Actresses. ")

1236 Gilburt, Naome. "To Be Our Own Muse: The Dia-
        lectics of a Culture Heroine. " Women and Film
        2(1972):25.
            Reflections on First International Festival of
Women's Films.

1237 Gilliatt, Penelope. Sunday Bloody Sunday. The Script
        of the John Schlesinger Film. New York: Viking,
        1971.
            Script of John Schlesinger film written by Gil-
liatt.

1238   . Sunday Bloody Sunday. New York: Grove
        Press, 1972.
            Script of Penelope Gilliatt's screenplay. (Film
directed by John Schlesinger, produced by Joseph
Janni for U. A.)

1239   Gimbel, Peter. "Blue Water, White Death. " Ameri-
            can Cinematographer 52, 9(September, 1971):872.
            Film-maker Peter Gimbel describes how he and
    his underwater experts, Valerie and Ron Taylor, made
    a film about a hunt for a great white shark. (The
    Taylors are now perhaps better known for their under-
    water cinematography in the film "Jaws. ")

1240   "Girls Who Failed as Actresses and Made Good in
            Other Film Channels. " Photoplay 29(March, 1926):
            28-29, 136.

1241   Glyn, Anthony, Elinor Glyn: a Biography. London:
            Hutchinson, 1968.
            Novelist, screenwriter, journalist, early and un-
    successful British film producer. She invented "It"
    for Clara Bow. She wrote 39 books.

1242   Glyn, Elinor. Romantic Adventure (autobiography).
            New York: E. P. Dutton and Co. , Inc. , 1937.
            Early screenwriter of the 1920's talks of her
    work of assisting in production of her novel, Three
    Weeks and others of her books made into film. (Also
    wrote Man and Maid. London: Duckworth and Co. ,
    1922.)

1243   Gonzales, J. A. "Conversación con Jorge Silva y
            Martha Rodriguez. " Cine Cubano (Havana) 86-88
            (1973):69-77.
            An interview. Jorge Silva and Martha Rodriguez
    talk about filming their documentaries "Cincales" and
    "Testimonio indigena sobre Planas, " and the existence
    of a militant cinema in Colombia.

1244   Gordon, Ruth. Myself Among Others. New York:
            Atheneum, 1971.
            "Kind of" autobiography of screenwriter and
    Academy Award supporting actress (1968-"Rosemary's
    Baby").

1245   _____ and Garson Kanin. Adam's Rib. New York:
            Viking Press, 1949.
            Screenplay of the Hepburn-Tracy, Cukor film by
    husband and wife screenwriting team of Gordon and
    Kanin.

1246   Gow, Gordon. "The Underground River. " Films and
            Filming 16, 6(March, 1970):6-13.

An interview with Agnes Varda.   Her films discussed.

1247   Gray, M. "Women in Film Making."   Goodbye to All
       That, Vol. 20(October, 1971):12.

1248   Greenbaum, Connie. "Musidora."   Women and Film
       2, 7(1975):4.
       An article on the organization of the First Women's Film Festival in Paris.

1249   Greene, Linda. "Politics of a Feminist Fantasy."
       Jump Cut No. 6(March-April, 1975):13.
       A review of Nelly Kaplan's film, "A Very Curious Girl."

1250   Greenfield, Amy. "Dance as Film."   Filmmakers'
       Newsletter 4, 1(November, 1970):26.

1251   Gregory, Muriel. "Toward Greater Efficiency in
       Handling Production Paperwork."   American Cinematographer 51, 3(March, 1970):234.
       Ms. Gregory, head of Stenographic Services at
       Universal Studios, tells another part of film production
       story.

1252   Grilikhes, Alexandra. "Films by Women: 1928-1971."
       Film Library Quarterly 6, 1(Winter, 1972-73):8.
       An article about Philadelphia's first International
       Festival of films by women. "Since media provide
       the most powerful socializing force in society, and
       constantly mold us in myriad ways, we had better take
       note that all of the images surrounding us are images
       conceived and made by men; we are never allowed to
       see how women perceive the world." Discusses film
       industry's notorious prejudice against woman directors.
       Films define women in all-too-familiar roles of: women as mother, or nurse to their husbands; women as
       harpies, or angels with their children; women as sexual objects; women as narcissists, preening themselves;
       women as props, sexual and other.   The festival provided concentrated framework within which to study images created by women and to see how different from
       men women perceive themselves, men and the world.
       First evening: Germaine Dulac, Leontine Sagan,
       Marie Menken. Dulac--"The Seashell and the Clergyman," 1928; "The Smiling Madame Beudet," 1922;
       (2nd French woman director).   Menken--"Notebook,"

1962-63; "Glimpse of the Garden," 1956; "Arabesque
for Kenneth Anger," 1961; "Lights," 1964-66; "Visual
Variations on Noguchi," "Hurry, Hurry" and "Mood
Mondrian." Sagan--"Maedchen in Uniform," 1931.
Second day: Maya Deren (only six films in her
lifetime)--"Meshes of the Afternoon," 1943; "A Study
in Choreography for Camera." Vera Chytilova--
"Something Different," 1964.
Third day: Storm DeHirsch.
Fourth day: Agnes Varda and Joyce Wieland.
Fifth day: Nelson and Wiley, and Julia Reichert.

1253   Griswold, J. B. "Mrs. Gale Henry East Trains Dogs
        for the Movies." American Magazine 126(August,
        1938):16-17, 60.

1254   Grunberger, Richard. The 12-Year Reich. New York:
        Holt, Rinehart and Winston, 1971.
        A study of Nazi Germany's social history. Chap-
        ters on relationship between culture and politics show
        the deadly effects of Hitlerite ideology on both film
        production and the creative spirit of those who did not
        flee their subverted homeland. Leni Riefenstahl is
        mentioned.

1255   Gunston, David. "Leni Riefenstahl." Film Quarterly
        14, 1(Fall, 1960):4-19.
        Riefenstahl's films with Arnold Fonch, her rela-
        tionship with Hitler, and her own films.

1256   Hahnert. "Amazon Media Project/Women for Women."
        Off Our Backs 4, 3(February, 1974):17.
        About a women's film festival.

1257   "Halas and Batchelor." International Film Guide 2
        (1965):175.
        On Joy Batchelor.

1258   "Halas and Batchelor; profile of a partnership." Film
        4(March, 1955):15.
        On Joy Batchelor.

1259   Harmetz, Aljean. "Why Won't They Let Haskell and
        Stella Be Directors?" New York Times Vol. 122,
        Sec. 2 (August 12, 1973):11.
        An article on Haskell Wexler (male) director of
        "Medium Cool" and accomplished cinematographer,

who states that the rigid society in Hollywood, "for all
its looseness, types its contributors and moving to a
new craft is not easy," and Stella Stevens, a fourteen
year acting veteran, who tells of the difficulties she
has encountered in trying to direct a film of her own.

1260 "Harriet Parsons: Biography." Current Biography
      14(January, 1953):44-47.
      Motion picture producer.

1261 "Harriet Parsons: Biography." Current Biography
      Yearbook 1953):470-73.
      Motion picture producer.

1262 Harris, Kay. "Interview with Nelly Kaplan." Women
      and Film No. 2(1972):33.
      In conjunction with First International Festival of
      Women's Films.

1263 Hartman, Charles. "The New and Independent Film-
      maker." Film Society Review (November, 1967):
      27-31.
      Discusses important independent film-makers in
      the U.S., including Shirley Clarke.

1264 Haskell, Molly. "Film: Half a Man Is Better Than
      One." Village Voice 17,25(June 22, 1972):73.
      Discussion of First International Festival of Wo-
      men's Films in New York. Wide range of films--old
      and new, feature and short, avant garde and narrative
      by women. Included in festival were panels on women
      in acting, screenwriting, TV, etc. and on whether
      there is a uniquely feminine film aesthetic and what its
      characteristics are. Several films are discussed by
      the writer.

1265   . From Reverence to Rape. New York:
      Holt, Rinehart and Winston, 1974.
      Scattered throughout are references to women
      film-makers.

1266   . "Moviemaking Without Men." Village Voice
      18(May 10, 1973):83.

1267   . "We've Yet to Catch Up with 'Adam's Rib,'"
      Village Voice 16,42(October 21, 1971):78, 90.
      Eleanor Perry, Kitty Winn, Barbara Loden, Susan

Martin, Nadine Trintignant and the author, Molly Has-
kell--panel discussion on Women in Film.

1268   Havas, E. "Ultimul tur de manivela: Zestrea. "
       Cinema (Bucharest) 10, 7(July, 1972):34.
       An interview. The Rumanian director, Letitia
Popa, talks about her film, "Zestrea. "

1269   Head, Edith. "A Costume Problem: From Shop to
       Stage to Screen. " Hollywood Quarterly 2, 1(October,
       1946):44.

1270   _____. "Head on Fashion. " Holiday 53(January,
       1973):24+ .

1271   _____ and Jane Kessner Ardmore. The Dress
       Doctor. Boston: Little, Brown, 1959.
       An autobiography. "A potpourri on designing
clothes. " (Books on costume design for film are rare
--therefore this one is valuable.)

1272   "Helen Winston: Obituary. " New York Times (Aug-
       ust 26, 1972):28.
       Actress and producer.

1273   Hellman, Lillian. The North Star. New York: Vik-
       ing, 1943. (Director, Lewis Milestone) Script of
       1943 film.

1274   Hennebelle, G. "Sambizanga. " Ecran (Paris) 15(May,
       1973):69-71.
       A film review of "Sambizanga" and interview
with its directress, Sarah Maldoror.

1275   _____ and M. Martin. "Situation du cinéma belge. "
       Ecran (Paris) 19(November, 1973):42-49.
       An interview. André Delvaux and producer Jac-
queline Pierreux talk about their commitment to Bel-
gian cinema.

1276   Henning-Jensen, Astrid. "Biographical Note. " Inter-
       national Film Guide 6(1969):61.
       Female director.

1277   Henshaw, Richard. "A Festival of One's Own: Review
       of Women Directors. " The Velvet Light Trap
       6(Fall, 1972):39.

A discussion of the First International Festival
of Women's Films in New York City.

1278 _____ . "Women Directors: 150 Filmographies. "
Film Comment 8, 4(November-December, 1972):33-
45.
With a fascinating introduction--history of women
directors. This is the place to begin research into
women directors. Includes: Reiniger, Dulac, Riefenstahl, Deren, Varda, Chytilova, Elaine May, Alice
Guy-Blaché, Dorothy Arzner, Lois Weber.

1279 Hepnerová, E. "Anna Karinová o svém filmu Zit
spolu. " Film a Doba (Prague) 19, 8(August, 1973):
434-35.
An interview. Directress Anna Karina talks
about her first film "Vivre ensemble. "

1280 _____ . "11-eh. " Film a Doba (Prague) 19, 11
(November, 1973):610-11.
A brief note on the films of directress, Lina
Wertmüller.

1281 _____ . "Mladi francouzsti reziséri o filmu a o
sobe. " Film a Doba (Prague) 19, 4(April, 1973):
202-06.
A filmography. Five young French film directors: Pascal Aubier, Guy Cavagnac, René Gilson,
Michel Mitrani, Annie Tresgot speak about their work
and their opinions.

1282 Hill, G. "Hollywood's Beautiful Bulldozer. " Colliers
127(May 12, 1951):18.
Ida Lupino.

1283 Hinsdale, Harriet. "Writing for Stage and Screen. "
Films in Review 2, 1(January, 1951):25-28.

1284 Hitchens, Gordon. "Interview with a Legend. " Film
Comment 3, 1(Winter, 1965):4.
An interview with Leni Riefenstahl, a German
film-maker who made "Triumph of the Will" and
"Olympia, " two films which help rank her among all-
time great documentary film-makers. The first was
a piece of Nazi propaganda (1937), the other on the
1939 Olympics.

1285   _____ . "Leni Riefenstahl Interviewed October 11,
            1971, Munich. " Film Culture 56-57(Spring, 1973):
            94-121.
                    An interview.   Leni Riefenstahl speaks of her
            films, her life in the past and present, contradicts
            some articles written about her, discusses her current
            project, a film made in Africa.

1286   _____ , K. Bond and J. Honhardt.   "Henry Jawor-
            sky, Cameraman for Leni Riefenstahl, Interviewed. "
            Film Culture 56-57 (Spring, 1973):122-61.
                    Henry Jaworsky tells of his experiences working
            with Leni Riefenstahl and discusses her methods and
            talents; also speaks of other German film-makers of
            the Nazi period.

1287   "Holiday Awards for 1950. "   Holiday 9(January, 1951):
            79.
                    (Ida Lupino.)

1288   "Hollywood Dress Designers. "   Photoplay 53(September,
            1939):28-29, 82.
                    The work of Adele W. Fletcher is discussed.

1289   "Hollywood's Scenarists Demand Greater Recognition
            and More Security. "   Literary Digest 120(August
            10, 1935):24, 26.

1290   "Home Sweet Hmoe. "   Avant-Scène du Cinéma (Paris)
            137(June, 1973):51-54.
                    A synopsis of the film "Home Sweet Home. "
            (1972).   Bio-filmographic information on directress
            Liliane de Kermadec.   An interview with de Kermadec
            in which she discusses her films.

1291   Houston, Penelope.   "After the Strike. "   Sight and
            Sound 29,3(Summer, 1960):108-112.
                    The strikes of the Screen Actors' Guild and the
            Writers' Guild of America.

1292   _____ . "Cukor and the Kanins. "   Sight and Sound
            24,4(Spring, 1955):186-191, 220.
                    Comic collaborations between director Cukor and
            Ruth Gordon and her husband, Garson Kanin.

1293   _____ . "Scripting. "   Sight and Sound 19,9(January,
            1951), 19, 11(March, 1951) and 21, 1(August/Septem-

ber, 1951).
Brief reviews of films based on their screenplays.

1294   "How Twelve Famous Women Scenario Writers Succee-
        ded. " Photoplay (August, 1928):47.

1295   Howard, Clifford. "Hollywood Notes. " Close-Up 2
        (April, 1928):54-55.
        About Dorothy Arzner, film director.

1296   Howard, J. "Merry, Angry Mother Hen. " Life 57
        (November 27, 1964):59.
        On Joan Littlewood, director.

1297   Hrbas, J. "Vera Plivová-Simkova-Svet detskÿch her. "
        Film a Doba (Prague) 19,4(April, 1973):182-191.
        The work and personality of Czech directress,
        Vera Plivová-Simkova, who specializes in films for
        children.

1298   Hunt, Julie L. "The Women Who Are Not Actresses. "
        Photoplay 50(September, 1936):50-51, 92.

1299   Hutchins, Patricia. "Cine Camera in Gaeltacht. "
        Sight and Sound 14,55(October, 1945):86-87.
        Film-maker discusses making a documentary in
        Ireland.

1300   Hyland, Peggy. "The Gentle Art of Make-Up. " Mo-
        tion Picture Classic 3, 6(February, 1917):15+ .
        Vitagraph actress tells how she makes up for
        the screen.

1301   Ibranyi-Kiss, A. "Women in Canadian Films. " Cin-
        ema Canada (Toronto) 5(December-January, 1972-73):
        26-31.
        (See entry under "Images. ")

1302   "Ida Lupino. " Films in Review 16, 1(January, 1965):
        61-62.
        TV filmography of director, Lupino.

1303   "Ida Lupino: Biography. " Current Biography (1943).
        (Ida Lupino)

1304   "Independent Women's Cinema: Reviews. " Women and

Film 1, 5-6(1974):77.
"Jemina, Daughter of the Mountains" by Anielle
Weinberger and Ginette Gablot.   "The Point Is to
Change It" by Claudia Alemann.   "Put Yourself in My
Place" by Francine Winham.   "Womanhouse" by Joanna
Demetrakas.   "Women of the Rhondda" by Esther
Ronay.   "Women Against the Industrial Bill" by Esther
Ronay.   "Sylvia, Fran, and Joy" by Joan Churchill.
"A 7-1/2 Minute Film" by Marnie McCormack.   A
review and compilation of films at the Ann Arbor Wo-
men's Film Festival (February, 1974).

1305   "Independent Women's Cinema: Reviews. " Women and
           Film 2, 7(1975):80.
           Information and brief reviews of some new fem-
inist films: "Plumb Line" by Carolee Schneemann.
"Self-Health" by Catherine Allen, Judy Irola, Allie
Light, Joan Musante.   "Tub Film" by Mary Beams
Phillips.   "The End of the Art World" by Alexis Kra-
silovsky.   "What's the Matter Sally?   The Roof Needs
Mowing" by Gillian Armstrong.   "Home" by Robynne
Murphy, Margot Knox, Barbara Levy, Leoni Crennan.
"Woman to Woman" by Donna Deitch.   "A Film About
a Woman Who" by Yvonne Rainer.   Chick Strand pro-
ductions "Legacy" by Karen Arthur.   "The Amazing
Equal Pay Show" by Linda Dove.   "Metroliner" by
Victoria Hochberg.   "Old-Fashioned Woman" by Martha
Coolidge.

1306   "Interview. " Women and Film 1(n. d.):30.
           On Judy Smith.

1307   "An Interview with Christiane Rochefort. " Women and
           Film 1, 3-4(1973):7.
           An interview with Christiane Rochefort who wrote
the screen play for "Les Stances à Sophie" and the
novel on which it was based.

1308   "Irene Thirer: Obituary. " New York Times (Febr-
           uary 20, 1964):29.
           Motion picture editor and critic.

1309   "Isabel Dawn: Obituary. " New York Times (June 30,
           1966):39.
           Actress and screenwriter.

1310   "Isobel Lennart: Obituary. " New York Times (Jan-

uary 26, 1971):36.
Obituary of dramatist and motion picture screenwriter.

1311   Israel, Lee. "Women in Film: Saving an Endangered
       Species. " Ms III, 8(February, 1975):51.
       Author examines 200 films between the years
       1968 and 1974 and discovers the lack of women artists
       in films. Contributions of women include three writers
       (Carole Eastman, Eleanor Perry, Elaine May), two co-
       producers (Julia Phillips, "The Sting"; Eleanor Perry,
       "The Man Who Loved Cat Dancing"), one director
       (Elaine May). Essay generalizes on the implications
       of these facts.

1312   Iverson, Lucille. "Feminist Critic of the First An-
       nual Erotic Film Festival (New York, 1972). " Wo-
       men and Film 1, 3-4(1973):23.
       Discusses the kind of entries in the festival and
       gives a brief description and evaluation of a few of
       them.

1313   Jaffe, Patricia. "Editing Cinéma Vérité. " Film Com-
       ment 3, 3(Summer, 1965):43-47.
       Film editor Jaffe discusses her work.

1314   "Janet Wood Carse: Obituary. " New York Times
       (March 24, 1971):46.
       Film editor.

1315   Janis, Elsie. So Far, So Good! New York: Dutton,
       1932.
       Actress, scenarist, co-author, collaborator,
       writer-consultant.

1316   Jeancolas, F. "Femmes à la caméra. " Jeune Cine-
       ma (Paris) 61(February, 1972):1-6.
       Analysis of 3 films directed by women.

1317   Jennings, Talbot, et al. The Good Earth, A Script
       of the 1937 Film by Talbot Jennings, Tess Sle-
       singer, and Claudine West. New York: Crown
       Publishers, 1943.
       Director, Sidney Franklin.

1318   "John Lennon and Yoko Ono: Our Films. " Film-
       makers Newsletter (Marblehead) 6, 8(June, 1973):25-
       27.

Lennon and Ono discuss the origin and content of
their films, with special attention to "Imagine. "

1319   Johnson, Albert. "The Dynamic Gesture: New Amer-
        ican Independents. " Film Quarterly 19,4(Summer,
        1966):6-11.
        Refers to Mary Ellen Bute ("Finnegans Wake")
        and Vic Morrow ("Deathwatch").

1320   _____. "The Negro in American Films: Some Re-
        cent Works. " Film Quarterly 18,4(Summer, 1965):
        14-30.
        "Lilies of the Field"-Nelson; "Pressure Point"-
        Cornfield; "Guns of the Trees"-Mekas; "Affair of the
        Skin"-Maddow; "The Intruder"-Carman; "Gone Are the
        Days"-Webster; "Nothing But a Man"-Raemer and
        Young; "The Cool World"-Shirley Clarke; "One Potato,
        Two Potato"-Pierce.

1321   Johnson, J. L. "A Lady General of the Picture
        Army. " Photoplay 8,1(June, 1915):42.
        On Lois Weber.

1322   Johnston, Claire, ed. "Notes on Women's Cinema. "
        Screen, pamphlet No. 2, 1973. Society for Educa-
        tion in Film and Television, 1973.

1323   _____, ed. The Work of Dorothy Arzner. London:
        British Film Institute, 1975.
        Pamphlet contends that Arzner's films are signi-
        ficant because they were directed by a woman and be-
        cause their structures "raise crucial questions for fem-
        inist film-makers and critics. " Includes two essays,
        an interview, and a filmography.

1324   "Joyce O'Hara: Obituary. " New York Times (Janu-
        ary 10, 1953):17.
        Motion picture executive.

1325   Jungmeyer, J. "Team of Wildlife Naturalist-Photo-
        graphers. " Audio-Visual Guide 22(November, 1955):
        30.
        A portrait of Elma and Alfred Milotte.

1326   Kalmar, S. "Demokrati. " Font (Oslo) 7,1(1973):54-
        57.
        An appeal to Norwegian film-makers to help

the Colombian directors Carlos and Julia Alvarez,
who have been imprisoned for their political films.

1327   Kanfer, S.   "Difficult but Triumphant. "   Time 98
          (September 27, 1971):82-83.
          A portrait of Penelope Gilliatt, motion picture
critic and screenwriter.

1328   Kaplan, Dora.   "Selected Short Subjects. "   Women and
          Film 2(1972):37.
          Discussion of selected films shown at the First
International Festival of Women's Films.   (Amalie
Rothchild, Claudia Weill.)

1329   _____ .   "A Woman Looks at the S. F. I. F. F. "   Wo-
          men and Film 1(1972):46.
          A woman's perspective of the 15th San Francisco
International Film Festival, "a (male) cultural event
of the greatest magnitude.... "

1330   Kaplan, E. Ann.   "Popcorn Venus: Analyzing the
          Fantasy. "   Jump Cut 3(September-October, 1974):
          21.
          Review of Marjorie Rosen's book.

1331   Kaye, Karyn and Gerald Peary.   "Dance, Girl,
          Dance. "   Velvet Light Trap 10(Fall, 1973): 26.
          In depth analysis of the Arzner film.

1332   _____ .   "Features and Directors: Dorothy Arzner. "
          Film Comment (n. d.):6.
          A brief biographical sketch of the directress and
analysis of her films.

1333   Keats, P.   "Ida Takes Over in No-Woman's Land. "
          Silver Screen 20, 8(June, 1950):36.
          Ida Lupino.

1334   Keller, Marjorie.   "Report from Knokke: Exprmentl-
          5. "   Women and Film 2, 7(1975):28.
          Report on the Fifth International Experimental
Film Competition, Belgium, December 25, 1974-Jan-
uary 1, 1975.

1335   Kemp, Jeffery.   "Write What the Film Needs. "   Sight
          and Sound 43, 4(Autumn, 1974):203.
          An interview with Elisabeth Lutyens, composer

of music for films, age 69.   Claims chief problem
of being a woman composer is "Man's prejudice!"
First film score, 1944, "Jungle Mariners." Interview
highlights some frustrations of her career.

1336   Kent, L.   "What Makes Susan Sontag Make Movies."
       New York Times Bio. Ed. (October 11, 1970).
       On Susan Sontag.

1337   Kevles, B. L.   "Interview."   Film Culture 38(Fall,
       1965):15.
       With Joan Chaffee, director.

1338   Kleinhans, Chuck.   "Interview: Julia Reichart and
       Jim Klein."   Jump Cut 5(January-February, 1975):
       11.
       An interview with two radical activists and film-
       makers.

1339   _____.   "Lives of Performers."   Women and Film
       1, 5-6(1974):52.
       A review of the film "Lives of Performers,"
       directed by Yvonne Rainer, one of America's leading
       dancers/choreographers.

1340   Klumph, Inez and Helen Klumph.   Screen Acting.
       Falk Publishing Co. , Inc. , 1922.
       A discussion of make-up.

1341   Knox, Donald.   The Magic Factory; How MGM Made
       "An American in Paris." New York: Praeger
       Publishers, 1973.
       This interesting account of a classic in movie
       musicals is constructed from recollections by the ma-
       jor contributors to the film.   Included are statements
       by actresses Leslie Caron and Nina Foch, editor
       Adrienne Fazan, script timer Honore (Nora) Janney,
       literary consultant Lilly Messinger, dress designer
       Mary Ann Nyberg, costume designer Irene Sharoff,
       publicist Emily Torchia.

1342   Kopanevová, G.   "7/gk."   Film a Doba (Prague) 18, 5
       (May, 1972):235.
       The Soviet script writer, Katerina Vinogradskaja,
       talks about her experiences.

1343   _____.   "Tvurci dvojice bulharského filmu: Irina

Aktasevová a Christo Piskov. " <u>Film a Doba</u>
(Prague) 18, 12(December, 1972):642-44.
An interview with the directress, Irina Aktaseva,
and her co-director, Hristo Piskov; discusses their
film, "Kato pesen. "

1344   Kopkind, A.   "Hollywood--Under the Influence of Wo-
        men?"   <u>Ramparts</u> 13(May, 1975):56-60.

1345   Kustow, L.   "Women in the Trade Unions. "   <u>Film and</u>
        <u>TV Technician</u> 39(January, 1973):20-21.
        On women's rights.

1346   Lacassin, Frances.   "Out of Oblivion: Alice Guy-
        Blaché. "   <u>Sight and Sound</u> 40, 3(Summer, 1971):151-
        54.
        Taken from a forthcoming book: "Le Septieme
        Art au Feminin: Les Femmes et la Mise-en-scene
        de 1895 a 1930. " Introduction includes statement:
        " ... enough women filmmakers now for it to be easy
        to forget just how recent a phenomenon they are ...
        only in 50's ... began to come into their own.   Until
        1939 only a dozen women directors in the world.
        From 1915-1925, you could count them on fingers of
        one hand.   In 1914 ... two ... before that one ...
        Alice Guy. " Brings one up to date on Alice Guy-
        Blaché, 97 years old as of the writing of the article
        (in 1971).   The article tells of this woman, the only
        woman present at the birth of cinema.

1347   "Lady of Many Titles. "   <u>American Magazine</u> 145(April,
        1948):119.
        A portrait of Margaret Ann Young, motion pic-
        ture title expert.

1348   Langlois, G.   "A propos de 'Feu de paille.'"   <u>Téléciné</u>
        (Paris) 178(March, 1973):32.
        An interview.   Volker Schlondörff and Margarethe
        von Trotta discuss their film "Strohfeuer. "

1349   "Latogatás rendezöi műhelyekben (II.). "   <u>Filmkultura</u>
        (Budapest) 6(November-December, 1972):9-14.
        Six Hungarian directors speak of their attitudes
        to their work.   Included is a statement by Livia
        Gyarmathy and Márta Mészáros.

1350   Leacock, Ricky.   "Remembering Frances Flaherty. "

Film Comment 9, 6(November-December, 1973):38.
A remembrance of Frances Flaherty, wife of
Robert Flaherty, documentary director.

1351   Lebouc, G.   "Entretien avec Jacqueline Pierreux,
        productrice. " _Cinéma_ (Paris) 174(March, 1973):
        92-97.
        An interview.   Producer Jacqueline Pierreux,
speaks of her work and the present situation of cinema
in Belgium.

1352   Leisen, E.   'Dans les coulisses d'Olympia. " _Ecran_
        (Paris) 19(November, 1973):13-14.
        Details of the financing of the films on the Ber-
lin Olympic Games which contradict Leni Riefenstahl's
statements.

1353   "Leni Riefenstahl. "   _Film Comment_ 3, 1(Winter, 1965):
        12.
            A biographical sketch of Leni Riefenstahl.   "The
Future Is Entirely Ours, " p. 16 (Outline of T/W):
"Triumph of the Will, " pp. 22-23 (reviews of her
work); "A Comeback for Leni Riefenstahl, " p. 24, by
Ulrich Gregor; "Can the Will Triumph, " p. 28, by Ro-
bert Gardner.

1354   "Leni Riefenstahl. "   _Film Culture_ 56-57(Spring, 1973).
        (Entire Issue).
            "Leni Riefenstahl Interviewed" by Gordon Hitch-
ens, p. 94; "Propaganda as Vision--'Triumph of the
Will'" by Ken Kelman, p. 168; "Production Credits
for 'Triumph of the Will'" on p. 172; 'Nazi Critical
Praise for 'Triumph of the Will'" on p. 174; "The
Production of the Olympia Films.   Incorrect Statements
and their Reputation" by Leni Riefenstahl, p. 176;
"Olympiad 1936"--Discussion by Andrew Sarris and
Dick Schaap p. 181; "Production Credits for 'Olympia'"
on p. 194; 'Nazi Critical Praise for Olympia" on p.
196; 'Why I Am Filming 'Penthesilea'" by Leni Riefenstahl, p. 198; Leni Riefenstahl's letter to Hitchens,
p. 223; Filmography of Leni Riefenstahl, p. 226.

1355   Lerman, L.   'International Movie Report. " _Mademoi-_
        selle 64(February, 1967):116.
            On Mai Zetterling, Swedish actress and director.

1356   _____ .   "People Are Talking About ... " _Vogue_ 164

(October, 1974):221.
An article on Lina Wertmuller, Italian motion
picture director.

1357   Lesage, Julia. "Whose Heroines. " Jump Cut 1(May-
        June, 1974):22.
        A review of Joan Mellen's book, Women and
Their Sexuality in the New Film.

1358   Lester, Elenore. "At Last: A Festival of Women's
        Films. " Ms. 1,4(October, 1972).
        A discussion of the First International Festival
of Women's Films, which ran sixteen days in New
York, Summer, 1972. Names some of women film-
makers and responses by some of the viewer/critics.
Includes Mai Zetterling, "The Girls" (Swedish); Vera
Chytilova, "Something Different" (Czech); Nelly Kaplan,
"A Very Curious Girl" (French); Barbara Loden,
"Wanda" (American); Marta Meszaros, "The Girl"
(Hungarian). Oldies: Arzner's first talkie for Para-
mount "The Wild Party"; "Mädchen in Uniform" (Ger-
man, 1931) ("the" lesbian film); Lina Wertmuller's
"The Lizards" (about men).

1359   "Letters. " Film Comment 3,3(Summer, 1965):82-87.
        Several letters about the Riefenstahl special
issue, Film Comment 3,1(Winter, 1965).

1360   Levitin, Jacqueline. "Mother of the New Wave: An
        Interview with Agnes Varda. " Women and Film 1,
        5-6(1974):62.
        Includes an interview with and filmography of
the French film-maker.

1361   Leyda, Jay. "The Evil That Men Do. " Film Culture
        2,1(1956):21-23.
        Comparison of "Boris Godunov" by Vera Stroyeva,
Russian directress, and "Richard" by Laurence Olivier.

1362   "Lili, Barono Hatvany: Obituary. " New York Times
        (November 13, 1967):47.
        Hungarian-American dramatist and screenwriter.

1363   Linder, H. , ed. "Leni Riefenstahl. " Filmkritik
        (Munich) 16,8(August, 1972):393-441.
        A filmography (special issue).

1364   Lippard, Lucy R.   "Yvonne Rainer on Feminism and
        Her Film. "   The Feminist Art Journal 4, 2(Summer,
        1975):5.
            Rainer talks about her film, "Film About a Wo-
        man Who. "

1365   "Listing of Films. "   Film Culture 37(Summer, 1965):
        7.   Filmmaker's Cooperative Catalogue # 3.
        Linda Talbot.

1366   Littera, G.   "Muzica Ochiului. "   Cinema (Bucharest)
        10, 8(August, 1972):22.
            Brief information on Germaine Dulac.

1367   _____.   "Pasiunea autobiografica. "   Cinema (Bu-
        charest) 10, 8(August, 1972):25.
            On the work of the Polish director, Wanda Jaku-
        bowska.

1368   Littlejohn, Josephine.   "Mrs. Thomas G. Winter:
        Interview with 'Lady Czar of the Movies. '"   Motion
        Picture 40(December, 1930):66, 112.

1369   "Littlewood's War. "   Newsweek 64(October 12, 1964):
        104.
            Joan Littlewood, director.   Article discusses
        her play, "Oh What a Lovely War. "

1370   "Lois Weber Talks Shop. "   Moving Picture World 28,
        9(May 27, 1916):1493.

1371   Loos, Anita.   A Girl Like I.   New York: Viking,
        1966.
            Autobiographical.

1372   _____.   Kiss Hollywood Good-by.   New York: Bal-
        lantine Books, 1974.

1373   _____.   No Mother to Guide Her.   New York: Mc-
        Graw-Hill, 1961.

1374   _____ and Edna Ferber.   "Good Bad Pictures and
        Those Just Bad. "   Theatre 46(July, 1927):41.

1375   Love, Bessie.   "On Working Behind the Camera. "
        Film and Filming 8, 10(July, 1962):16, 44.
            Learning to be a script girl after being a well-
        known actress.

1376   Loveland, Kay and Estelle Changas. "Eleanor Perry:
       One Woman in Film. " Film Comment 7, 1(Spring,
       1971):64.
           An interview with screenwriter who has avoided
       being trapped with women's specialty films. The no-
       velist and playwright's screen credits include "David
       and Lisa" and "Diary of a Mad Housewife. " Includes
       a filmography.

1377   Lovett, Josephine. "The Tortures of Cutting. " Mo-
       tion Picture Classic 28, 10(November, 1924):86-87.
           She edits films for her husband, director John
       S. Robertson.

1378   Lowell, Sondra. "Women in Film. " Take One 3, 5
       (May-June, 1971):32-33.
           A discussion about the preparation of and reac-
       tion to a "Women and Film" lecture.

1379   _____ . "Women in Film. " Take One 3, 4(March-
       April, 1971):43, 45.
           The article discusses improving opportunities
       for women as film-makers. Specific reference to
       film-maker Joan Churchill's difficulties in getting ac-
       cepted by unions.

1380   _____ . "Women in Film. " Take One 3, 7(Septem-
       ber-October, 1971):41-42.

1381   Luft, H. G. "The Screen as a Propaganda Weapon. "
       Journal Producers Guild of America 15, 2(June,
       1973):11-14.
           A survey of propaganda films made in Germany
       under Hitler. Includes those by Leni Riefenstahl.

1382   Lupino, I. "I Cannot Be Good. " Silver Screen 19, 8
       (June, 1949):42.

1383   _____ . "Me, Mother Directress. " Action 2, 3
       (May-June, 1967):14.

1384   _____ . "My Fight for Life. " Photoplay 28, 3(Feb-
       ruary, 1946):58.

1385   _____ . "My Secret Dream. " Photoplay 23(Octo-
       ber, 1943):54.

1386   _____ . "New Faces in New Places, They Are

Needed Behind the Camera, Too. " Films in Review
1,9(December, 1950):17.
She talks of how new talents have been discovered and encouraged by her production company.

1387   . "The Trouble with Men Is Women. " Silver
Screen 17, 6(April, 1947):36.

1388   . "Who Says Men Are People?" Silver
Screen 18, 8(June, 1948):22.

1389   Maas, Willard. "The Gryphon Yaks. " Film Culture
29(Summer, 1963):46-54.
A filmography of Marie Menken. Thoughts on
experimental film-makers and film-making; "Image in
the Snow, " which the author made with Menken and
"George of the Body, " Menken.

1390   Macauley, C. Cameron. "Women's Films: A New
Category in EMC Films 1973-1974. " Lifelong Learning (University of California Extension Media Center,
Berkeley--Newsletter) 42(March 5, 1973):1.
In presenting the new category of women's films
in the University of California Extension Media Center,
Macauley gives a brief history of women in films, including films about World War I women made between
1914-17 and the suffrage movement made in the 20's.
The 30's and 40's were a blank period for women in
films.

1391   McClary, J. "The Gaffer Is a Lady. " Making Films
in New York 7(August, 1973):7-9+ .
Lighting woman is discussed.

1392   McCormick, Ruth. "Magazines. " Cinéaste 5, 2(Spring,
1972):41-42.
Discusses recent issues of three periodicals
(Film Library Quarterly, Take One, Women and Film)
which deal with the question of women and films.

1393   . "Women's Liberation Cinema. " Cinéaste
5, 2(Spring, 1972):1-7.
Reviews nearly a dozen recent films made by
and for women.

1394   MacDonald, M. I. "Alice Brady Talks About Dress
and Make-Up. " Moving Picture World 33(July 21,

1917):426.
The star gives pointers on preparing for a screen role. (Makes a picture every four weeks.) Voices the opinion that cameraman is more important than the director, that she dresses for the character she is to play, and must buy her own costumes. How she does her eye make-up, but not why "the unnecessary and ugly daubing for ... close-ups."

1395   MacDowell, Josephine. "Lois Weber Understands Girls." Cinema Art 5, 18(January, 1927):38-39.
On the director, Lois Weber.

1396   McGary, Eileen. "Documentary Realism and Women's Cinema." Women and Film 2, 7(1975):50.

1397   MacGilluray, Greg and Jim Freeman. "A Life with 'Jonathan.'" American Cinematographer 54, 12(December, 1973):1530.
Film-makers discuss the filming of "Jonathan Livingston Seagull." Brief mention is made of their camera assistant, Cindy Huston.

1398   MacKay, Tanya Ballantyne. "Women on Women in Films." Take One 3, 2(November-December, 1970): 10.

1399   McLucas, Leroy (photographs by). "Shirley Clarke Shooting 'The Cool World.'" Film Culture 27(1962-63):37.

1400   MacMahon, H. "Women Directors of Plays and Pictures." Ladies Home Journal 37(December, 1920): 12-13, 140, 143-4.

1401   Madison Women's Media Collective. "Barbara Loden Revisited." Women and Film 1, 5-6(1974):67.
The film, "Wanda," is re-examined seven years after its original release, through an interview with its director, Barbara Loden.

1402   "Mai Zetterling at the Olympic Games." American Cinematographer 53, 11(November, 1972):1277, 1320-21.
Mai Zetterling discusses her role in the filming of the official film on the Twentieth Olympiad.

1403   Malverne, P.   "Interview."   Motion Picture Classic
        16(May, 1923):60.
        On Lois Weber.

1404   Manoiu, A.   "Contra curentului."   Cinema (Bucharest)
        10, 8(August, 1972):25.
        A survey of the films of Agnes Varda.

1405   _____.   "Nu am orgolii, am doar ambitii ... "
        Cinema (Bucharest) 11, 4(April, 1973):13-14.
        An interview.   Elisabeta Bostan discusses her
        films, in particular, "Veronica."

1406   _____.   "Seninatatea Feminitatii."   Cinema (Bucha-
        rest) 10, 8(August, 1972):23.
        On the work of Rumanian director, Elisabeta
        Bostan.

1407   _____.   "Un Eisenstein Femeie? Tot ce se poate!"
        Cinema (Bucharest) 10, 8(August, 1972):22-23.
        Opportunities available to women to become film
        directors.

1408   Manvell, Roger.   "Ideas from Britain."   Films and
        Filming 1, 7(April, 1955):11.
        The animation tradition in the United Kingdom.
        Joy Batchelor and her partner, John Halas, are dis-
        cussed.

1409   "Marie Menken: Obituary."   New York Times (Decem-
        ber 31, 1970):26.
        Artist and film-maker.

1410   "Marie Menken: Obituary."   New York Times Bio.
        Ed. (December 31, 1970).

1411   Marion, Frances.   How to Write and Sell Film Sto-
        ries.   New York: Covici, Friede, 1937.
        Hollywood screenwriter discusses her work.
        The book contains complete shooting script for "Marco
        Polo" by Robert E. Sherwood.

1412   _____.   Off with Their Heads.   New York: Mac-
        millan, 1972.
        "A serio-comic tale of Hollywood" by famous
        screen writer of the 20's and 30's.   Autobiography.

1413   . Valley People. Freeport, New York:
Books for Libraries Press, 1971.
      Short story.

1414   Markopoulos, Gregory. "Beyond Audio Visual Space;"
Filmography. " Vision 1, 2(Summer, 1962):54.
      On Mary Ellen Bute, director.

1415   . "The Films of Mary Ellen Bute: Beyond
Audio Visual Space. " Vision 1, 2(Summer,
1962):52.
      Two writers discuss the "seeing sound" audio-
visual rhythms of the film-maker. Lists her filmography on p. 54.

1416   . "Three Filmmakers. " Film Culture 35
(Winter, 1964-65):23-24.
      Included is a discussion of Storm DeHirsch's
film, "Goodbye in the Mirror. "

1417   Martin, A. "From 'Wop' Parts to Bossing the Job. "
Photoplay 10, 5(October, 1916):95.
      On Jeanie MacPherson.

1418   Martin, M. "Breve rencontre avec Martha Rodriguez
et Jorge Silva. " Ecran (Paris) 16(June, 1973):33-
34.
      An interview. Documentary film-makers Martha
Rodriguez and Jorge Silva talk about their recent work,
especially "Chircales" and "Planas-testimonio de un
etnocidio. "

1419   . "Djamilia. " Ecran (Paris) 6(June, 1972):
60-61.
      A film review of the film "Djamilja, " combined
with an interview with the directress, Irina Poplavskaja.

1420   Martineau, Barbara. "'La Femme du Ganges,' or,
as the French Say, Who Is Marguerite Duras?"
Jump Cut 5(January-February, 1975):13.
      Review of Duras' film.

1421   . "The New York Women's Film Festival. "
Cinema Canada 5(December-January, 1972-73):34-
36.
      Festival Report.

1422   _____ . "Paris/Chicago: Women's Film Festivals
1974. " Women and Film 2, 7(1975):10.
Introduction by Martineau but remainder of the
article includes observations by other film-makers
and writers.

1423   _____ . "Women vs. Cannes. " Cinema Canada 9
(August-September, 1973):50-52.
Cannes from the point of view of a feminist film
critic. Special reference to the films by women shown
there this year.

1424   _____ . "Women's Film Daily. " Women and Film
1, 5-6(1974):36.
Account of festivals, films pertaining to women.
Also brief answers to "Why study women's films?"
and "how study women's films?"

1425   "Maya Deren: Program Notes on Three Early Films. "
Film Culture 39(1965):1.

1426   Meade, M. "Prime of Ms. Perry. " McCall's 99
(June, 1972).
A portrait of Eleanor Perry, screenwriter.

1427   Mekas, Jonas. "The Experimental Film in America. "
Film Culture 1, 3(May-June, 1955):15-20.
Characteristics of experimental film in U. S.
(ref. New American Cinema). Includes list of "most
representative American Film Poets and Cineplasts. "

1428   _____ . "Films by Yoko Ono and John Lennon. "
Village Voice 16, 1(January 7, 1971):51.
Discusses: "Apotheosis, " "Legs, " "Rape. "

1429   _____ . "In Praise of Marie Menken and Willard
Maas. " Village Voice 12, 44(August 17, 1967):23.
Ref. "Orgia" and "Excited Turkeys. "

1430   _____ . "Interview. " Village Voice 9, 39(July 16,
1964):12.
An interview with Storm DeHirsch. Discusses
her films.

1431   _____ . "Interview. " Village Voice 10, 10(December 24, 1964):12.
An interview with film-maker, Naomi Levine,

and discussion of her career.

1432   . "Interview." Village Voice 12, 17(February 9, 1967):29 and 12, 18(February 16, 1967):27.
Interviews with Susanah Campbell, John Cavanaugh, Barbara Rubin regarding their film-making.

1433   . "Interview." Village Voice 13(December 21, 1967):10.
An interview with Naomi Levine, film-maker.

1434   . "Marie Menken and Willard Maas: In Memoria." Village Voice 16, 2(January 14, 1971): 59.

1435   . "New Films About Women." Village Voice 16, 15(April 15, 1971):67.
"Growing Up Female" by Klein and Reichart; "Pigs" by Warhol; "The Women's Film" by Smith, et al.

1436   . "Notes on Some New Movies and Happiness." Film Culture 37(Summer, 1965):16.
Mentions film-makers Naomi Levine, Marie Menken, Barbara Rubin.

1437   . "Notes on Some Women Experimental Film-makers." Village Voice 8, 40(July 25, 1963):13.
Naomi Levine, Storm DeHirsch, Barbara Rubin, Linda Talbot.

1438   . "Notes on the New American Cinema." Film Culture 24(Spring, 1962):6.
On Shirley Clarke and Marie Menken, directors.

1439   . "Shirley Clarke: Retrospective at the Museum of Modern Art, New York." Village Voice 16, 20(May 20, 1971):63, 72.

1440 Mekas, Marie. "Marie Menken's Films Is Poetry." Village Voice 7, 11(January 4, 1962):11-12.

1441 Melton, Ruby. "Barbara Loden on 'Wanda': An Environment that Is Overwhelmingly Ugly and Destructive." Film Journal 1, 2(Summer, 1971):11.
An interview with Barbara Loden.

1442   "Membership Figures of Women in Filmmaking Unions
          and Guilds. " Women and Film 1(1972):74.
              Lists the number of women compared to total
        membership of women working in the following areas:
        costumers, grips, electricians/gaffers, still photo-
        graphers, art directors, cartoonists, scenic and title
        artists, film technicians, studio projectionists, script
        supervisors, studio teachers, publicists, writers, pro-
        ducers, directors, assistant film directors, associate
        directors/stage managers (TV).

1443   "Membership Roster: American Cinema Editors. "
          American Cinemeditor 24, 1(Spring, 1974):19.
              List of members of honorary film editors' soci-
        ety includes: Dede Allen, Marjorie Fowler, Eve New-
        man, Rita Roland, Barbara McLean, Irene Morra,
        Eda Warren.

1444   Michishita, Kyoko. "Tokyo--New York Video Ex-
          press. " Women and Film 1, 5-6(1974):86.
              Videotapes by Shigeka Kubota, Susan Milano,
        Julie Geiger, Shirley Clarke, Woody and Stella Vas-
        ulka, Nam Jun Paik, and Joan Jonas were presented
        at the three-day video showing and the videos are
        briefly described.

1445   Mickelson, Annette. Art Forum 10(March, 1972):60-
          82.
              An article on Dziga Vertov's wife, Yelizaveta
        Svilova, an editor.

1446   Millstein, G. "Harrison Horror Story. " New York
          Times Magazine (July 21, 1957):44.
              A portrait of Joan Harrison, English motion pic-
        ture producer.

1447   Minoff, P. "Non-Private Lives?" Cue 26, 3(January,
          19, 1957):12
              Ida Lupino.

1448   "Misguided Genius. " Newsweek 84(September 16,
          1974):91.
              A portrait of Leni Riefenstahl, German actress
        and motion picture director.

1449   "Miss Dunham Trains Dancers for New Film. " Ebony
          13(October, 1958):121-22.

Katherine Dunham does choreography for movie
"Green Mansions." Woman choreographer.

1450   "Mr. Duff and Ida." T.V. Guide 5, 22(June 1, 1957):
       17.
       On Ida Lupino.

1451   Morella, Joe, et al. Those Great Movie Ads. New
       Rochelle, N.Y. : Arlington House Publishers, 1972.
       Well-documented survey of Hollywood publicity
       techniques. Some 1000 reproductions of outstanding
       ads and text includes statements by publicity experts
       Eleanor Clark, Joe Morella and Ed Epstein.

1452   "Mother Cutter; V. Fields." Newsweek 84(October
       28, 1974):96+.
       Film editor V. Fields.

1453   "Mother Lupino." Time 81(February 8, 1963):42.
       Ida Lupino. At this time a director for 12 years
       already. A discussion of ther direction of an episode
       in a TV serial, "The Untouchables." Brief, sketchy
       rundown on her directing credits.

1454   Mount, Laura. "Mlle. Gabrielle Chanel to Design
       Clothes for the Movies and the Stars." Collier's
       87(April 4, 1931):21, 60.

1455   Myers, Louis Budd. "Marie Menken Herself." Film
       Culture 45(Summer, 1967):37-39.
       Discussion of "Image in the Snow" (Menken);
       "Narcissus" (Maas); "Life of Juanita" (Warhol).

1456   "Natalie Mabelle (Dunfee) Kalmus: Obituary." New
       York Times (November 18, 1965):47.
       Motion picture photographer.

1457   "Natalie Mabelle (Dunfee) Kalmus: Obituary." Time
       86(November 26, 1965):100.
       Motion picture photographer.

1458   Naumburg, Nancy, ed. We Make the Movies. New
       York: Norton, 1937.
       "Cutting the Film," Anne Bauchens, pp. 199-215.
       Takes readers to studio to show how motion picture
       is made. The book moves from producer to presen-
       tation. Articles are written by outstanding contributors

to their field.   For our purposes two articles are of
interest: "The Actress Plays Her Part" by Bette
Davis and "Cutting the Film" by Anne Bauchens, cutter for C. B. DeMille, Paramount Pictures.   Her introduction is interesting: discusses quality of Hollywood motion pictures.   Nancy Naumburg studies dramatic production.   Motion picture and still photographer.   Photographed and co-directed "Sherriffed"
(1934) and "Taxi" (1935).

1459   [No entry]

1460   Nelson, K.   "Keep It Simple!"   Silver Screen 18, 12
          (October, 1948):44.
              On Ida Lupino.

1461   Nemser, Cindy.   "Editorial: Rainer and Rothschild,
          an Overview. "   The Feminist Art Journal 4, 2(Sum-
          mer, 1975):4.
              Editorial on Yvonne Rainer, dancer, choreogra-
       pher and film-maker, and Amalie R. Rothschild, film-
       maker.

1462   "The New American Cinema Group, the First State-
          ment of the NAC Group. "   Film Culture 22-23(Sum-
          mer, 1961):130-33.
              Lists members.   Manifesto of NAC.

1463   "A New Twist. "   T. V. Guide 5, 28(July 13, 1957):28.
              On Ida Lupino.

1464   Newman, Joyce.   "Super-8 News. "   Women and Film
          1, 5-6(1974):95.
              Discusses Super-8 women film-makers and teach-
       ers.

1465   _____ .   "Super-8 News. "   Women and Film 2, 7
          (1975):110.
              Brief sketches of some Super-8 film-makers.

1466   "Newsreel, Newsreel, Newsreel. "   Film Quarterly
          22, 2(Winter, 1968-69):43-48.
              Comments on Newsreel by Newsreel film-makers:
       Norm Fruchter, Marilyn Buck, Karen Ross, Robert
       Kramer.

1467   "Nicole Vedrès: Obituary. "   Sight and Sound 35

(Spring, 1966):100.

(Portrait of French author, essayist, and producer.

1468 "The Night Porter." Films and Filming 19, 12(September, 1973):33.

Résumé of the career of Liliana Cavani, Italian directress, with special reference to her latest film, "The Night Porter."

1469 Nin, Anaïs   The Diary of Anais Nin. 4 vols. Edited and with a preface by Gunther Stuhlmann. Vol. I. New York: The Swallow Press and Harcourt Brace Jovanovich, Inc., 1966; Vols. II-IV, 1967.

Personal record of Nin's struggles and pleasures as a woman and an artist. Vol. IV covers the period of her life from 1944-47 and covers her critical breakthrough as a writer and friendship with Maya Deren, experimental film-maker and film theorist.

1470 Noble, Lorraine, ed.   Four Star Scripts: Actual Shooting Scripts and How They Are Written.   Garden City, N.Y.: Doubleday, Doran and Co., 1936.

Includes scripts: "Lady for a Day"; "It Happened One Night"; "Little Women"; "Story of Louis Pasteur."

1471 Nolan, J. E.   "Ida Lupino."   Films in Review 16, 1 (January, 1965):61.

Letter to editors updating Ida Lupino's filmography, with the directing she's done for TV.

1472 _____.   "Ida Lupino, Director; Directing Filmography."   Film Fan Monthly 89(November, 1968):8.

1473 "Nominees for Eddie Awards."   American Cinemeditor 23, 4(Winter, 1973-74):10.

Nominees for editing awards for 1973 include: Marjorie Fowler for "The Blue Knight," a TV film.

1474 "Non-Olympian."   Time 102, 12(September 17, 1973): 96.

Mai Zetterling.   Review of the film "Visions of Eight," impressions of the 1972 Olympics directed by 8, including Mai Zetterling.   Consists of "cliches of contemporary film making."   "Most abused device" is Mai Zetterling's ironic cross cutting.

1475   [No entry]

1476   Nugent, F. S.   "Work of Wardrobe Department at
            MGM Studio. " Good Housekeeping 122(January,
            1946):12-13, 128.

1477   O'Brien, G.   "Interview with Ruth Gordon. " Inter/
            View 20(March, 1972):32-33, 43.
                Ruth Gordon talks about films and writing for
        films.

1478   _____ and L. Gerard.   "Anita Loos, Gentlemen
            Prefer Genius. " Inter/View 23(July, 1972):20-26.
                A discussion with scriptwriter and author Anita
        Loos.

1479   Ono, Yoko.   "Yoko Ono on Yoko Ono. " Film Culture
            48-49(Winter-Spring, 1970):32-33.
                Discusses "Film No. 4, " "Film No. 5" and
        "Rape. "

1480   "Opening the Old Kit Bag. " Time 82(July 5, 1963):
            64.
                On Joan Littlewood, director.

1481   Orme, Michael.   "The Continuity Girl. " Illustrated
            London News 188(April 18, 1936):690.

1482   Orth, M.   "How to Succeed: Fail, Lose, Die. "
            Newsweek 83(March 4, 1974):50-51.
                Gives figures on number of women film-makers.

1483   "The Pacific Film Archive. " Women and Film No. 2
            (1972):70.
                (See entry under "Images. ")

1484   Parent, Gail.   Sheila Levine Is Dead and Living in
            New York.   New York: Putnam, 1972.
                Novel and screenplay.

1485   Parker, F.   "Approaching the Art of Arzner. " Action
            8, 4(July-August, 1973):9-14.
                Discusses the career of director Dorothy Arzner,
        with special reference to her pre-1935 films.

1486   _____.   "Discovering Ida Lupino. " Action 8, 4(July-
            August, 1973):19-23.
                The directing career of Ida Lupino.

1487   Parsons, Mrs. Louella Oettinger. How to Write for
        the Movies. Chicago: A. C. McClurg and Co.,
        1915.
        (Same Louella.)

1488   "Pasolini, Varda, Allio, Sarris, Michelson." Film
        Culture 42(Fall, 1966):96-101.
            Their concepts of film-making. Includes direc-
        tress Agnes Varda; critic Annette Michelson.

1489   Patterson, Frances Taylor. Cinema Craftsmanship;
        a Book for Photo Playwrights. New York: Har-
        court, Brace and Howe, 1920.
            Included in this discussion of the art and science
        of photoplaywriting by this Columbia professor is the
        script of the film "Witchcraft" by Miss Margaret Turn-
        bull, one of the foremost scenarists of her day.

1490   Peary, Gerald. "Czarina of the Silent Screen: So-
        lax's Alice Blaché." Velvet Light Trap 6(Fall,
        1972):2-7.
            Based on Lacassin's article above and on
        Blaché's articles in the Moving Picture World. In-
        cludes a reprint of one of Blache's articles from Mo-
        ving Picture World from 1914.

1491   _____. "Dorothy Arzner." Cinema (Beverly Hills)
        34(1974):2.
            "A survey of the career of an important and in-
        sufficiently discussed director, with special emphasis
        on her 1933 'Christopher Strong,' followed by an ex-
        tensive interview (with Karyn Kay) and a filmography."
        Many photos.

1492   _____. "Sanka, Pink Ladies, and Virginia Slims."
        Women and Film 1,5-6(1974):82.
            Some notes about early women film-makers:
        Alice Guy-Blaché, Miriam Nesbitt, Ruth Bryan Owen
        (Wm. Jennings Bryan's daughter); Frances Marion,
        Grace Cunard, Zelda Sears, Dorothy Arzner, Dorothy
        Farnum, Dorothy Davenport (Mrs. Wallace Reid),
        Margaret J. Winkler (film distributor), Elizabeth Pic-
        kett, Katherine Eggleston (editor), Lois Weber, Ida
        Lupino, Wanda Tuchock. Notes: Arzner was only
        woman director in Hollywood, 1928-49, when Ida Lu-
        pino appeared. One exception, Wanda Tuchock who
        co-directed one film.

1493 _____ and K. Kay. "Dorothy Arzner: Interview."
Cinema 34(1974):10-17.

1494 Pedersen, Vibeke. "Danish Letter." Take One 3, 2
(November-December, 1970):35-37.
Women in Danish film. Article lists a number
of outstanding Danish films by and/or about women.
Includes description and analysis.

1495 Peltret, E. "On the Lot with Lois Weber." Photoplay 12, 5(October, 1917):89.

1496 "People Are Talking About ... " Vogue 156(September 1, 1970):375.
A portrait of Eleanor Perry, screenwriter.

1497 Perry, Eleanor. The Swimmer. New York: Stein
and Day, 1967.
A novelized script of 1967 film directed by Frank
Perry.

1498 _____ and Frank Perry and Truman Capote. Tri-
logy; An Experiment in Multimedia. New York:
Macmillan, 1969.
"Notes on Adaptation" by E. Perry giving screen-
writing, adaptations for screen. 3 stories (Capote),
3 people, 3 media (print, TV, film). A study of the
process by which the stories found expression in the
three different media.

1499 "Phoebe Ephron: Obituary." New York Times (October 14, 1971):48.
A portrait and obituary of the dramatist and motion picture screenwriter.

1500 Picard, L. "Holly Solomon." Inter/View 23(July,
1972):38, 45.
An interview and discussion with film-maker
Holly Solomon.

1502 "Plants and Animals." Newsweek 67(June 13, 1966):
114-15.
On Agnes Varda, French director.

1501 "Poetry and Form: A Symposium with Maya Deren,
Arthur Miller, Dylan Thomas, Parker Tyler," in
Film Culture Reader, P. Adams Sitney, ed. New

York: Praeger Publishers, 1970.   171+ pp.

1503   Polt, Harriet.   "Interview with Shirley Clarke."   Film
       Comment 2, 2(Spring, 1964):31-32.
            The director tells of her films and how she be-
       gan her career.   Also tells what it's like to be a wo-
       man film director.

1504   Praunheim, R. von.   "Film der Welt."   Filmkritik
       (Munich) 16, 2(February, 1972):78.
            The making of a new film in America and Asia,
       reported by the film-maker, Rosa von Praunheim.
       Includes cineastic impressions of the different countries
       visited.

1505   "Problemy kino FRG."   Iskusstvo Kino (Moscow) 6
       (June, 1973):148-52.
            An interview.   Volker Schlöndorff and Margarethe
       von Trotta discuss the cinema of West Germany.

1506   "Problemy-vyhlidky-otazniky."   Film a Doba (Prague)
       19, 10(October, 1973):540-42.
            An interview.   Volker Schlöndorff and Margarethe
       von Trotta talk about the problems of film production
       in the German Federal Republic.

1507   "Producer."   New Yorker 44(January 4, 1969):25-27.
            Mag Bodard, Italian-French producer.

1508   "Program and General Attendance Facts: Filmex
       1974."   American Cinematographer 55, 6(June, 1974):
       708.
            List of the films and film-makers participating
       in the 1974 Los Angeles International Film Exposition.
       One entry is by film-makers: Morgan Fisher, Pat
       O'Neill, Jo Carson, Peggy Wolff, Roberta Friedman,
       Adam Beckett, Thom Anderson.

1509   "Program at the 2nd Los Angeles International Film
       Exposition."   American Cinematographer 53, 11 Nov-
       ember, 1972):1292.
            Mentions a special program on "Women and Wo-
       men Film-makers."   Includes: "Angela," a feature-
       length film by Yolande DeLuart, and "Judy Chicago
       and the California Girls," by Judith Donkoff.

1510   Pryor, William Clayton and Helen Sloman Pryor.

<u>Let's Go to the Movies.</u>   New York: Harcourt,
Brace, 1939.
Views on costumes and make-up, pp. 96-113.

1511   Pugh, Sally.   "Home Born Baby. "   <u>Women and Film</u>
       1, 3-4(1973):102.
       A discussion of the cinema vérité documentary
       on natural childbirth.

1512   Pulliam, Rebecca.   "Newsreel: Radical Film-
       makers. "   <u>The Velvet Light Trap.</u>   4(Spring, 1972).

1513   Pyros, J.   "Notes on Women Directors. "   <u>Take One</u>
       3, 2(February, 1972):a special issue.

1514   Queval, Jean.   "Nicole Vedrès. "   <u>Sight and Sound</u>
       35, 2(Spring, 1966):100.
       In memoriam to the French documentary direc-
       tor.

1515   Queyrel, P.   "Digne.   Le Cinéma différent n'a laissé
       personne indifférent. "   <u>Cinéma</u> (Paris) 178-179 (July-
       August, 1973):25-27.
       The account of a meeting in Digne where Mar-
       guerite Duras presented her latest film "La femme
       du Ganges. "

1516   "Radical American Film Questionnaire--Part II. "
       <u>Cinéaste</u> 6, 1(1973):14-21.

1517   Ransohoff, Doris.   "Film Editing in a Large Studio:
       Every Cut Counts. "   <u>Californian</u> 1(May, 1946):70-
       71.

1518   Raymond, Alan and Susan.   "An American Family. "
       <u>American Cinematographer</u> 54, 5(May, 1973):590+
       How husband and wife team filmed the twelve-
       part documentary series that became the most talked-
       about program on public TV.

1519   Read, Jan.   "Pregnant with Jeopardy. "   <u>Hollywood</u>
       Quarterly 4, 4(Summer, 1950):354-59.
       British scriptwriters' struggle for existence.

1520   "Reel Life at Last--Women and Film. "   <u>Ms.</u>   11, 2
       (August, 1973):95.
       Lists new outstanding film-makers and their

films. (See entry under "Images. ")

1521 Reid, Alison. "Canadian Women Directors. " Take
      One 3, 2(February, 1972):Special Issue.

1522 _____ . Canadian Women Film Makers. Canadian
      Film Institute, 1972.

1523 Reid, Janet. "From Telephone Operator to Motion
      Picture Producer. " Motion Picture Magazine (May,
      1923):66.
           About 22-year-old Grace Hoskins, producer. At
      this time the only previous woman producer was Lois
      Weber. This article was written after the completion
      of her first film.

1524 Reiniger, Lotte. "Scissors Make Films. " Sight and
      Sound 5, 17(Spring, 1936):13-15.
           Her technique in making puppet films.

1525 Remont, F. "Sketch. " Motion Picture 15(May, 1918):
      59.
           On Lois Weber.

1526 "Replies to a Questionnaire. " Sight and Sound 23, 2
      (October-December, 1953):99-104, 112.
           Catherine de la Roche, Freda Bruce Lockhart,
      and Dilys Powell answer questions on the role of the
      critic and the relationship between film-maker and
      critic.

1527 "Replies to a Questionnaire. " Sight and Sound 26, 4
      (Spring, 1957):180-85.
           Iris Murdoch and Colin Wilson answer questions
      concerning the role of the artist and of the critic.

1528 [No entry]

1529 "Reviews. " Take One 3, 2(November-December, 1970):
      28-35.
           (See entry under "Images. ")

1530 "Reviews. " Women and Film 1(1972):66+
           "Three Lives" directed by Kate Millett (Susan
      Rice); "Dirty Mary" directed by Nelly Kaplan (Brenda
      Roman); "Les Stances à Sophie" Christine Rochefort
      and Moshe Mizraki. (Everywoman.) "Vivre Sa Vie, "
      Godard (Siew-Hwa Beh).

1531   Rice, Susan. "Shirley Clarke: Image and Images. "
        Take One 3, 2(November-December, 1970):20-22.
        An interview with Shirley Clarke. Includes a
        filmography.

1532   _____. "Some Women's Films. " Take One 3, 2
        (February, 1972):30-31.
        Includes "It Only Happens to Others" by Nadine
        Trintignant, "L'Opera-Mouffe" by Agnes Varda.

1533   Richardson, Brenda. "Women, Wives, Film-makers:
        An Interview with Gunvor Nelson and Dorothy Wi-
        ley. " Film Quarterly 25, 1(Fall, 1971):34-40.
        Two women film-makers discuss themselves in
        their many roles.

1534   Riefenstahl, Leni. "Notizen zu Penthesilea. " Film-
        kritik (Munich) 16, 8(August, 1972):416-25.
        Riefenstahl's unrealized project for a film on
        the legend of Penthesilea.

1535   _____. "Statement on Sarris/Gesner Quarrel about
        'Olympia'. " Film Comment 4, 2-3(Fall-Winter,
        1967):126.

1536   Ring, Frances K. "Story Analysts: the Case of the
        Cream Puffs. " Hollywood Quarterly 2(October,
        1946):30-34.

1537   Ringgold, Gene. "Constance Bennett. " Films in Re-
        view 16, 8(October, 1965):472-95.
        A filmography and career sketch of the stage
        and screen actress and film producer.

1538   Rivkin, Allen and Laura Kerr. Hello Hollywood! The
        Story of the Movies by the People Who Make Them.
        New York: Doubleday and Co. , 1962.
        "Pseudo-documentary account--very good for 'le-
        gends. '"--Manchel.

1539   Robinson, Martha. Continuity Girl, a Story of Film
        Production. London: Oxford University Press,
        1946.

1540   Rock, Gail. "Pacific Polemic, Political Tour. " Ms.
        1, 8(February, 1973):32.
        Review of the film "Crocodile Tears: the Year

of the Woman, " the first feature film produced, written, directed, photographed and edited by an all-woman
staff (with the exception of the co-producer, Porter
Bibb). Poet-novelist and now film-maker, Sandra
Hochman's cinematic poem about what she saw,
thought, felt in Miami Beach at the 1972 Democratic
Convention. (See entry under "Images. ")

1541   _____. "Play It As It Lays. " Ms. 1, 7(January,
1973):41.
Review of film "Play It As It Lays" based on
novel by Joan Didion and adapted to screen by her.
(See also entry under "Images. ")

1542   Rogoff, G. "Joan and the Good Guys. " Reporter 31
(November 19, 1964):52.
On Joan Littlewood, director.

1543   Rosen, Marjorie. "Shirley Clarke: Videospace Ex-
plorer. " Ms. III, 10(April, 1975):107.
Dancer, film-maker, is interviewed and discusses
her new interest in video.

1544   _____. "Three Films in Search of a Distributor. "
Ms. IV, I(July, 1975):30.
Discussion of three films by and/or about women
which have had distribution difficulties: "Other Half
of the Sky" by Shirley MacLaine and directed by Claudia Weill; "Coup pour Coup" and "Hester Street" directed by Joan Micklin Silver.

1545   _____. "Women, Their Films and Their Festival. "
Saturday Review (August 12, 1972):32.

1546   Rosen, Steve. "SOS--Save Our Sea. " American Cinematographer 52, 9(September, 1971):888.
High school film-makers serve as crew in the
making of this successful ecology documentary film.
Includes young female film-makers Linda Olmstead
and Maureen Goff.

1547   Rosenberg, Bernard and Harry Silverstein. Real Tin-
sel. New York: Macmillan, 1970.
A portrait of Anita Loos, screenwriter, is con-
tained on pp. 401-11.

1548   Rosenheimer, A. , Jr. "Review: Maya Deren's Ana-

gram of Ideas on Art, Form and Film. " Theatre
Arts 31(January, 1947):68.

1549   Roth, W. and G. Pflaum. "Gespräch mit Danièle
       Huillet und Jean-Marie Straub. " Filmkritik (Mun-
       ich) 17, 2(February, 1973):66-79.
           An interview. Discussion about the film "Ges-
       chichtsunterricht, " made by Danièle Huillet and her
       husband, Jean-Marie Straub.

1550   Roud, Richard. "Conversation with Marguerite Du-
       ras. " Sight and Sound 29, 1(Winter, 1959-60):16-17.
           A discussion of her scenario and dialogue for
       "Hiroshima Mon Amour. "

1551   _____. "The Left Bank. " Sight and Sound 32, 1
       (Winter, 1962-63):24-27.
           Agnes Varda, Marker and Resnais compared and
       contrasted.

1552   St. John, A. R. "Story of Ida Lupino. " Cosmopoli-
       tan 114, 46(January, 1943) and following issues.

1553   Sarachild, Kathie. "Women's Films: The Artistic Is
       Political. " Feminist Art Journal 2, 2(Winter, 1972):
       6-8+.

1554   Sarris, Andrew, ed. Interviews with Film Directors.
       Indianapolis: Bobbs-Merrill, 1967.
           A portrait of Leni Riefenstahl, director, pp.
       387-402.

1555   _____. "Oddities and One Shots. " Film Culture
       28(Spring, 1963):45.
           On Ida Lupino.

1556   _____. The Primal Screen. New York: Simon
       and Schuster, 1975.
           Barbara Loden's "Wanda, " p. 170. Some ob-
       servations about women directors in general and Loden
       in particular--"instinctual" abilities characterize Loden

1557   _____. "Run-down on Women Directors. " Village
       Voice 16, 11(March 18, 1971):65.
           Ref. Barbara Loden's "Wanda. "

1558   _____. "Women Directors. " Village Voice 16, 11

(March 18, 1971):65.
>Rundown of women directors.   Refers to Barbara
Loden.

1559   Sashi.   "I Seen It in a Picture Show. " Women and
>Film 1, 3-4(1973):100.
>>A discussion of one event at "Women's Week"
held at UCLA, April, 1973, which included various
feminist speakers and programs.   50 women in film
and TV organized and participated in a panel discussion about the influence of the media on society.

1560   Sava, V.   "Marturii de pe platou: Veronica. " Cin-
>ema (Bucharest) 10, 7(July, 1972):33.
>>The Rumanian director, Elisabeta Bostan, talks
about the shooting of her new film, "Veronica. "

1561   Sayers, Dorothy.   "Detective Stories for the Screen. "
>Sight and Sound 7, 26(Summer, 1938):49-50.
>>Asserts that detective novelist is best detective
scriptwriter.

1562   "Schloendorff.   Feu de paille. " Jeune Cinéma (Paris)
>67(December-January, 1972-73):17-18.
>>An interview.   Volker Schlöndorff and Margare-
the von Trotta speak of their film "Strohfeuer" and
the problems of women in the German Federal Republic today.

1563   Scholar, Nancy.   "Maedchen in Uniform. " Women and
>Film 2, 7(1975):68.
>>Review of Leontine Sagan's 1931 release, "Maed-
chen in Uniform. "

1564   Scott, Audrey.   I Was a Hollywood Stunt Girl.   Phila-
>delphia: Dorrance, 1969.

1565   Secteur, P.   "Jeunes Cinéastes, au feminin: les '5a7'
>de Michka, Gorki. " Cinéma Pratique (Paris) 122
>(April, 1973):39-41.

1566   Seider, Norman R.   "New East German Cinema: An
>Interview with Gitta Nickel. " Women and Film 1,
>5-6(1974):48.
>The East German director is interviewed.

1567   Shadegy, Stephen C.   Clare Booth Luce; a biography.

New York: Simon and Schuster, 1970.
Primarily a playwright, but some plays adapted
for films.

1568   "She Cuts the Kisses. " American Magazine 147(January, 1949):99.
On Barbara McLean, film editor.

1569   Silber, Irwin and Bill Nichols.   "Confronting the Consciousness Industry: Two Analyses of Women's
Role in the Media. " Women and Film 1(1972):34.
Two differing views of how women can help to
shape a new consciousness.

1570   "Silver Anniversary Eddie Awards. " American Cinemeditor 25, 1(Spring, 1975):10.
Awards for outstanding achievement in film editing as determined by editing society are listed.   Women nominated were: Dorothy Spencer, "Earthquake";
Jodie Copelan, TV show, "The Word Is Persistence. "

1571   Sitney, P. Adams.   "Imagism in Four Avant Garde
Films. " Film Culture 32(Winter, 1963-64):15-23.
A discussion.   Single-central-image films, in-
cluding "Choreography for Camera" by Maya Deren.

1572   "Sketch. " Film 51(Spring, 1968):33.
On Vera Chytilova, director.

1573   "Sketch. " Motion Picture 53(April, 1937):22.
On Dorothy Arzner.

1574   "Sketch. " Movie Classic 11(December, 1936):64.
On Dorothy Arzner.

1575   Sloan, William.   "A Discussion of 'Troublemakers'
and 'A Time for Burning. '" Film Comment 4, 2-3
(Fall-Winter, 1967):54-56.
"A Time for Burning, " directed by Wm. C.
Jersey and Barbara Connell.

1576   Smith, B. H.   "A Perpetual Leading Lady. " Sunset,
the Pacific Monthly 32, 3(March, 1914):634.
Lois Weber.

1577   Smith, F. L.   "Alice Guy-Blaché. " Films in Review
15, 4(April, 1964):254.

A letter to the magazine about the female director.

1578   Smith, Frederick Y., ed. ACE Second Decade Anni-
        versary Book. Los Angeles: American Cinema
        Editors, Inc., 1971.
             American Cinema editors anniversary book in-
        cludes membership lists, award winners. Photo and
        brief biography and filmography of each member. Wo-
        men include: Marjorie Fowler, Eve Newman, Viola
        Lawrence, Barbara McLean, Irene Morra, Eda War-
        ren. Also includes a list of feature film titles with
        editing credits.

1579   Smith, Sharon. "The Image of Women in Film: Some
        Suggestions for Future Research." Women and
        Film 1(1972):13.
             (See entry under "Images.")

1580   _____. "Women Who Make Movies." Women and
        Film 1, 3-4(1973):77.
             A condensed version of Smith's later book. Ar-
        ticle gives a brief survey of women directors includ-
        ing biographical and filmographical information. For
        more complete and inclusive information on women
        directors, refer to Smith's book in reference section.

1581   Solanas, Fernando and Octavio Getino. "Toward a
        Third Cinema." Cinéaste 4, 3(Winter, 1970-71):1.
             Encourages a movement to new cinema, including
        "feminist," to fight the System.

1582   Sontag, Susan. Brother Carl; A Screenplay. New
        York: Farrar, Straus and Giroux, 1973.

1583   _____. Duet for Cannibals. New York: Farrar,
        Straus, and Giroux, 1970.
             Script of 1970 film written and directed by Susan
        Sontag.

1584   [No entry]

1585   "Special Report: the Woman Director." Action 8, 4
        (July-August, 1973):7-23.
             A special issue. A series of articles discuss
        the role of the woman-filmmaker and her place in the
        development of the motion picture industry.

1586   Starr, C.   "Animation: Abstract and Concrete. " Sa-
            turday Review 35(December 13, 1952):46.
                On Mary Ellen Bute, director.

1587   _____.   "Movie-making Mother. " Saturday Review
            36(August 8, 1953):36-38.
                On Judith Rosemary (Sparks) Crawley, Canadian
        motion picture producer.

1588   Starr, Helen.   "Putting It Together. " Photoplay 14
            (July, 1918):52-54.
                Describes the art of cutting.   Refers to Rose
        Smith, early editor.

1589   "Statements by Curtis Harrington, Maya Deren, Ed
            Emshwiller, Robert Brier, Carmen D'Avino. " Film
            Culture 29(1963):69.
                Film-makers Deren and D'Avino.

1590   Steed, Judy.   "It's No Secret that Oil and Gas and
            Film Festivals Are Related. " This Magazine 3
            (August, 1973):3-5
                The author and film-maker argues that recent
        International Film Festival in Toronto and other media
        projects are run and organized by Americans, both
        men and women.

1591   Steen, Mike.   Hollywood Speaks.   New York: Putnam,
            1974.
                The book includes sections on Ruth Burch, mo-
        tion picture casting director (pp. 354-63), and Catalina
        Lawrence, script supervisor (pp. 345-53).

1592   Sternberg, Janet.   "Movies That Remember Mama. "
            Ms. III, 9(March, 1975):38.
                (See entry under "Images. ")

1593   "Strasberg-on-Avon. " Time 76(October 31, 1960):62.
                Joan Littlewood, stage director and film director
        for "Sparrows Can't Sing, " 1963.

1594   "Straub om den Sprakløse Film. " Fant (Oslo) 6, 3
            (1972):28-43.
                Jean-Marie Straub and his wife, Danièle Huillet,
        discuss their film "Les yeux ne veulent pas en tout
        temps se fermer" and the problems of film aesthetics
        in general.

1595   Struck, Karen. "Weg von den Müttern." Der Spiegel
          48(November 26, 1973):163-66.
          The writer criticizes the First International Wo-
       men's Film Festival in Berlin which included discus-
       sion groups as well as films by women. Viewpoint of
       the films was too simplistic and narrow; a small num-
       ber of media women claimed to speak for all--women
       from privileged backgrounds for working class women.
       In films, women were self-sufficient, active, self-
       assured career women, not women with problems.

1596   "Sue Schapiro, Lady Movie Producer." Sepia 19(Aug-
          ust, 1970):32-36.

1597   Sullivan, Beth. "Bed and Sofa/Master of the House."
          Women and Film No. 1(1972):21.
          (See entry under "Images.")

1598   Sullivan, Pat. "The Second Annual New York Women's
          Video Festival." Women and Film 1, 5-6(1974):96.
          Festival held in New York City, September 28-
       October 14, 1974, is discussed.

1599   Tadros, J.-P. "Marie-Claire Blais et Claude Weisz
          répondent à Jean-Pierre Tadros." Cinéma Québec
          (Montreal) 2:6-7(March-April, 1973):32-33.
          An interview. Marie-Claire Blais and Claude
       Weisz explain how they worked together to make the
       film "Une saison dans la vie d'Emmanuel."

1600   "Talks on Her Movie, 'It Only Happens to Others.'"
          Show 2, 10(December, 1971):36.
          On Nadine Trintignant.

1601   Tallmer, Jerry. "For Maya Deren." Village Voice
          6, 52(October 19, 1961):11, 16.
          In memoriam.

1602   "Ten Super Women Achievers." Mademoiselle 76(Feb-
          ruary, 1973):118.
          A portrait of Amalie Rothschild, motion picture
       film-maker.

1603   "They Stand Out from the Crowd." Literary Digest
          118(November 3, 1934):12.
          On Dorothy Arzner.

1604   "Third World Perspectives: Focus on Sarah Maldor-
       or. " Women and Film 1, 5-6(1974):71.
       The French/Angolese film-maker is interviewed
and her films reviewed.

1605   "Third World Perspectives: Reviews. " Women and
       Film 2, 7(1975):76.
       Reviews of: "Introduction to the Enemy" direc-
ted by Christine Burrill, Jane Fonda, Tom Hayden,
Haskell Wexler, Bill Yahrans; "Memories of Under-
development" by Thomas Gutierrez Alea.

1606   Tildesley, A. L.   "She Stepped Down to Step Up. "
       Independent Woman 32(November, 1953):402-3+ .
       On Dorothy Arzner, director.

1607   Tildesley, R. M.   "Dorothy Arzner; Director. " Wo-
       mans Journal 14(February, 1929):25.

1608   "Top Lyricists Seek Oscar No. Two. " Biography
       News 1(May, 1974):494.
       Marilyn Bergman and J. Alan Haber; portrait
of film lyricists.

1609   Tournès, A.   "Liliana Cavani. " Jeune Cinéma (Paris)
       63(May-June, 1972):20-24.
       A film review of "I Cannibali" and interview with
the director, Liliana Cavani.

1610   Trojan, J.   "Who's Who in Filmmaking: Beginnings
       ... Martha Coolidge. " Sightlines 6(May/June,
       1973):11-12.
       New film-maker is discussed.   (N. Y. -Ed'l.
Film Lib. Assoc.)

1611   Tuckman, Mitch.   "Interview with Judy Smith. " Wo-
       and Film No. 1(1972):30.
       An interview with the film-maker, Judy Smith,
and discussion of her film, "The Women's Film. "

1612   Turnbull, Margaret.   The Close-Up.   New York:
       Harper and Bros. , 1918.
       The author was a famous screenwriter.

1613   "Twelve Women Who Did Something: Mademoiselle
       Awards. " Mademoiselle 78(February, 1974):104.

Includes a portrait of Claudia Weill, motion picture photographer and executive.

1614 "Twelve Women Working to Make Things Better." Mademoiselle 81(February, 1975):123. Jill Godmilow, film-maker, is one.

1615 Tynan, K. "Joan of Cockaigne." Holiday 36(November, 1964):113. On Joan Littlewood, director.

1616 Van Dongen, Helen. "Robert Flaherty, 1884-1951." Film Quarterly 18, 4(Summer, 1965):2-14. Her experiences editing "The Land" and "Louisiana Story."

1617 Van Loon, H. H. "Lois the Wizard. A Chat with Lois Weber." Motion Picture 11, 6(July, 1916):41.

1618 Van Wert, William. "Germaine Dulac: First Feminist Film-maker." Women and Film 1, 5-6(1974):55. Most important and prolific French director between 1920 and 1930. Her "Film style proceeded from psychological realism and symbolism through surrealism to documentaries and attempts at transposing musical structures to film.... "

1619 _____. "Love, Anarchy, and the Whole Damned Thing." Jump Cut No. 4(November-December, 1974):8. Review of Lina Wertmuller's "Love and Anarchy."

1620 Verdi, E. "Entretien avec Liliana Cavani." Cinéma (Paris) 167(June, 1972):144-47. Liliana Cavani talks about her latest film, "I Cannibali."

1621 Vermilye, Jerry. "Ida Lupino." Films in Review 10, 5(May, 1959):266-83. A filmography and career sketch.

1622 Viertel, Salka. The Kindness of Strangers. New York: Holt, Rinehart and Winston, 1969. An autobiography of the actress-turned-writer. The author arrived in Hollywood in 1929. She worked with all of Garbo's films. She was involved with the Hollywood Ten and the hearings in the 1950's.

1623   Vinson, James, ed. Contemporary Dramatists. New
         York: St. Martins, 1973.
         Elaine May is discussed on pp. 519-20.

1624   Visart, Natalie. "Designing Costumes for the Actors. "
         Collier's 104(August 5, 1939):17, 46.

1625   Vogel, Amos. "I Made a Glass Hammer." Village
         Voice 16, 25(June 24, 1971):65, 74.
         Includes an interview with Yoko Ono and John
         Lennon. They discuss making films together. Ref.
         "Apotheosis, " "Fly. "

1626   _____. "Reviews. " Village Voice 16, 11(March
         18, 1971):71.
         A review of Gunvor Nelson and Dorothy Wiley
         films, "My Name is Oona, " "Schmeerguntz, " "Fog
         Pumas. "

1627   "Vyvyan Donner: Obituary. " New York Times (June
         29, 1965):32.
         Motion picture editor (and fashion critic).

1628   Walker, Anne. "Dressing the Movies. " Woman's
         Home Companion 48(May, 1921):24.
         Discusses Claire West, costumer for C. B. De-
         Mille and Sophie Wachner for Goldwyn Studios.

1629   _____. "The Girls Behind the Screen. " Woman's
         Home Companion 48(January, 1921):14, 50-51.

1630   Ward, M. "The Making of 'An American Family. '"
         Film Comment 9, 6(November-December, 1973):24-
         31.
         An interview with Susan Raymond, Alan Raymond
         and John Terry. The film-makers discuss the film-
         ing and editing of "An American Family. "

1631   Ward, Martha E. and D. A. Marquardt. Authors of
         Books for Young People. 2nd ed. Metuchen, N. J. :
         Scarecrow Press, 1971.
         Includes a portrait of Doris Ransohoff, script
         writer, on pp. 424-25.

1632   "Wardrobe Mistress, A Day with Nance Monde. " Mo-
         tion Picture Magazine 15(August, 1918):58-59.

1633   Warfel, Harry Redcay.   American Novelists of Today.
        N. Y. : American Book, 1951.
        Includes a portrait of Elizabeth Chevalier, author
        and film editor, on pp. 88-89.

1634   Watts, Stephen, ed.   Behind the Screen; How Films
        Are Made.   London: Arthur Barker, Ltd. , 1938.
        "The Cutter, " Margaret Booth, pp. 147-53.

1635   Wayne, Pamela.   "The Social Secretary, One of the
        Most Fascinating Jobs in Hollywood. " Cosmopoli-
        tan 107(October, 1939):32-33, 68, 70.

1636   Weigel, H.   "Interview mit Leni Riefenstahl. " Film-
        kritik (Munich) 16, 8(August, 1972):395-410.
        Riefenstahl discusses her work and career.

1637   _____ .   "Randbemerkungen zum Thema. " Film-
        kritik (Munich) 16, 8(August, 1972):426-41.
        A filmography.   Bibliography.   Critical notes
        on Leni Riefenstahl and her work.

1638   Weinberg, Gretchen.   "Interview with Mary Ellen
        Bute. " Film Culture No. 35(1964-65):25.

1639   Weinberg, Herman.   "Reflections on the Current
        Scene. " Take One 3, 2(November-December, 1970):
        37-38.
        In praise of Nelly Kaplan, film-maker.

1640   Weiner, P.   "New American Cinema; filmography. "
        Film 58(Spring, 1970):22.
        On Shirley Clarke and Marie Menken.

1641   Weiss, Marion.   "Interview with Eleanor Perry. "
        Women and Film 2, 7(1975):44.

1642   West, Jessamyn.   To See the Dream.   New York:
        Harcourt, 1957.
        Her journal while scriptwriter of "Friendly Per-
        suasion" for Wm. Wyler.

1643   "What Directors Are Saying. " Action 4, 5(September-
        October, 1969):32.
        On Ida Lupino.

1644   "Where Are They Now?" Newsweek 72(October 28,

1968):26.
A portrait of Leni Riefenstahl.

1645   Whitcomb, J.   "Girls Behind Disney's Characters. "
        Cosmopolitan 136(May, 1954):50.

1646   Whitney, D.   "Follow Mother, Here We Go Kiddies. "
        TV Guide 14,41(October 8, 1966):14.
        On Ida Lupino.

1647   "Who's Who in Audio-Visual Education. " Audio Visual
        Guide 16(January, 1950):22.
        A portrait of May Field, English educational film
        producer.

1648   Wieland, Joyce.   "North America's Second All-Woman
        Film Crew. " Take One 1, 8(1967-68):14-15.

1649   Wikarska, Carol.   "Attica. " Women and Film 2, 7
        (1975):60.
        A review of the film "Attica" directed by Cinda
        Firestone.

1650   _____.   "San Francisco--FILMEX. " Women and
        Film 2, 7(1975):113.
        A brief description of the film festival in San
        Francisco, with particular mention of those films
        made by women.

1651   Winetrabe, Maury.   "How Do You Edit an Earthquake?"
        American Cinemeditor 24, 3-4(Fall-Winter, 1974-
        75):6.
        Film editor Dorothy Spencer is interviewed re-
        garding her award-winning work in "Earthquake. "

1652   Wise, Naomi.   "The Hawksian Woman. " Take One
        3, 3(April, 1972):17-19.   (Reprinted in Filmkritik
        (Germany) 17(May-June, 1973):256-64).

1653   "A Woman's Place: Review of Film 'Antonia: A Por-
        trait of the Woman. '" Time 104, 17(October 21,
        1974):4.
        Women's film directed by Judy Collins and Jill
        Godmilow.   (See also entry under "Images. ")

1654   "Women and Film International Festival. " Cinema
        Canada No. 8(June-July, 1973):9.

1655-7   [No entries]

1658   "Women Directors. " Women and Film No. 1(1972):75.
         Reprint of a page from Andrew Sarris' book,
The American Cinema.   Commentary under the reprint
points out that Sarris discusses every male director
but with Ida Lupino he simply lists her films, and as
an afterthought adds the names of all the women directors he can think of, dismissing them in a short
condescending manner.

1659   "Women Directors of Plays and Pictures. " Ladies
         Home Journal (December, 1920):12.

1660   "Women for Equality in Media. " Everywoman 2, 12
         (August 20, 1971):4.

1661   "Women in Film. " Film Library Quarterly 5, 1(Win-
         ter, 1971-72).   Special issue.
         Includes reviews of films by and about women.
An interview with Madeline Anderson, director of "I
Am Somebody, " pp. 39-41.   A commentary by profes-
sional women on their experiences working in film.
"Maya Deren and Germaine Dulac: Activists of the
Avant Garde. "   An article by Regina Cornwell, pp.
29-38.

1662   "Women in Film. " Take One 3, 2(February, 1972):1-38.
         Special issue. Women (Including: Eleanor Perry,
Anita Loos, Sylvia Spring, Tanya Ballantyne MacKay
and Stephanie Rothman) discuss "Women in Film. " Filmographies of women directors (Canadian and International).   An interview with Shirley Clarke; Interview with
Joyce Wieland; reviews.

1663   Women in Media Collective.   "The Berkeley Women
         and Media Conference. " Women and Film 1, 5-6
         (1974):92.
         Conference is described and discussed by the
Collective.

1664   "Women in Music and Movies, Women Artists Today,
         Building a Revolution with Art. " Women: A Jour-
         nal of Liberation.   Vol. 2, No. 1.

1665   [No entry]

1666   "Women on Women in Films. " Take One 3, 2(Novem-
        ber-December, 1970):10-15.
            A symposium. Sylvia Anderson, Tanya Ballan-
        tyne McKay, Stephanie Rothman, Sylvia Spring, Eleanor
        Perry, Betty Box, Anita Loos, Mary Borer, Polly
        Elliott.

1667   "Womens Film Coop. " Off Our Backs 2, 2(October,
        1971):33.
            On films and film-makers.

1668   Wood, C. "TV Personalities Biographical Sketch-
        book. " T. V. Personalities (1957):16.
            On Ida Lupino.

1669   "Writers' Roost. " Vogue 160(October 1, 1972):146-
        49.
            A portrait of Joan Didion.

1670   Young, Colin and Gideon Bachmann. "New Wave--or
        Gesture?" Film Quarterly 14, 3(Spring, 1961):6-
        14.
            Discusses problems and similarities of U. S. in-
        dependent film-makers. Includes Shirley Clarke.

1671   Zec, Donald. Some Enchanted Egos. New York:
        St. Martin's, 1973.
            A portrait of Edna O'Brien, Irish screenwriter,
        on pp. 128-31.

1672   Zimmerman, P. D. "Passionate Assassin. " News-
        week 83(April 29, 1974):98-99.
            A portrait of Italian motion picture director,
        Lina Wertmuller.

1673   Zsugan, I. "Változott-e és Miért a dokumentumfilm
        az Elmult Evtizedben?" Filmkultura (Budapest)
        4(July-August, 1972):5-11.
            Discussion; young film-makers Judit Elek and
        Livia Gyarmathy discuss documentary production in
        Hungary.

1674   Zwerdling, Shirley. Film and TV Festival Directory.
        New York: Backstage Publications, Inc. , 1970.
            World-wide listing and full details of nearly 400
        festivals in 50 countries. Does not mention any wo-
        men's film festivals.

Chapter 3

IMAGES OF WOMEN

A. Reference and Historical Works

1675   Barry, Iris. Let's Go to the Movies. New York:
       Arno Press, 1972. (Reprint of 1926 ed. publ. by
       Payson and Clark).
       (See annotation under "Actresses," entry No. 5.)

1676   Baxter, John. Hollywood in the Sixties. (Internation-
       al Film Guide Series.) New York: A. S. Barnes
       and Co., 1972.

1677   _____. Hollywood in the Thirties. (International
       Film Guide Series.) New York: A. S. Barnes and
       Co., 1968.

1678   Bibliography of Articles on Women and Film. British
       Film Institute, 81 Dean Street, London W1, England.
       (See listing under "Film-makers.")

1679   Billings, Pat and Allen Eyles. Hollywood Today.
       (International Film Guide Series.) New York: A.
       S. Barnes and Co., 1971.

1680   Cameron, Ian Alexander. Dames. New York: Prae-
       ger, 1969.
       (Also see entry under "Actresses.")

1681   Dawson, Bonnie. Women's Films in Print: An An-
       notated Guide to Six Hundred Films Made by Wo-
       men. San Francisco: Bootlegger Press, 1975.

1682   Durgnat, Raymond. The Crazy Mirror. London:
       Faber, 1969.
       (See entry under "Actresses.")

1683   Eyler, Allen. American Comedy Since Sound. New
       York: A. S. Barnes, 1970.
       (See entry under "Actresses. ")

1684   Gedlund, Carolyn. "Defining Women's Films. " Uni-
       versity of California Extension Media Center Sup-
       plement 42, 21(September 16, 1974):16-20.

1685   Gillman, Barbara. Photoplay Treasury. New York:
       Crown Publications, Inc. , 1973.
       (See entry under "Actresses. ")

1686   Gow, Gordon. Hollywood in the Fifties. (Internation-
       al Film Guide Series.) New York: A. S. Barnes
       and Co. , 1971.

1687   Griffith, Richard. The Talkies. New York: Dover
       Publications, 1971.
       (See annotation under "Actresses. ")

1688   Higham, Charles and Joel Greenberg. (International
       Film Guide Series) Hollywood in the Forties. New
       York: A. S. Barnes and Co. , 1968.

1689   Hughes, Langston and Milton Meltzer. Black Magic:
       A Pictorial History of the Negro in American En-
       tertainment. Englewood Cliffs, N. J. : Prentice-
       Hall, 1967.

1690   Jerome, Victor Jeremy. The Negro in Hollywood
       Films. New York: Masses and Mainstream, 1950.
       (See listing under "Actresses. ")

1691   Kanin, Garson. Hollywood: Stars and Starlets, Ty-
       coons and Flesh-Peddlers, Moviemakers and Money-
       makers, Frauds and Geniuses, Hopefuls and Has-
       Beens, Great Lovers and Sex Symbols. New York:
       Viking Press, Inc. , 1974.

1692   Kleinhans, Chuck. "Seeing Through Cinema Vérité. "
       Jump Cut 2(July-August, 1974):14.
       Reviews of "Wanda" and "Marilyn Times Five. "
       Includes a list of Resources on Women and Film.

1693   Knight, Arthur and Hollis Alpert. Playboy's Sex in
       the Cinema. 3 vols. Chicago: Playboy Press,
       n. d.

1694   Kobal, John. Romance and the Cinema. London:
              Studio Vista, 1973.
                    Discusses the romantic notion that Hollywood ex-
              udes Gods and Godesses. Fan magazine pictures.
              Images projected from screen.

1695   McCarthy, Todd and Charles Flynn. Kings of the B's.
              New York: E. P. Dutton and Co., Inc., 1975.
              (See listing under "Film-makers.")

1696   McClure, Arthur F. The Movies: An American Id-
              iom. Rutherford, N. J.: Fairleigh Dickinson Uni-
              versity Press, 1971.
                    Bibliography. Readings in the Social History of
              the American Motion Picture. Contains an especially
              good article by Olivia de Havilland, her role in "Gone
              with the Wind," type of character she portrayed, Me-
              lanie, as a symbol of spiritual values of a nation.
              Other articles make references to women as well, es-
              pecially "Films of Postwar Decade," "The Celluloid
              Safety Valve," Bob Newhart's "June Allyson Never
              Kicked Anyone in the Shins."

1697   Mapp, Edward. Blacks in American Films: Today
              and Yesterday. Metuchen, N. J.: Scarecrow Press,
              1972.
                    Old and new stereotypes, emerging black stars.

1698   Morgan, Robin, ed. Sisterhood Is Powerful. New
              York: Vintage Books, 1970.
                    List of feminist films, p. 582.

1699   Null, Gary. Black Hollywood: The Negro in Motion
              Pictures. New York: Citadel Press, 1974.

1700   Pines, Jim. Blacks in the Cinema: The Changing
              Image. London: Education Dept., British Film
              Institute, 1971.
                    (See listing under "Actresses.")

1701   Robinson, David. Hollywood in the Twenties. (Inter-
              national Film Guide Series) New York: A. S.
              Barnes and Co., 1968.

1702   Ross, Theodore T. Film and the Liberal Arts. New
              York: Holt, Rinehart and Winston, 1970.
                    Contains some material on Blacks in motion pic-
              tures.

1703   Sadoul, Georges. The Cinema in Arab Countries.
       Beirut-London: Interarab Centre of Cinema and
       Television, 1966.
       History of Arab cinema.

1704   _____. The French Film. London: The Falcon
       Press, 1953.
       History of French cinema.

1705   Schickel, Richard. The Stars. New York: The Dial
       Press, 1962.
       (See entry under "Actresses. ")

1706   Sennett, Ted. Lunatics and Lovers. New Rochelle,
       N. Y. : Arlington House, 1973.
       On screwball and romantic comedies. Analysis
       of comedies of the 30's. He examines: "The Cinder-
       ella Syndrome, " Chap. 2; the relationship between
       "Wife, Husband, Friend, Secretary, " Chap. 3; "Poor
       Little Rich Girls, " Chap. 4; "Boss Ladies and Other
       Liberated Types, " Chap. 8. Includes appendices on
       players, directors, and writers of these comedies.
       Many actresses listed, no directors. Some screen
       writers including Frances Goodrich, Gladys Lehman,
       Katherine Scola, Lynn Starling, Virginia Van Upp.
       Includes a filmography of all films discussed.

1707   Slide, Anthony. Early American Cinema. New York:
       A. S. Barnes and Co. , 1970.

1708   Smith, Sharon. Women Who Make Movies. New
       York: Hopkinson and Blake, 1974.
       (See listing under "Film-makers. ")

1709   Sprecker, Daniel, ed. Guide to Films About Negroes.
       Alexandria, Va. : Serina, 1970.

1710   Wagner, Robert W. , editor. "Special Issue: Women
       in Film. " Journal of the University Film Associa-
       tion. 26, 1-2(1974). Department of Photography
       and Cinema, 156 W. 19th Ave. , Ohio State Univer-
       sity, Columbus, Ohio 43210

1711   Wheeler, Helen. Womanhood Media: Current Re-
       sources About Women. Metuchen, N. J. : Scare-
       crow Press, 1972. Suppl. , 1976.
       Contains a section on film resources.

1712   "Women in Film. " Film Quarterly 5, 1(Winter, 1971-
        72). 65 pp. Special issue.
              Includes critical reviews and a list of films deal-
        ing with subject of modern women.

1713   Women's History Research Center, Inc. Films By
        and/or About Women. Berkeley: Women's History
        Research Center, Inc. , 1972.
              (See entry under "Film-makers. ")

1714   "Women's Studies Films and Video Tapes. " Women:
        A Select Bibliography. University of Michigan:
        University Library, 1975.
              (See listing under "Film-makers. ") Listing of
        films available at U. M.

B. Catalogues

1715   Ahlum, Carol and Jacqueline M. Fralley. "Feminist
        Resources for Schools and Colleges: A Guide to
        Curricular Materials. "
              (See listing under "Film-makers. ")

1716   Art and Cinema. Visual Resources, Inc. , One Lin-
        coln Plaza, New York City 10023.
              Triennial publication lists visual resources; $35/
        yr.

1717   Artel, Linda J. and Kathleen Weaver. Film Program-
        mer's Guide to 16mm Rentals. 1972. Reel Re-
        search, P. O. Box 6037, Albany, California 94706.

1718   Bartlett, Freude. Serious Business Catalog, 1609
        Jaynes St. , Berkeley, California 94703. 1974.
              Free catalog lists films distributed by Serious
        Business.

1719   Bishop, Anne. "Women on Film. " Lifelong Learning
        (U. C. Extension Media Center, Berkeley--News-
        letter) 42(March 5, 1973):2-5.
              Bishop presents a short filmography of current
        films on women which she helped preview for inclusion
        in the media center's collection. She reviews films
        on the socialization of women, job discrimination,
        child care, abortion, Third World Women, portraits
        of women and historical studies.

1720   Canyon Cinema Catalog. Industrial Center Bldg. ,
        Room 220, Sausalito, California 94965.
        Free catalog lists films available for distribution.

1721   Cinema Femina, 250 West 57th Street, New York,
        New York 10019.
        A referral service for film-makers and indivi-
        duals who wish to program women's films.

1722   Dawson, Bonnie. Women's Films in Print: An An-
        notated Guide to Six Hundred Films Made by Wo-
        men. San Francisco: Booklegger Press, 1975.

1723   _____, and Cynthia Montilla. Women and Film.
        Albany, N. Y. : State Department of Education,
        1973.

1724   Filmmakers Cooperative Catalog. 175 Lexington Ave. ,
        New York, N. Y. 10016.
        Catalog lists films for distribution. $2 donation.

1725   Films by Women. Toronto: Canadian Film-makers'
        Distribution Centre, 406 Jarvis St. , Toronto, On-
        tario.
        (See listing under "Film-makers. ")

1726   Freude. "Films by Women: A Suggested Program. "
        Canyon Cinemanews No. 4/5(September-October,
        1973):14.
        Filmographies.

1727   Grimstad, Kirsten and Susan Rennie. The New Wo-
        man's Survival Catalog. New York: Coward, Mc-
        Cann and Geoghegan; Berkeley Publishing Co. ,
        1973.
        Catalog list includes: Amalie R. Rothschild,
        Liane Brandon, Joyce Chopra, Claudia Weill, Julia
        Reichert and James Klein, Jill Foreman Hultin, Faith
        and John Rubley, Jan Oxenberg, Harriet Kriegel, Jean
        Shaw, Judith Shaw Acuna, Marie Celine Canfield, Su-
        zanne Armstrong, Jane Warren Brand, Barbara Brown,
        Nancy Greiner, Lorraine McConnel, Ann Weiner, Helen
        Zaglew, Ariel Daugherty, Sheila Page, Louise Alaimo,
        Judy Smith, Ellen Sorrin.

1728   Hart, Lois B. A Feminist Looks at Educational Soft-
        ware Materials. Everywomen's Center, Munson

Hall, University of Massachusetts, Amherst, Mass.
01002.
Evaluation of educational materials used in ele-
mentary and secondary schools.

1729   Lesage, Julia. "Resources: Blue Collar Movies. "
        Jump Cut No. 2(July-August, 1974):15.
            A filmography of films with working class themes.
        Includes films in the general categories of: Films de-
        picting actual work; Strike films; Innovative cinematic
        approaches; Portraits of working class youth; Women's
        position, sexual politics; Prostitution; Racism; Psycho-
        logical Portraits; Urban Life; Working Class Melodra-
        mas; Comedy; Athletes and Entertainers; At War;
        Lumpen Chase Films.

1730   Maynard, Richard A. "Women on Film. " Scholastic
        Teacher (May, 1973):21-22.
            A popular approach to study of discrimination
        against women is the analysis of women's roles in
        American commercial films.   Lists films to sensitize
        high school students to the negative images of women
        projected in films: followed by values-oriented dis-
        cussions of: "The Goddess, " "The Hired Hand, "
        "Rachel, Rachel, " "The Pumpkin Eater, " "The Wo-
        men, " "I'm No Angel. " Sources of information on
        women directors and distributors of the films listed
        are included.

1731   Mendenhall, Janice.   Films on the Women's Move-
        ment.   Federal Women's Program Coordinator,
        General Services Administration, Washington, D. C.
        20405.
            Annotated list of about 90 films, mostly shorts.

1732   Museum of Modern Art Film Rental Catalog.   11 West
        53rd St. , New York, N. Y.   10019.
            Free catalog includes films by/about women a-
        vailable for rental.

1733   New Day Films Catalogue.   P. O. Box 315, Franklin
        Lakes, N. J.   07417.
            Lists their available films.

1734   Newsreel Catalogue.   322 7th Ave. , N. Y.   10001, or
        Antioch Union, Yellow Springs, Ohio.
            Has available a number of films concerning wo-
        men's movement.

1735   Whole Film Catalogue.   Films, Inc., 1144 Wilmette,
         Wilmette, Illinois.
         Includes a number of films by and about women.

1736   Women and Film: A Resource Handbook. The Pro-
         ject on the Status and Education of Women, Assoc.
         of American Colleges, 1818 R Street, N.W., Wash-
         ington, D. C. 20009.
         (See entry under "Film-makers. ")

1737   Women and Film--La Femme et la Film, 1896-1973.
         International Festival Program. 4 Maitland St.,
         Toronto, Ontario, M4Y 1C5, Canada.
         An access catalog which lists distributors and
       films.

1738   Women in Film: A Bibliography. Women in the Arts,
         Albany Area NOW, Box 6064, Albany, N.Y. 11568.
         Lists variety of films by and about women.

1739   Women Make Movies, Inc. Catalogue.   257 W. 19th
         St., New York, N.Y. 10011.
         Distributor's catalogue.

1740   Women Make Movies Poster-Catalog.   107 West 26th
         St., New York, N.Y. 10001.
         Free catalog.

1741   Women's Film Co-op Catalog. c/o Valley Women's
         Center, 100 Main St., Northhampton, Ma. 01060.
         Films by women which are available for distri-
       bution are listed. $1.50.

1742   Women's Films--A Critical Guide. Bloomington, Ind.:
         Indiana University Audio-Visual Center, 1975.
         Reference guide to recent women's films. Use-
       ful for women's studies. Listing of films available
       for rental or purchase from University of Indiana and
       elsewhere. Film notes by Carolyn Geduld. Not com-
       prehensive.

C.   Specific Works

1743   Abet, A. "La femme chez Marcel Carné." Cahiers
         de la Cinémathèque (Perpignon) 5(Winter, 1972):22-
         23.

Women in the films of Marcel Carné.

1744   "Ain't Beulah Dead Yet? Or Images of the Black Wo-
        man in Film." Essence 4(May, 1973):61.

1745   Alexander, A. J. "A Modern Hero: the Nongenue."
        Film Culture No. 22-23(Summer, 1961):81.
            New character emerging in film--not a female
        character in a story but "a woman of heroic character,
        a female hero." Her development in "Private Proper-
        ty," "The Savage Eye," "The Lovers," "Look Back in
        Anger." Fullest portrait: "Room at the Top"; "The
        Fugitive Kind"; "Hiroshima, Mon Amour."

1746   Alexandrescu, M. "B. B. -contestata de Bardot." Cin-
        ema (Bucharest) 11, 4(April, 1973):36.
            Brigitte Bardot objects to the myth which she
        has acquired.

1747   "Antonia: A Portrait of the Woman." New Republic
        171(October 26, 1974):20+.

1748   Apon, A. "Sylvana Mangano." Skrien (Amsterdam)
        28(January, 1972):16-18.
            (See listing under "Actresses.")

1749   Armatage, Kay. "Women in Film." Take One 3, 11
        (May/June, 1972):45-48. Pub. (September, 1973)
            A discussion of a number of major women's
        film festivals being held. "What Is One to Think?"

1750   _____ and Barbara Martineau. "Women in Film;"
        Take One 3, 8(November-December, 1971):35-38.
            The Women's Film Event at the Edinburgh Fes-
        tival.

1751   Atkins, Thomas R. Sexuality in the Movies. Bloom-
        ington: Indiana University Press, 1975.
            A collection of essays on eroticism in film and
        a discussion of six recent films and what they repre-
        sent as artistic or cultural landmarks in the screen
        treatment of sexuality. Most are new essays. Few
        have appeared in Film Journal (author is founder/edi-
        tor-publisher of Film Journal).

1752   Atlas, Jacoba. "Beauty/Enigma/Mother: Women in
        'Children of Paradise,' 'Jules and Jim,' and 'Alice's
        Restaurant.'" Women and Film 1, 3-4(1973):38.

An analysis of women in the three films.

1753   "B. B. --Mythe ou femme?" Cinéma (Paris) 176(May,
       1973):15.
              Criticism of a TV interview with Brigitte Bardot.

1754   Bachmann, G.   "Bernardo Bertolucci: 'Every Sexual
       Relationship Is Condemned. '"   Film Quarterly 26, 3
       (Spring, 1973):2-9.
              Bertolucci discusses the sexual and political
       overtones of "Last Tango in Paris. "

1755   "Background: Female Directors. " Film Series 2,
       No. 1(April, 1973):24.   British Federation of Film
       Societies, 81 Dean Street, London, W1V 6AA.

1756   "A Bad Black Image in Film. " Essence 4(May, 1973):
       70.

1757   Bargowski, Dolores.   "Moving Media: 'The Exor-
       cist. '" Quest: A Feminist Quarterly 1, 1(Summer,
       1974):53.
              A discussion of the film.

1758   Bataille, Gretchen.   "Preliminary Investigations: Ear-
       ly Suffrage Films. " Women and Film 1, 3-4(1973):
       42.
              An analysis of six early suffragette films.

1759   Bazin, Andre.   What Is Cinema? Vol. II.   Trans. by
       Hugh Gray.   Berkeley: University of California
       Press, 1971.
              Film theorist discusses the "Entomology of the
       Pin-Up Girl" on p. 158.   He contends the pin-up girl
       is a "specific erotic phenomenon" and "embodies the
       sexual ideal of the future. "

1760   Beauvoir, Simone de.   Brigitte Bardot and the Lolita
       Syndrome.   New York: Arno Press, 1960.
              (See annotation under 'Images. ")

1761   [No entry]

1762   Beh, Siew Hwa.   "The Image of Women in the Cine-
       ma. " 1972 Oberlin Film Conference: Selected Es-
       says and Discussions Transcription, V. II.   Oberlin
       College: Christian Koch and John Powers, eds.

1763 _____. "Red Detachment of Women." Women and
    Film No. 1(1972):43.
    A discussion of the recent Chinese film, "The
Red Detachment of Women."

1764 _____. "Reflections on Recent Trends in Hollywood
    Films." Women and Film No. 2(1972):16.
    Recent films show an "Upsurge of hostile and
dangerous reaction toward the feminist movement and
other revolutionary concerns."

1765 _____. "The Woman's Film." Film Quarterly 25,
    1(1971):48-49.

1766 Belfrage, Cedric. "Psyching the Hollywood Blond."
    Motion Picture Classic 31, 5(July, 1930):51.
    Starlet June Clyde is "psycho-analyzed." The
article is amusing but is hardly telling of Hollywood
blondes. The idyllic presentation of Miss Clyde is
good fan magazine writing but poor psychology and
even poorer biography.

1767 Belkin, M. "Scarlett O'Hara and Me." Up From Un-
    der 1, 3(January, 1971):18.

1768 Bergen, Polly. Polly's Principles. New York: Ban-
    tam Books, 1975.
    Polly tells "truth" about show business, the beau-
ty trap and herself.

1769 Bergman, Andrew. We're in the Money; Depression
    America and Its Films. New York University,
    1971.

1770 Betancourt, Jeanne. "High School Women and Film:
    A Report from New York City." Women and Film
    No. 2(1972):56.
    (See entry under "Film-makers.")

1771 _____. "Report from New York: Women's Video
    Festival at 'The Kitchen.'" Women and Film 1, 3-
    4(1973):97.

1772 _____. Women in Focus. Dayton, Ohio: Pflaum
    Publishing, 1974.
    (See entry under "Film-makers.")

1773   Biskind, Peter. "Lucía." Jump Cut No. 2(July-August, 1974):7.
        A review of Humberto Solas' film.

1774   Bodeen, DeWitt. "Theda Bara." Films in Review 19,
        5(May, 1968):266-87.
        A filmography and career of early silent "vamp."

1775   Bogle, Donald. Toms, Coons, Mulattoes, Mammies,
        and Bucks. New York: Viking Press, 1973.
        (Intrep. history of Blacks in American Films)
        Ways in which Black females have been typecast in
        movies--mammies, aunt jemima--and also fascinating
        readings on personal and public life of famous and
        not-so-famous Black actresses: Hattie MacDaniel,
        Butterfly McQueen, Dorothy Dandridge.

1776   Bond, Frederick W. The Negro and the Drama. College Park, Md. : McGrath Publishing Co. , 1969.
        (See listing under "Actresses.")

1777   Bourget, Jean Loup. "Romantic Dramas of the Forties." Film Comment 10, 11(January-February,
        1974):46.
        An analysis.

1778   Brackett, Leigh. "A Comment on the Hawksian Woman." Take One 3, 6(July-August, 1971):19-20.
        A scriptwriter who collaborated on scripts for
        Hawks offers support for Naomi Wise's article.

1779   _____. "Ein Kommentar zu 'The Hawksian Woman.'" Filmkritik 17(May/June, 1973):265-67.

1780   Brakhage, Jane. "The Birth Film," in Film Culture
        Reader, edited by P. Adams Sitney. New York:
        Praeger Publishers, 1970.
        On p. 230 Jane Brakhage describes the film
        made by her husband, Stan, about the birth of their
        first child, and how at one point she herself filmed
        the event.

1781   Braucourt, G. "Les Cannibales et propos de Liliana
        Cavani." Ecran (Paris) 6(June, 1972):68-69.
        (See listing under "Film-makers.")

1782   Braudy, Susan. "Film." Ms. III, 7(January, 1975): 34.

Subtitle: "Bang! A Little Gift from Hollywood. "
A movie review of "Alice Doesn't Live Here Any
More. " Also lists women who worked on the film:
actress Ellen Burstyn, editor Marcia Lucas, art director Toby Rafelson, associate producer Sandy Weintraub, co-producer Audrey Maas. (Also listed under
"Film-makers. ")

1783   Bruno, Michael. Venus in Hollywood: The Continen-
tal Enchantress from Garbo to Loren. New York:
Lyle Stuart, 1970.
(See entry under "Actresses. ")

1784   Burrell, Walter. "The Black Woman as a Sex Image
in Films. " Black Stars 2(December, 1972):32-39.

1785   Busby, M. "Enchantresses on the Screen. " Photoplay
37(March, 1930):36-37, 131.

1786   Calendo, J. "Dietrich and the Devil. " Inter/View 26
(October, 1972):26-30, Part I; 27 (November, 1972):
23, 45, Part II.
(See listing under "Actresses. ")

1787   Campbell, Marilyn. "RKO's Fallen Women: 1930-
1933. " The Velvet Light Trap No. 10(Fall, 1973):
13.

1788   Černev, G. "Predi 'Tjutjun. '" Kinoizkustvo (Sofia)
28, 1(January, 1973):36-44.
A survey of the lyrical heroines created by Bul-
garian actress Nevena Kokanova between 1957 and
1961.

1789   Changas, Estelle. "Slut Bitch Virgin Mother: The
Role of Women in Some Recent Films. " Cinema
(Los Angeles) 6, 3(Spring, 1971):43-47.
Deals primarily with "The Grasshopper" and
"Diary of a Mad Housewife. "

1790   Child, Abigail. "The Girls. " Women and Film 1, 3-
4(1973):73.
(See entry under "Film-makers. ")

1791   Citron, Michelle. "Feminist Criticism: What It Is
Now; What It Must Become. " Velvet Light Trap
6(Fall, 1972):43-44.

Calls for criticism that will create a "more realistic self image" for women.

1792   Cohen, S.   "Marilyn Chambers 99-44/100% Pure."
       Inter/View 36(September, 1973):8-9.
       (See entry under "Actresses.")

1793   Confino, B.   "Interview with Agnes Varda." Saturday
       Review 55(August 12, 1972):35.
       (See entry under "Film-makers.")

1794   Cook, Pam and Claire Johnston.   "The Place of Women in the Cinema of Raoul Walsh," in Raoul
       Walsh, edited by Phil Hardy. Edinburgh Film Festival, 1974.

1795   Cooper, K.   "Kate Millett's Three Lives." Filmmakers' Newsletter 5, 3(January, 1972):28-33.
       An interview. Kate Millett discusses how and
       why she made "Three Lives"; Louva Irvine and Susan
       Kleckner discuss the production.

1796   Corliss, Richard.   Village Voice 15, 24(June 11, 1970):
       56, 59.
       Radley Metzger and Russ Meyer as the best of
       the sexploitationists.

1797   Cornwell, Regina.   "'True Patriot Love': The Films
       of Joyce Wieland." Art Forum Vol. 10, No. 1.

1798   Crawford, Joan.   "They Made Me a Myth." Sight and
       Sound 21, 4(April-June, 1952):162-64.
       Career notes.

1799   Crowther, Bosley.   "Where Are the Women?" New
       York Times Sec. 2(Sunday, January 23, 1966):11.

1800   Cruse, Harold.   The Crisis of the Negro Intellectual.
       New York: Wm. Morrow and Co., Inc., 1967.
       See: Film Industry and Movie Industry sections.

1801   Dalton, Elizabeth.   "Women at Work: Warners in the
       Thirties." Velvet Light Trap No. 6(Fall, 1972):
       15-20.
       The image of women in 1930's films.

1802   Davidon, A. M.   "A Great Man Who Humiliates Wo-

men?" Village Voice 18(March 29, 1973):70.
Women in film.

1803   Davidson, Carol. "'Letter to Jane': A Critique."
       Women and Film 1, 3-4(1973):52.
       Critique of the film, "Letter to Jane"--a "filmic
       letter" to Jane Fonda--by Godard and Gorin.

1804   Davis, John. "The Tragedy of Mildred Pierce." The
       Velvet Light Trap No. 6(Fall, 1972):27.
       A variation of the "woman's film" genre, it cri-
       ticized accepted values in 1945.

1805   Dee, Ruby. "The Tattered Queens: Some Reflections
       on the Negro Actress." Negro Digest 15(April,
       1966):32-36.

1806   de Laurent, Yves. "The Public as Vanguard of the
       People: A Women's Liberation and the Avatars of
       Madame Prometheus." Cinéaste IV, 4(Spring, 1971).

1807   Deming, Barbara. Running Away from Myself. New
       York: Grossman, 1969.
       A dream portrait of America drawn from the
       films of the 40's. It deals with images of males and
       females as projected on the screen. Written in 1950
       but not "publishable" because of its negative commen-
       tary. Our world has been in part shaped by our mo-
       vie screens.

1808   Denby, D. "Men Without Women, Women Without
       Men." Harper's 247(September, 1973):51-54.

1809   Donnie. "Bondage Series." Women and Film No. 2
       (1972):61.
       A discussion of three current political films:
       "Women in Cages," "The Big Doll House," and "The
       Hot Box."

1810   _____. "The Movie Channel." Women and Film
       1, 3-4(1973):102.
       An analysis of the 1961 film, "Something Wild,"
       which deals with masculine power and rape.

1811   Durgnat, Raymond. "B. B." Films and Filming 9, 4
       (January, 1963):16-18.
       Brigitte Bardot as a sex symbol.

1812   _____. "Eroticism in Cinema. " 8-part series.
        Films and Filming 8, 1(October, 1961); 8, 8(May,
        1962).

1813   Dyer, Peter John. "The Face of the Goddess. "
        Films and Filming 5, 9(June, 1959):13-15+.
        "The Myth of the Woman in the American cinema
        of the Thirties, from Garbo and Dietrich to Crawford
        and Bette Davis. "

1814   _____. "Some Silent Sinner. " Films and Filming
        4, 6(March, 1958):13-15, 34.
        Causes and effects of personal and sociological
        silent films. Refers to crime films and feminist per-
        sonal drama through vamps.

1815   Eckert, Charles. "The Anatomy of a Proletarian
        Film: Warner's 'Marked Woman.'" Film Quart-
        erly 17, 2(Winter, 1973-74):10-24.

1816   _____. "Shirley Temple and the House of Rocke-
        feller. " Jump Cut No. 2(July-August, 1974):1.
        A discussion of Temple and her films.

1817   Edwards, Clara. "Women and Better Films. " Films
        in Review 7, 3(March, 1956):111-13.
        Women viewers work for more wholesome films.
        Movement toward "cleaner, " family films.

1818   Edwards, N. "Women and Film Festivals. " Cinema
        Canada 9(August-September, 1973):14-18.
        Includes a report from some of the cities in
        Canada where the Festival was sent on tour.

1819   Ehrenstein, David. "Anna Karina. " Film Culture
        48, 49(Winter/Spring, 1970):52-53.
        Karina on Godard's films.

1820   Ellis, Robert. "Ida Lupino Brings New Hope to Holly-
        wood. " Negro Digest 8(August, 1950):47-49.

1821   Ellis, Shirley. The Negro in American Film. New
        York: U. S. Information Service, 1957.

1822   Embree, Alice. "Media Images I: Madison Avenue
        Brainwashing--the Facts, " in Sisterhood Is Power-
        ful, edited by Robin Morgan. New York: Vintage

Books, 1970.

An anthology of women's writings includes this essay on p. 175 which has reference to women in film. Complains that the creation of an "Undifferentiated Mass" while good for consumerism is deadly to all, but especially to women, "the neglected orphans of the technological age." Special emphasis on television, the favorite child of technological America, but message is applicable to film images.

1823   Erens, Patricia. "Interview with Jill Godmilow." Women and Film 2, 7(1975):34.
(See listing under "Film-makers.")

1824   _____. "Love and Anarchy." Jump Cut No. 2 (July-August, 1974):8.
An analysis and review of Lina Wertmuller's film.

1825   _____. "Making and Distributing 'Nana, Mom and Me.'" The Feminist Art Journal 4, 2(Summer, 1975):12.
(See listing under "Film-makers.")

1826   Evans, Peter. Bardot: Eternal Sex Goddess. New York: Drake Publishers, Inc., 1973.
(See entry under "Actresses.")

1827   "Excerpts from the Transcript of Godard-Gorin's 'Letter to Jane.'" Women and Film 1, 3-4(1973):45.
(See entry under "Actresses.")

1828   Farber, Stephen. "Film Noir: the Society Violence and the Bitch Goddess." Film Comment 10, 6(November-December, 1974):8.
A discussion of one of the kinds of thrillers and the image of women projected ("gangster film is a dark parody of national myth--variant of American rugged individualist"). Strong women presented as monsters, harpies.

1829   "Feedback." Take One 3, 4(March-April, 1971):4.
Letters and additional information on Take One Vol. 3, No. 2, the Women's Issue.

1830   La Femme and Le Film: Women and Film. Toronto International Festival, 1973, 9a Charles Street

West, Toronto, Ont. M4Y 1R4, Canada.
(See listing under "Film-makers. ")

1831   Fenin, George.   "M. M. "   Films and Filming 9, 4(Jan-
        uary, 1963):23-24
        Marilyn Monroe as a sex symbol.

1832   "Filmex Announces Extraordinary Success of Second
        Exposition. " American Cinematographer 54, 1(Jan-
        uary, 1973):61.
           A description of 2nd Los Angeles International
        Film Exposition.   Eleven-day non-competitive event.
        Mentions screenwriter Kay Kanin's participation in
        International Screenwriters Conference; special tribute
        to Myrna Loy; special short programs including one
        on "Women and Film" followed by a panel discussion.

1833   "Films by and about Women. "   Film Library Quarterly
        5, 1(Winter, 1971-72):46-59.
           (See also entry under "Film-makers. ")

1834   Finkle, D.   "Random Thoughts on a First Viewing of
        'The Women. '"   Filmograph 3, 4(1973):2-6.

1835   Fisher, J.   "Three Paintings of Sex: The Films of
        Ken Russell. "   Film Journal 2, 1(1972):32-43.

1836   Flinn, Tom.   "Joe, Where Are You?" Velvet Light
        Trap 6(Fall, 1972):9.
           Article in the "Sexual Politics" issue on the
        Sternberg-Dietrich relationship.

1837   Ford, April.   "Hawks' Women: Don't You Think I
        Could Know a Girl?" Women and Film No. 1(1972):
        26.
           A discussion of female roles in Howard Hawks'
        films.

1838   "Forum: What Is Female Imagery?" Ms. 3, 11(May,
        1975):62.
           A group of women artists, including film-maker
        Royanne Rosenberg, discuss female imagery in the
        arts.

1839   Fothergill, Bob.   "Cowards, Bullies and Clowns. "
        Canadian Forum (January, 1973):22-24.
           The English Canadian male as represented on

film can be seen in three roles: coward, bully and
clown. In each of these roles the male fails to gain
the female's respect. French Canadian films project
a similar vision. Canadian film directed by a woman
("Madeline Is" by Sylvia Spring) also confirms this
imagery of maleness. Stereotype of men as over-
grown children has been emerging in life as well as
art, but one exception, the film "Proxy Hawks" (1972),
transcends the stereotypes and suggests males and females may be able to work something out.

1840   Fox, J. "Maureen O'Hara: the Fighting Lady."
        Films and Filming 19, 3(December, 1972):32-40.
        (See listing under "Actresses.")

1841   Francis, M. "Sexism and Film." Great Speckled
        Bird 3, 30(July 27, 1970):4.

1842   French, Michael L. "Sex in the Current Cinema."
        Kansas Quarterly 4(Spring, 1972):39-46.
            Current films, more cerebral and less physical
        regarding sex, center on sexual politics, sex as sub-
        limated violence (and vice versa), and the anxieties of
        sexual hang-ups. This is done through attempts at
        self-revelation, graphic language, and the presentation
        of the dual possibilities of sex: healing and destruc-
        tion. "Carnal Knowledge," "Klute," and "McCabe and
        Mrs. Miller" are discussed.

1843   Freyer, E. "Film: Three Films on Women." Craft
        Horizons 34(April, 1974):13+.

1844   Frohde, L. "Filmen og Kjønnsrollene." Fant (Oslo)
        7, 2(Summer, 1973):59-60.
            Several films are discussed from the point of
        view of the roles played by women.

1845   Gant, Liz. "Ain't Beulah Dead Yet? Or Images of
        Black Women in Film." Essence 4(May, 1973):
        60-61+.
            Tracing the characterization of black women in
        films, one finds three basic stereotypes: the tragic
        mulatto, the mammy (earth-mother variation) and the
        red hot mama. Only recent films such as "Melinda"
        and "Sounder" show black women expressing a full
        range of feelings.

1846   Gardiner, H. C. In All Conscience. Plainview,
         N. Y. : Books for Libraries, Inc. , n. d. (Reprint of
         1959 edition.)
              Includes essay, "Bardot and the Admen," on pp.
         221-22.

1847   Gauthier, G. "La femme dans le cinéma québécois. "
         Image et Son (Paris) 267(January, 1973):10-17.
         (See entry under "Film-makers. ")

1848   Geduld, Carolyn. "Defining Women's Films. " Univer-
         sity of California Extension Media Center Supplement
         42, 21(September 16, 1974):16-20.

1849   Geng, Veronica. "Film: Holly Woodlawn Melts Alla
         Nazimova. " Ms. 2, 8(February, 1974):81.
              A discussion of two films--the silent "Salomé, "
         made in 1923, with Alla Nazimova showing woman as
         bitch, and the modern Warhol "Broken Goddess" with
         Holly Woodlawn as woman as martyr. The romantic
         alternatives for women.

1850   Geraghty, Christine. "Film Culture: an Article. "
         Screen 15, 4(Winter, 1974-75):89.
         (See listing under "Critics. ")

1851   Gerard, Lillian N. "Belles, Sirens, Sisters. " Film
         Library Quarterly 5, 1(Winter, 1971-72):14-21.
              The degradation of women in "McCabe and Mrs.
         Miller, " "Carnal Knowledge, " "Sunday, Bloody Sun-
         day. "

1852   Giddis, Diane. "The Divided Woman: Bree Daniels
         in 'Klute. '" Women and Film 1, 3-4(1973):57.
              A discussion of the major character in the film,
         "Klute. "

1853   Gilburt, Naome. "To Be Our Own Muse: the Dialec-
         tics of a Culture Heroine. " Women and Film No.
         2(1972):25.
              Reflections on the First International Festival of
         Women's Films.

1854   Gillette, D. C. "Hollywood-Image-Wreckers. " Jour-
         nal of the Producers Guild of America (Los Angeles)
         15, 2(June, 1973):3-6, 17.
              Fan magazines and their lack of conscience in

harming or destroying the careers of actors and actresses.

1855   Girls Who Do Stag Movies. Los Angeles: Holloway
       House Publishing Co. , n. d.
       No author; paperback, but American Cinemato-
      grapher book reviewer claims "surprisingly articulate
      views expressed by these women of problems peculiar
      to these films reveal unsuspected professionalism and
      a grasp of the socioethical issues involved. "

1856   The Goddess, A Script of the 1958 Film, by Paddy
       Chayefsky. Directed by John Cromwell. New York:
      Simon and Schuster, 1958.

1857   Gornand, A. "Evelyne Dress, actrice.... " Image et
       Son (Paris) 266(December, 1972):53-56.
      (See listing under "Actresses. ")

1858   Gough-Yates, Kevin. "The Heroine--Part One. "
       Films and Filming 12, 8(May, 1966):23-27; "Part
      Two. " 12, 9(June, 1966):27-32; "Part Three. " 12,
      10(July, 1966):38-43; "Part Four. " 12, 11(August,
      1966):45-50.

1859   [No entry]

1860   Gow, Gordon. Hollywood in the Fifties. New York:
       A. S. Barnes and Co. , 1971.

1861   Granlund, Nils Thor, with Sid Feder and Ralph Han-
       cock. Blondes, Brunettes and Bullets. New York:
      McKay, 1957.

1862   Gray, M. "Women in Film Making. " Goodbye To
       All That 20(October, 1971):12.

1863   Greenbaum, Connie. "Musidora. " Women and Film
       2, 7(1975):4.
      An article on the organization of the First Wo-
      men's Film Festival in Paris.

1864   Greene, Linda. "Politics of a Feminist Fantasy. "
       Jump Cut No. 6(March-April, 1975):13.
      (See listing under "Film-makers. ")

1865   Grilikhes, Alexandra. "Films by Women: 1928-1971. "

Film Library Quarterly 6, 1(Winter, 1972-73):8.
     Philadelphia's First International Festival of films
by women. (See entry under "Film-makers.")

1866   Groark, Steven. "George Cukor's 'Sylvia Scarlet.'"
          Velvet Light Trap 3(Winter, 1972):19.

1867   Hagen, Ray. "The Day of the Run-Away Heiress."
          Films and Filming 12, 7(April, 1966):40-43.
               Unrealistic, glittery portrayals of life. Refers
          to portrayals of women in Hollywood films of the 30's.

1868   Hahnert. "Amazon Media Project/Women for Women."
          Off Our Backs 4, 3(February, 1974):17.
               About women's film festival.

1869   Hall, Gladys. "Samuel Goldwyn Chooses Women
          Trained to Please Men." Motion Picture Magazine
          36(October, 1928):50-51, 106.

1870   Hardwick, Leon. "Negro Stereotypes on the Screen."
          Hollywood Quarterly 1, 2(January, 1946):234-36.

1871   Harmetz, A. "Rape--An Ugly Movie Trend." New
          York Times 122(September 30, 1973):Sec. 2, p. 1+.

1872   Harrington, Curtis. "The Erotic Cinema." Sight and
          Sound 22, 2(October-December, 1952):67-74, 96.
               A history and analysis.

1873   Haskell, Molly. "Film: Half a Man Is Better Than
          One." Village Voice 17, 25(June 22, 1972):73.
               (See listing under "Film-makers.")

1874   _____. From Reverence to Rape. New York:
          Holt, Rinehart and Winston, 1974.
               Discusses treatment of women in movies, women
          in moving-pictures.

1875   _____. "Howard Hawks--Masculine Feminine."
          Film Comment 10, 2(March-April, 1974):34.
               Discusses Hawks' themes: male-female compe-
          tition, sexual inversion, struggle between adolescent
          and maturity in grown man's soul. Contends there is
          an evolution in his view of women and that his view
          is precariously divided between male and female prin-
          ciples.

1876 _____. "Sources, Themes, Actors, Actresses for
Truffaut's Films. " Village Voice 15, 16(April 16,
1970):57, 61, 63.
Refers to "Mississippi Mermaid. "

1877 _____. "We've Yet to Catch Up With 'Adam's
Rib. '" Village Voice 16, 42(October 21, 1971):78,
90.
Includes Eleanor Perry, Kitty Winn, Barbara
Loden, Susan Martin, Nadine Trintignant, and Molly
Haskell--panel discussion on women in film.

1878 _____. "The Woman in the 'All-man' Legend. "
Village Voice 18(June 21, 1973):85.

1879 _____. "Woman Wins in Some New Movies. "
Vogue 159(April, 1972):66.

1880 _____. "'Women's Films'/Reviving What Custom
Staled. " Village Voice 17, 15(April 13, 1972):81+.
Discusses the lack of traditional women's films
lately.   The reason may be that sex roles are vanish-
ing but the author suspects TV is filling the demand
via soap operas.   The author contends Women's Lib
movement has not resulted in the creation of new female models, but, instead, has bequeathed to males
all the feminine qualities; that sex differences are not
only cultural, and that images of women in films are
projections of male fantasies or women's reactions
against those fantasies via their own fiction.

1881 Henshaw, Richard.   "A Festival of One's Own: Re-
view of Women Directors. " The Velvet Light Trap
No. 6(Fall, 1972):39.
First International Festival of Women's Films,
New York, N. Y.

1882 Hirschfeld, Bert. Diana. New York: Domino Pocket
Books, 1963.
About Hollywood "goddesses. "

1883 Houser, Arnold.   "The Film as a Product of Society. "
Sight and Sound 8, 32(Winter, 1939-40):129-32.
Film subjects determined by bourgeois society
and economics.

1884 Houston, Beverle and Marsha Kinder.   "Odd Couple:

Woman and Manchild in 'Harold and Maude,' 'Minnie and Moskowitz, 'Murmur of the Heart'." Women and Film No. 2(1972):16.
An analysis of three films.

1885   Houston, Penelope. The Contemporary Cinema. New York: Penguin Books, 1963.
An account of films of the late 1950's and early 1960's.

1886   _____. "Scripting." Sight and Sound 19,9(January, 1951); 19,11(March, 1951); 21,1(August-September, 1951).
Brief reviews of films based on their screen-plays.

1887   Howes, Elizabeth. Anything but Love. New York: Rinehart, 1948.
Rules for feminist behavior from birth to death in print, film, radio.

1888   Hoyt, Edwin P. Marilyn: The Tragic Venus. New edition. Radnor, Pa.: Chilton Book Co., 1973.

1889   Huff, Theodore. "40 Years of Feminine Glamour." Films in Review 4,2(February, 1953):49-63.
Trends in Feminine film glamour.

1890   Hurley, Neil P. Toward a Film Humanism. New York: Dell Publishing Co., Inc., 1970.
Original title: Theology Through Film. The book includes articles: "Toward a Cinematic Theology of Sex" which deals with the way love/sex are depicted on the screen; "Screen's Theology of Sacrificial Love"; 'Marguerite Duras," screenwriter for "Hiroshima Mon Amour. Discusses puritanical conditioning of women and Bergman's remarkable ability to represent female viewpoint in love affairs.

1891   Ibrányi-Kiss, A. "Women in Canadian Films." Cinema Canada (Toronto) 5(December-January, 1972-73):26-31.
Brief reviews of some recent Canadian films a-bout women, followed by an interview with Mireille Dansereau about "La vie révée."

1892   "The Ideological Massage: Reviews of Commercial

Cinema. " Women and Film 1, 5-6(1974):85.
Reviews of: "Summer Wishes, Winter Dreams. "

1893   "Independent Women's Cinema: Reviews. " Women
       and Film 2, 7(1975):80.
       (See listing under "Film-makers. ")

1894   "Independent Women's Cinema: Reviews. " Women
       and Film 1, 5-6(1974):77.
       (See entry under "Film-makers. ")

1895   "An Interview with Christiane Rochefort. " Women and
       Film 1, 3-4(1973):7.
       (See entry under "Film-makers. ")

1896   "Interview with Robert Aldrich. " Movie 8(April,
       1963):8-10.
       Themes in Aldrich's films.

1897   Israel, Lee. "Women in Film: Saving an Endangered
       Species. " Ms. III, 8(February, 1975):51.
       (See annotation under "Film-makers. ")

1898   Iverson, Lucille. "Feminist Critic of the First An-
       nual Erotic Film Festival (New York, 1972). " Wo-
       men and Film 1, 3-4(1973):23.
       (See entry under "Film-makers. ")

1899   James, Sibyl. "The Movie's Over. " Women and
       Film 1, 3-4(1973):54.
       A poem.

1900   Jarvie, I. C. "Recent Films About Marriage. " Jour-
       nal of Popular Film 2, 3(Summer, 1973):278-99.
       Discusses films from the 1960's and 70's dealing
       with marital relationships, showing how they reflect,
       and perhaps contribute to, significant changes in so-
       ciety's attitudes.

1901   Jeancolas, F. "Femmes à la caméra. " Jeune-
       Cinéma (Paris) 61(February, 1972):1-6.
       An analysis of three films directed by women.

1902   Jebb, Julian. "Scenes from a Marriage. " Sight and
       Sound 44, 1(Winter, 1974-75):57.
       Review of Bergman's film. Bergman explains
       hypocrisies and passions of sexual and domestic life.
       High-class soap-opera "a first draft. "

1903   . "Truffaut: The Educated Heart. " Sight
——— and Sound 41, 3(Summer, 1972):144-45.
         Contrasts the heroines of "Two English Girls"
and "Mississippi Mermaid, " locating the failure of "Two
English Girls" in Truffaut's failure to understand Muriel's self-absorption. The women in Truffaut's films
share an intense and often uncomplicated responsive-
ness to life. "Les gens sont formidables, " says one
character. Truffaut's films are a testament to this
belief.

1904 Johnson, Albert. "Beige, Brown or Black. " Film
         Quarterly 13, 1(Fall, 1959):38-43.
         Depictions of Blacks in Hollywood films of the
50's: "Edge of the City, " "Island in the Sun, " "Kings
Go Forth, " "Night of the Quarter Moon, " "Imitation
of Life, " "The World, the Flesh and the Devil. "

1905   . "The Negro in American Films: Some Re-
——— cent Works. " Film Quarterly 18, 4(Summer, 1965):
         14-30.
         (See entry under "Film-makers. ")

1906 Johnson, William. "Alice Doesn't Live Here Any-
         more. " Film Quarterly XXVII, 3(Spring, 1975):55.
         A review of the film.

1907 Johnston, Claire. "Film Culture: an Article. "
         Screen 15, 4(Winter, 1974-75):82.
         A discussion of BBC serial on the Women's Suf-
frage Movement, "Shoulder to Shoulder. " Six 75-
minute plays.

1908   . Women's Cinema as Counter Cinema.
——— British Film Institute publication.

1909   , ed. "Notes on Women's Cinema. " Screen,
——— Pamphlet No. 2, 1973. Society for Education in
         Film and Television, 1973.

1910   , ed. The Work of Dorothy Arzner. London:
——— British Film Institute, 1975.
         (See listing under "Film-makers. ")

1911   with Paul Willeman. "Penthesilea, Queen of
——— the Amazons: Interview with Laura Mulvey and
         Peter Wollen. " Screen 15, 3(Summer, 1974):120.

1912   Jungmann, R.   "Notes for My Son. " Cinema Canada
        8(June-July, 1973):80-81.

1913   Kael, Pauline.   "Morality Plays Right and Left. "
        Sight and Sound 24, 2(October-December, 1954):67-
        73.
          Films as advertising ways of life.   Refers to
        pro- and anti-communist propaganda.

1914   Kagan, Norman.   "Black American Cinema: A Pri-
        mer. " Cinema 6, 2(Fall, 1970):2-7.
          Pre-1940 Black films made by Black American
        film-makers.

1915   Kane, Joe.   "Beauties, Beasts, and Male Chauvinist
        Monsters. " Take One 4, 4(Mar. -April, 1973):8.
          Women in horror films--always a victim, never
        a star.

1916   Kaplan, Dora.   "Selected Short Subjects. " Women and
        Film No. 2(1972):37.
          A discussion of selected films shown at the First
        International Festival of Women's Films.

1917   _____. "A Woman Looks at the S. F. I. F. F. " Wo-
        men and Film No. 1(1972):46.
          15th San Francisco International Film Festival.

1918   Kaplan, E. Ann.   "The Importance and Ultimate Fail-
        ure of 'Last Tango in Paris. '" Jump Cut No. 4
        (November-December, 1974):1.
          A review.

1919   _____. "Popcorn Venus: Analyzing the Fantasy. "
        Jump Cut No. 3(September-October, 1974):21.
          A review of Marjorie Rosen's book, Popcorn
        Venus.

1920   Kay, Karyn.   "The Revenge of Pirate Jenny. " Velvet
        Light Trap 9(Summer, 1973):46-49.
          Part I about "A Very Curious Girl. " See Wald-
        man (entry 2013) for Part II.

1921   _____. "Sisters of the Night. " The Velvet Light
        Trap No. 6(Fall, 1972):20.
          A discussion of the film, "Marked Woman, "
        loosely based on the Lucky Luciano versus Thomas A.

Dewey court case in which prostitutes' testimony a-
gainst the gangster resulted in his conviction.   "Defies
every stereotype. "

1922   .   "You Can Get a Man with a Gun: or the
         True Story of Annie Oakley. "   Velvet Light Trap
         8(1973):11-13.
         Compares two film versions with biographies by
Swarthout, Havighurst, and Fields.

1923   and Gerald Peary.   "Dorothy Arzner's
         'Dance, Girl, Dance. '" The Velvet Light Trap 10
         (Fall,   1973).
         An in-depth analysis of the Arzner film.

1924   Keeler, Ruby.   "Hooray for Busby Berkeley. "   Films
         in Review 24, 8(October, 1973):471-73.
         Reminiscences of and tribute to B. B.   Reprinted
from The Busby Berkeley Book by Jim Terry and Tony
Thomas.

1925   Keller, Marjorie.   "Report from Knokke: Exprmentl
         -5. "   Women and Film 2, 7(1975):28.
         A report on the 5th International Experimental
Film Competition, Belgium, December 25, 1974-Jan-
uary 1, 1975.

1926   Keneshea, Ellen.   "Sirk: 'There's Always Tomorrow'
         and 'Imitation of Life. '" Women and Film No. 2
         (1972):51.
         Director Douglas Sirk's films are analyzed.

1927   Kinder, Marsha.   "Scenes from a Marriage. "   Film
         Quarterly 28, 2(Winter, 1974-75):48.
         Possibilities of growth and change particularly
for women.

1928   .   "Woman and Manchild in the Land of Bro-
         ken Promise. "   Women and Film 1, 3-4(1973):31.
         Reviews of Ken Russell's "Savage Messiah" and
Paul Morrissey's "Heat. "

1929   and Beverle Houston.   "Truffaut's Gorgeous
         Killers. "   Film Quarterly 17, 2(Winter, 1973-74):
         2-10.
         An analysis of central character in Truffaut's
films--profoundly seductive, seeped in mystery, who

uses her sexual liberation to destroy the sensitive or
needy hero or one who believes he can cope with her
rationally.

1930   Klein, Michael. "'Day for Night': A Truffaut Retrospective on Women and the Rhetoric of Film. "
Film Heritage 9, 3(Spring, 1974):21.
       Discusses Truffaut's concerns about the rhetoric
of film and his persistent semifeminist critique of sexual relationships.

1931   Kleinhaus, Chuck. "Two or Three Things I Know
About Her. " Women and Film 1, 3-4(1973):65.
       Discussion of the importance of Godard's film
in his development as a "feminist" film-maker.

1932   Klynne, K. "Ingmar Bergman's 'Kvinnosyn'. " Chaplin
(Stockholm) 14, 1(1972):28-29.
       Bergman's views on women as expressed in his
latest film, "The Touch. "

1933   Knoll, Robert F. "Women in Love. " Film Heritage
6, 4(Summer, 1971):1.
       Review of the film.

1934   Kopkind, A. "Hollywood--Under the Influence of Women?" Ramparts 13(May, 1975):56-60.

1935   Kwakernaak, E. J. "Madonna med barn. " Kosmorama 18, 110(September, 1972):261-63.
       The "passionate" woman character in later Berg-
man films, with emphasis on Karin in "The Touch. "

1936   Laver, James. "Some Thoughts on Pulchritude. "
Sight and Sound 19, 1(March, 1950):19.
       Fallacy of trying to cast beautiful women for all
parts.

1937   Lawson, John Howard. Film in the Battle of Ideas.
New York: Masses and Mainstream, 1953.
       Sections on: "The Degradation of Women, " pp.
60-71, and "Mother-Informer, " pp. 71-81.

1938   Lesage, Julia. "'The Green Wall': The Peruvian Woman and Us. " Women and Film 1, 3-4(1973):62.
       Discussion of Armando Robles Godoy's film,

"The Green Wall," which "presents the middle-class male myth of Peruvian womanhood and generally accepted Latin ideals of sexuality and the family."

1939 _____. "Whose Heroines." Jump Cut No. 1(May-June, 1974):22.
A review of Mellen's book.

1940 Lester, Elenore. "At Last: A Festival of Women's Films." Ms. 1,4(October, 1972.

1941 "Letter to an Unknown Woman, Namely Jack Smith by Ondine." Film Culture 45(Summer, 1967):21.
The New York Maria Montez cult.

1942 Lichtman, R. "The Rising of the Women/Past." Up From Under 1,3(January, 1971):56.

1943 Lindsey, Karen. "Elegy for Jayne Mansfield, July, 1967." In Sisterhood Is Powerful, edited by Robin Morgan. New York: Vintage Books, 1970.
A poem on p. 496.

1944 Lippard, Lucy R. "Yvonne Rainer on Feminism and Her Film." The Feminist Art Journal 4,2(Summer, 1975):1.
(See listing under "Film-makers.")

1945 Lippe, Richard. "Letter from an Unknown Woman." Velvet Light Trap 5(Summer, 1972):36.
Discusses Max Ophuls' film and the kind of female character portrayed in it.

1946 Lowell, Sondra. "Women in Film." Take One 3,4 (March-April, 1971):43,45.
(See entry under "Film-makers.")

1947 _____. "Women in Film." Take One 3,5(July, 1972):32-33.
(See listing under "Film-makers.")

1948 _____. "Women in Film." Take One 3,7(September-October, 1971):41-42. Published December, 1972.
Members of "Her-story Films" are interviewed. Marta Vivas, Patricia Bertozzi, Marion Hunter and their kind of films discussed.

1949   Macauley, C. Cameron. "Women's Films: A New
        Category in EMC Films, 1973-74." Lifelong Learn-
        ing (University of California, Extension Media Cen-
        ter, Berkeley, Newsletter) 42(March 5, 1973):1.
        (See listing under "Film-makers. ")

1950   McBride, Joseph and Michael Wilmington. "'Seven
        Women. '" Film Comment 8,1(Spring, 1972):56-60.
        Rebuts Wood's assertion that Ford's later works
        lack substance. Concentrates on Ford's attitude toward
        women in this and previous films. Discusses Ford's
        views of women.

1951   McClure, Michael. "In Defense of Jayne Mansfield. " in
        Film Culture Reader edited by P. Adams Sitney.
        New York: Praeger Publishers, 1970.
        Jane Mansfield section on p. 160.

1952   McCormick, R. "Magazines. " Cinéaste 5, 2(Spring,
        1972):41-42.
        (See listing under "Film-makers. ")

1953   _____. "Women's Liberation Cinema. " Cinéaste
        5, 2(Spring, 1972):1-7.
        Analyzes various attitudes within the women's
        liberation movement and discusses recent films em-
        bodying these attitudes.

1954   McCreadie, Marsha, ed. The American Movie God-
        dess. New York: Wiley, 1973.
        (See annotation under "Actresses. ")

1955   MacDougall, Allan. "Paris Cinemas of Yesteryear
        and Today. " Films in Review 1, 3(April, 1950):
        14-16, 48.
        Memories of Isadora Duncan and Paris movie
        theatres.

1956   McGarry, Eileen. "Documentary Realism and Women's
        Cinema. " Women and Film 2, 7(1975):50.

1957   McVay, Douglas. "The Goddesses: Part One. "
        Films and Filming 11, 11(August, 1965):5-9. "Part
        Two. " 11, 12(September, 1965):13-18.

1958   Madden, D. "Marble Goddesses and Mortal Flesh:
        Notes for an Erotic Memoir of the Forties. " The
        Film Journal 2, 1(1972):2-21.

1959   Madison Women's Media Collective.   "Barbara Loden
        Revisited. " Women and Film 1, 5-6(1974):67.
        (See entry under "Film-makers. ")

1960   Mallery, David.   "Von Sternberg and Dietrich. "   AFFS
        Newsletter (November, 1964):14-15.
        Dietrich with and without Sternberg.

1961   Mănoiu, A.   "Mitul Marilyn si Prăbusirea 'visului
        American,'" Cinema (Bucharest) 11, 10(October,
        1973):36-39.
        (See entry under "Actresses. ")

1962   Mapp, Edward.   "Black Women in Films. " The Black
        Scholar 4, 6-7(March-April, 1973).

1963   Martineau, Barbara.   "'La Femme du Ganges, ' or,
        as the French say, 'Who Is Marguerite Duras'?"
        Jump Cut No. 5(January-February, 1975):13.
        A review of Duras' film.

1964   _____ .   "The New York Women's Film Festival. "
        Cinema Canada 5(December-January, 1972-73):34-36.
        Festival report.

1965   _____ .   "Paris /Chicago: Women's Film Festivals
        1974. " Women and Film 2, 7(1975):10.
        (See listing under "Film-makers. ")

1966   _____ .   "Thoughts About the Objectification of Wo-
        men. " Take One 3, 2(February, 1972):15-18.
        Referring to the films of Garbo and Dietrich and
        with quotations from Doris Lessing's The Golden Note-
        book and other books, the article discusses the reduc-
        tion of women to objects.

1967   _____ .   "Women vs. Cannes. " Cinema Canada 9
        (August-September, 1973):50-52.
        (See entry under "Film-makers. ")

1968   _____ .   "Women's Film Daily. " Women and Film
        1, 5-6(1974):36.
        (See entry under "Film-makers. ")

1969   "Material Needed: Films on Women. " People's World
        33, 12(March 21, 1970):11.

1970   Mayersberg, Paul. "Robert Aldrich. " Movie 8(April,
        1963):4-5.
                Aldrich's themes.

1971   Maynard, R. A. "Women on Film. " Senior Scholas-
        tic: Scholastic Teacher, Jr/Sr High Teacher's
        Edition (May, 1973):21-22.

1972   Mazilu, T. "Obsesia frumusetii. " Cinema (Bucharest)
        11, 10(October, 1973):32-33.
                The evolution of the ideal of beauty in the stars
        of the cinema.

1973   Mekas, Jonas. "New Films About Women. " Village
        Voice 16, 15(April 15, 1971):67.
                "Growing Up Female" by Klein and Reichert;
        "Pigs" by Warhol; "The Women's Film" by Smith et al.

1974   Mellen, Joan. "Bergman and Women: Cries and
        Whispers. " Film Quarterly 27, 1(Fall, 1973):2-11
                Bergman's subject is women--(like Antonioni) he
        has a unique affinity for portraying and understanding
        the female psyche. Many of Bergman's films focus
        on women and how they come to terms with their lot
        in life.

1975   _____. "A Conversation with Bernardo Bertolucci. "
        Cinéaste 5, 4(1973):21-24.
                An interview. Bernardo Bertolucci discusses
        his films and the conceptions behind them.

1976   _____. "The Moral Psychology of Rohmer's
        Tales. " Cinema 7, 1(Fall, 1971):16-21.
                Reviews of Eric Rohmer's "Claire's Knee, " "La
        Collectionneuse, " "My Night at Maud's. "

1977   _____. "Sexual Politics and 'Last Tango in Paris'. "
        Film Quarterly 26, 2(Winter, 1972-73):9.
                A discussion of the political nature of Bertoluc-
        ci's film.

1978   _____. Voices from the Japanese Cinema. New
        York: Liveright, 1975.
                Japan--its cinema and images of its women.
        Feudal, authoritarian attitudes toward women--move-
        ment away from this by new film-makers. Statement
        by Sachiko Hidari acclaimed actress and wife of Susu-
        mu Hani.

1979   <u>   </u> . Women and Their Sexuality in the New
      Film. New York: Horizon Press, 1973.
         Examination of many significant recent films and
how women and their sexuality have been portrayed.

1980   Melton, Ruby. "Barbara Loden on 'Wanda': An Envi-
      ronment that Is Overwhelmingly Ugly and Destruc-
      tive. " Film Journal 1, 2(Summer, 1971):11.
         An interview with Barbara Loden.

1981   Merritt, M. "A Giant Step Sideways from 'Sapphire'
      to 'Billie. '" Village Voice 18(February 1, 1973):
      65.
         Black women in film.

1982   Michishita, Kyoko. "Tokyo-New York Video Express. "
      Women and Film 1, 5-6(1974):86.
         (See entry under "Film-makers. ")

1983   Miller, Loren. "Uncle Tom in Hollywood. " In The
      Negro in American History: Black Americans 1928-
      1968. Vol. I. Editors: Mortimer J. Adler, Char-
      les Van Doren, George Ducas. Encyclopaedia Bri-
      tannica Educational Corp., 1969.
         Discussion of the perpetuation of Black stereo-
types by Hollywood movies of the 30's.

1984   Milner, Michael. Sex on Celluloid. New York: Mac-
      fadden-Bartell Books, 1964.
         Images of women--Hollywood sex symbols.

1985   Mohanna, Christine. "A One-Sided Story: Women in
      the Movies. " Women and Film No. 1(1972):7.
         Male view dominates films and tells us directly
and indirectly what it means to be a man or woman
in our world. View has subtly changed in the past
seventy years. "Reality feeds the screen and is fed,
in turn, by its own reflection on that screen. " Article
briefly traces the subtle and not so subtle images of
women in film during the history of the cinema from
Méliès to the present.

1986   Morgan, James. "Coronation USA. " Sight and Sound
      23, 1(July-September, 1953):43-46.
         Filming of the Coronation of Queen Elizabeth II
of England.

1987   Mosher, Donald L. "Sex Differences, Sex Experi-
        ences, Sex Guilt, and Explicity Sexual Films. "
        Journal of Social Issues 29, 3(1973):95-111.
            A study of the differences between male and fe-
        male responses to sexual films shown to students in
        an introductory psychology class. Summary of the
        findings is reported and implication of the findings is
        discussed. Most significant is the lack of "disastrous
        consequences" on the viewers suggesting an end to
        censorship of sexual subjects.

1988   Nathan, George Jean. Passing Judgments.   New
        York: Knopf, 1935.
            About Mae West; 1890's figure appeals to 1930's
        audience, on pp. 266-68.

1989   Nau, P. "Filme zur Situation der Frau. " Filmkritik
        17(August, 1973):340-43.

1990   Neely, M. S. "From Reverence to Rape: Holt's
        Study of Women in Movies. " Publishers Weekly
        204(August 6, 1973):36.
            A review of Haskell's From Reverence to Rape.

1991   Nelson, Joyce. "Warner Brothers' Deviants, 1931-
        1933. " Velvet Light Trap 15(Fall, 1975):7.

1992   Noble, Peter. The Cinema and the Negro, 1905-1948.
        London: 1948.
            (See listing under "Actresses. ")

1993   _____ . The Negro in Films. London: Skelton
        Robinson, 1948. New York: Arno Press, 1970.
            (See entry under "Actresses. ")

1994   Noble, Robin. "Killers, Kisses and Lolita. " Films
        and Filming 7, 3(December, 1960):11-12, 42.
            An analysis of films of Stanley Kubrick.

1995   Nordstrom, Kristina. "Mae West in Venice. " Woman
        and Film 1, 3-4(1973):93.
            (See entry under "Actresses. ")

1996   O'Brien, G. "Interview with Cloris Leachman. "
        Inter/View 19(February, 1972):16.
            (See listing under "Actresses. ")

1997   Oldenburg, J.   "Favorite Film: 'Funny Face.'"
        Kosmorama 19(August, 1973):233-39.

1998   Orth, M.   "How to Succeed: Fail, Lose, Die."
        Newsweek 83(March 4, 1974):50-51.

1999   "The Pacific Film Archive." Women and Film No. 2
        (1972):70.
              A brief overview of the film collection in Berke-
        ley. Some films significant to women are noted.

2000   Parker, F.   "Approaching the Art of Arzner." Action
        8(July-August, 1973):9-14.
              On Dorothy Arzner.

2001   "The Passing of Beulah: Will Hattie McDaniel's Death
        Mark End of Long Era of 'Kitchen-Comedy' Roles
        for Negroes on Radio and Screen?" Our World 8
        (February, 1953):12-15.

2002   Patrichi, Gina.   "A Convinge cu sufletul." Cinema
        (Bucharest) 10, 3(March, 1972):49.
              (See listing under "Actresses.")

2003   Patrick, R. and W. Haislip.   "'Thank Heaven for Lit-
        tle Girls': An Examination of the Male Chauvinist
        Musical." Cinéaste 6, 1(1973):22-25.
              A short study of the American musicals seen as
        instruments of male chauvinism.

2004   Paul, W.   "The Reckless Moment." Film Comment
        7, 2(1971):65-66.

2005   Peary, Gerald.   "Dorothy Arzner." Cinema (Beverly
        Hills) 34(1974):2.
              (See listing under "Film-makers.")

2006   Pedersen, V.   "Danish Letter." Take One 3, 2(Feb-
        ruary, 1972):35-37.
              (See entry under "Film-makers.")

2007   Penley, Constance.   "Cries and Whispers." Women
        and Film 1, 3-4(1973):55.
              An analysis of Bergman's film.

2008   Perry, E.   "Women Still Get a Raw Deal in the Mo-
        vies." Vogue 162, 1(July, 1973):64.

2009   Petersen, Roberta. "Women and Myths. " Film Li-
          brary Quarterly 7, 2(1974):36.
               Reviews of three films concerning women:
          "Helen: Queen of the Nautch Girls, " about a film star
          in India; "Behind the Veil, " Arab women in Dukai; and
          "Magic Beauty Kit, " a cosmetics party in Queens,
          N.Y. Three different perspectives on the roles of wo-
          men in three different societies.

2010   Pile, S. , J. Moran and P. T. Close. "Getting Inti-
          mate with Edy Williams. " Inter/View 34(July,
          1973):16-18.
               An interview: Edy Williams talks about her ca-
          reer and the films of her husband, Russ Meyer.

2011   Powdermaker, Hortense. Hollywood, the Dream Fac-
          tory. London: Secker and Warburg, 1951.
               Subtitle: An anthropologist looks at the movie-
          makers. Some interesting observations and conclu-
          sions but some sections read like a fan magazine
          story. Hardly scholarly, refuses to identify specific
          names.

2012   "Program at 2nd Los Angeles International Film Ex-
          position. " American Cinematographer 53, 11(Nov-
          ember, 1972):1292.
               (See entry under "Film-makers. ")

2013   Pugh, Sally. "Home Born Baby. " Women and Film
          1, 3-4(1973):102.
               Discussion of the cinema vérité documentary on
          natural childbrith.

2014   Pulliam, Rebecca. "Newsreel: Radical Filmmakers. "
          The Velvet Light Trap, 4(Spring, 1972).

2015   Pyros, J. "Notes on Women Directors. " Take One
          3, 2(November-December, 1970):7.
               On Dorothy Arzner, Mary Ellen Bute, Shirley
          Clarke, Marie Menken, Lois Weber.

2016   Quart, Barbara and Leonard. "Cassavetes' Lunatic-
          Comic Pathos. " Jump Cut No. 5(January-February,
          1975):8.
               A review of "Woman Under the Influence. "

2017   Queyrel, P. "Digne. Le Cinéma différent n'a laissé

personne indifférent. " Cinéma (Paris) 178-179(July-
August, 1973):25-27.
  An account of a meeting in Digne where Margue-
rite Duras presented her latest film "La femme du
Ganges. "

2018   Raymond, Alan and Susan. "An American Family. "
       American Cinematographer 54, 5(May, 1973):590+.
       (See entry under "Film-makers. ")

2019   Reed, R. "Movies: Give them Back to Women. "
       Vogue 165(March, 1975):130-31.

2020   "Reel Life At Last--Women and Film. " Ms. II, 2
       (August, 1973):95.
         An article listing some recent films by outstand-
       ing women film-makers. Short descriptions of the
       films. Also lists organizations interested in helping
       women make films and helping them in every aspect
       of film.
         Topic: Roles We Learned to Play--And Why:
       "Anything You Want to Be, " Liane Brandon; "The Cab-
       inet, " Suzanne Bouman; "Crocus, " Susan Pitt Kraning;
       "Game, " Abby and Jon Childs; "The Gibbous Moon, "
       Nancy Ellen Dowd; "Growing Up Female: As Six Be-
       came One, " Julia Reichert and James Klein; "Schmeer-
       guntz, " Gunvor Nelson and Dorothy Wiley; "Three
       Lives, " Kate Millett, Louva Irvine, Susan Kleckner,
       Robin Mide.
         Topic: Portraits of Independent Women: "Angela:
       Portrait of a Revolutionary, " Yolande De Luart; "Fear
       Woman, " Elspeth MacDougall; "Gertrude Stein: When
       This You See Remember Me, " Perry Miller Adato;
       "Virginia Woolf: The Moment Whole, " Janet Sternberg.
         Topic: Finding New Patterns: "A to B, " Nell Cox;
       "Birth, " Susan Kleckner; "Day Care: Children's Li-
       beration, " Newsreel Collective; "Genesis 3:16, " Mau-
       reen McCue and Lois Ann Tupper; "How About You?"
       Bonnie Friedman, Deborah Shaffer, Marilyn Mulford;
       "I Am Somebody, " Madeline Anderson; "It Happens to
       Us, " Amalie Rothschild; "Janie's Janie, " Giri Achur,
       Peter Barton; "Joyce at 34, " Joyce Chopra, Claudia
       Weill; "Women Talking, " Midge MacKenzie; "Near the
       Big Chakra, " Anne Severson; "What I Want, " Sharon
       Hennessey; "Women and Children at Large, " Freude
       Bartlett; "The Women's Film, " Louise Alaimo, Judy
       Smith, Ellen Sorrin; "The Women's Happy Time
       Commune, " Sheila Paige.

2021   Reid, Alison. "Canadian Women Directors. " Take
       One 3, 2(February, 1972). Special Issue.

2022   "Reviews. " Take One 3, 2(November-December, 1970):
       28-35.
              Reviews of some recent women's films: "It Only
       Happens to Others, " "Growing Up Female, " "Wanda, "
       "Make a Face, " "Three Lives, " two Stephanie Rothman
       films, "Back Street" (reconsidered). Reviews are in-
       cluded in Take One's special issue on "Women in
       Film. "

2023   "Reviews. " Women and Film No. 1(1972):66+ .
       (See listing under "Film-makers. ")

2024   Reynolds, Lessie M. "The Journey Toward Liberation
       for Fellini's Women. " ERIC (Education Resources
       Information Center), 1973. 10 pp.
              The characterizations of women in three of Fel-
       lini's films can be used to demonstrate the process of
       self-actualization real women experience during the
       fulfillment of the promises of the women's liberation
       movement. "La Dolce Vita" and "8-1/2" portray tra-
       ditional stereotypes of women with traditional societal
       roles. However, in "Juliet of the Spirits" Fellini
       creates a female character with full personality dimen-
       sions.

2025   Rheubon, J. "Josef Von Sternberg: the Scientist and
       the Vamp. " Sight and Sound 42, 1(1972-73):34-40.

2026   Rhode, Eric. "Sensuality in the Cinema. " Sight and
       Sound 30, 2(Spring, 1961):93-95.
              The failure of the erotic in the cinema.

2027   Rice, Susan. "Image and Images: Interview. " Take
       One 3, 2(November-December, 1970):20.
              On Shirley Clarke.

2028   _____. Some Women's Films. " Take One 3, 2
       (November-December, 1970):30-31.
              (See entry under "Film-makers. ")

2029   Riefenstahl, L. "Out of Vogue--Bob Mizer Movies. "
       Advocate 4, 13(August 19, 1970):13.

2030   Ringel, Harry. "A Hank of Hair and a Piece of

Bone. " The Film Journal 2, 4(1975):14.
Image of women in horror films. Writer can-
didly chronicles his growing awareness of the attitudes
toward women implicit in these films.

2031   Rivers, C.   "Why Can't Hollywood See That 35 Is
        Beautiful, Too?" New York Times 122(April 1,
        1973), Sec. 2, p. 13.

2032   Robinson, David.   "20's Show People. " Sight and
        Sound 37, 4(Autumn, 1968):198-202.
        The 20's girls: refers to Marion Davies, Gloria
    Swanson.

2033   Rock, Gail.   "Cries and Whispers: A Film of Anguish
        and Insight. " Ms. I, 9(March, 1973):60.

2034   _____.   "Film: I Can't Believe I Watched the
        Whole Thing. " Ms. II, 2(August, 1973):27.
        A discussion of women characters in some re-
    cent films.

2035   _____.   "It Takes Two to Tango. " Ms. I, 10(April,
        1973):37.
        A review of Bertolucci's "Last Tango in Paris. "

2036   _____.   "Play It As It Lays. " Ms. I, 7(January,
        1973):41.
        (See also entry under "Film-makers. ")

2037   _____.   "Poetic Polemic, Political Tour. " Ms.
        I, 8(February, 1973):32.
        (See annotation also under "Film-makers. ")

2038   Ronan, M.   "Silver Screen Blues; Lack of Good Roles
        for Actresses. " Senior Scholastic 102(May 14,
        1973):30-31.

2039   Rosen, David N.   "King Kong: Race, Sex, and Rebel-
        lion. " Jump Cut No. 6(March-April, 1975):8.
        An interesting analysis of the film.

2040   Rosen, Marjorie.   "Film: Loved Message, Hated
        Movie. " Ms. 3, 3(September, 1974):42-44.
        Some hostile male attitudes toward women are
    explored in this review and in the movie "Going
    Places. "

2041   . "Film: The Return of the 'Women's Picture.'" Ms. II, 12(June, 1974):29-34.
     A discussion of "women's films" by foreign film-
makers and how they are redefining the genre. "Lu-
cia," "Love and Anarchy," "The Mother and the
Whore."

2042   . "Film: Who's Crazy Now? John Cassa-
vetes' 'A Woman Under the Influence.'" Ms. III, 8
(February, 1975):29.
     Cassavetes, America's major "woman's director."
Cassavetes, like Bergman, explores depths, torment,
isolation of individuals and relationships. A review of
"Women Under the Influence."

2043   . Popcorn Venus. New York: Coward, Mc-
Cann and Geoghegan, 1973.
     Women, movies and the American dream.

2044   . "Popcorn Venus: What Movies Have Done
to Women." Ms. II, 10(April, 1974):41.
     A condensation of the book, Popcorn Venus.

2045   . "Three Films in Search of a Distributor."
Ms. IV, 1(July, 1975):30.
     (See entry under "Film-makers.")

2046   . "Women, Their Films and Their Festival."
Saturday Review (August 12, 1972):32.

2047 Rosten, Leo Calvin. Hollywood: The Movie Colony,
     the Movie Makers. N.Y.: Arno Press, 1970.
     One excerpt from the book: "Movies: Boy Gets
Girl."

2048 Salber, Wilhelm. Film und Sexualität. Untersuchun-
     gen zur Filmpsychologie. Bonn: H. Bouvier, 1970.
     Sex in motion-pictures.

2049 Sarachild, Kathie. "Women's Films: The Artistic Is
     Political." Feminist Art Journal 2, 2(Winter, 1973):
     6-8+.

2050 Sarris, Andrew. "Garbo's Charisma." Village Voice
     9, 36(June 25, 1964):10.

2051   . "Women's Films." Village Voice 14, 44

(August 14, 1969):35.
    Similarities between "dope films" and soap opera.
Refers to "Easy Rider." Also definition of "woman's
picture" and comparison between it and soap opera.

2052   Sashi. "I Seen It in a Picture Show." Women and
          Film 1, 3-4(1973):100.
          (See entry under "Film-makers.")

2053   Scholar, Nancy. "Maedchen in Uniform." Women and
          Film 2, 7(1975):68.
          (See entry under "Film-makers.")

2054   Schumach, Murray. The Face on the Cutting Room
          Floor. New York: Wm. Morrow and Co., 1964.
          On movie censorship. Much information concern-
ing images of women which were cut when it was at-
tempted to portray them.

2055   Schwartz, Nancy. "Coming of Age: A Masculine
          Myth?" The Velvet Light Trap No. 6(Fall, 1972):
          33.
          A discussion of "Summer of '42" and "The Last
Picture Show" as films with "coming of age" themes.

2056   _____. "The Role of Women in 'Seven Women.'"
          The Velvet Light Trap 2(August, 1971):22-24.

2057   "Secret of a Movie Maid." Ebony 5(November, 1949):
          52-56.
          (See listing under "Actresses.")

2058   "Sex Symbols." Films and Filming 9, 4(January, 1963):
          16-24.
          Bardot, Cardinale, Dors, Monroe.

2059   "Sexism in Films." Kaleidoscope--Milwaukee 61(Aug-
          ust 7, 1970):7.

2060   Shapiro, L. "Women as Seen by Women." Phoenix
          3, 24(June 15, 1971):26.

2061   Shedlin, Michael. "Love, Estrangement, and Coadun-
          ation in Rossellini's 'Voyage to Italy.'" Women and
          Film No. 2(1972):46.
          A review of Rossellini film.

2062   Siclier, Jacques.   Le mythe de la femme dans le cin-
        éma américain; de "La Divine" à Blanche Duboise.
        Paris: Cerf, 1956.

2063   Silber, Irwin and Bill Nichols.   "Confronting the Con-
        sciousness Industry: Two Analyses of Women's
        Role in the Media. "   Women and Film No. 1(1972):
        34.
        (See listing under "Film-makers. ")

2064   Simon, John.   Private Screenings.   New York: Mac-
        millan, 1967.
        "Spotlight on the Nonwoman" on p. 297.   Discus-
        ses the image of femininity conveyed by American ac-
        tresses as not feminine.   Simon attacks Monroe, Tay-
        lor, Day.   Urges better role models for the young wo-
        men in our society, "for it is on our actresses that
        young women model themselves to a large extent.... "
        The rest of the book is a collection of Simon's reviews.

2065   Simsolo, N.   "Notes sur les Westerns de Sergio
        Leone. "   Image et Son (Paris) 275(September, 1973):
        15-50.
        A study of the Westerns of Sergio Leone, includ-
        ing the part played by women and the place of politics
        in the films.

2066   Sloan, Margaret.   "Film: Keeping the Black Woman
        in Her Place. "   Ms. II, 7(January, 1974):30.
        How the images of Black women, i. e. , "behind
        my Man-ers" and "Women Used to Find Himself and
        Manhood, " have remained virtually unchanged in re-
        cent movies.   But praises "Black Girl, " "Coffee, "
        "Cleopatra Jones. "

2067   Smith, Sharon.   "The Image of Women in Film: Some
        Suggestions for Future Research. "   Women and
        Film No. 1(1972):13.
        Suggests kinds of themes needed to portray wo-
        men more positively, but frankly admits the problems
        to be solved before such an idea becomes a reality.

2068   Solanas, Fernando and Octavio Getino.   "Toward a
        Third Cinema. "   Cinéaste 4, 3(Winter, 1970-71):1
        (See listing under "Film-makers. ")

2069   "Sophia Loren: Earth Mother. "   Cinema 2, 1(February-

March, 1964):20-25.
A picture essay.

2070   Sternberg, Janet. "Film and Fiction Help to Open the
       Door: Revealing Herself. " Film Library Quarterly
       5(Winter, 1971-72):7-12.
       The article is a reflection on the cross-fertiliza-
       tion of various media to find mutually complementary
       voices. The film "Growing Up Female: As Six Be-
       come One" and four novels, Up the Sandbox, Walking
       Papers, The Bluest Eye, and An American Girl, are
       discussed. The film focuses on the way a woman is
       manipulated to discard her early, intuitive self and to
       identify with a learned preconceived notion of her sex.
       Other themes in film and novels: women in a consu-
       mer society, mothers and daughters, the emerging
       expression of female sexuality.

2071   _____. "Movies that Remember Mama. " Ms. III,
       9(March, 1975):38.
       Reviews of Amalie Rothchild's film "Nana, Mom
       and Me, " Martha Coolidge's "Old-Fashioned Women, "
       and Mirra Bank's "Yudie. " All three independently
       produced, all autobiographical.

2072   _____. "Revealing Herself. " Film Library Quart-
       erly 5, 1(Winter, 1971-72):7-12+.
       Much on "Growing Up Female. "

2073   Stimpson, Catherine. "The Case of Miss Joan Didion. "
       Ms. 1, 7(January, 1973):36.
       An analysis of kinds of women Didion portrays
       in her writings.

2074   Strick, Philip. "Cries and Whispers. " Sight and
       Sound 42, 2(Spring, 1973):110.
       A review. Bergman's exploration of four women.

2075   Struck, Karin. "Weg von den Mütten. " Der Spiegel
       48(November 26, 1973):163-66.
       (See listing under "Film-makers. ")

2076   Stutz, Jonathan. "Sex and Character in 'Klute. '" The
       Velvet Light Trap No. 6(Fall, 1972):36.

2077   Suchianu, D. I. "Ingrid Bergman ... si dulcea ei
       seriozitate. " Cinema (Bucharest) 11, 4(April, 1973):

44-45.
An analysis of the roles played by Ingrid Bergman.

2078   Sullivan, Beth. "Bed and Sofa/Master of the House. "
        Women and Film No. 1(1972):21.
        An analysis of the two films which attempt to
deal with the position and treatment of women in society.

2079   Sullivan, Pat. "The Second Annual New York Women's
        Video Festival. " Women and Film 1, 5-6(1974):96.
        Festival held in New York City September 28-
October 14, 1974 is discussed.

2080   Taylor, Anne-Marie. "Lucía. " Film Quarterly 28, 2
        (Winter, 1974-75):53.
        A review of the film "Lucía. " Film is divided
into three sections. Each includes a protagonist named
Lucía, each documents a different period of history
and a different feminine attitude and explores the cultural and societal influences on a male-female relationship.

2081   Taylor, Judith. "Did She or Didn't She? Mystifying
        Women's Oppression. " Women and Film 2, 7(1975):
        106.
        Discussion of the made-for-TV film, "The Legend of Lizzie Borden. "

2082   _____. "The Rape of Women on TV. " Women and
        Film 1, 5-6(1974):88.
        Made-for-TV movies as well as some television
series in 1973-74 season deal with the problem of
rape. The films and programs are discussed.

2083   Thorp, Margaret. The Literature of Cinema. New
        York: Arno Press and New York Times, 1970.
        Selection from writings on cinema: Glamour--
sex, money; Cinema fashions--effect on women. Also
lists the Code restrictions on films which shaped
images of women.

2084   "Tinker Bell, Mary Poppins, Cold Cash. " Newsweek
        66(July 12, 1965):74.
        On Disney's characters.

2085   Tom, Lily. "Swashbuckling Swordswomen of the Sil-
            ver Screen. " Ms. I, 10(April, 1973).
            An analysis of the "sword movie, " a Chinese
        genre that projects an image of Oriental woman far
        different than that which Westerners usually imagine.
        She is heroic--usually righting some wrong--attrac-
        tive, charming, delicate, young and innocent but al-
        ways chaste and independent. Includes a list of re-
        commended titles in the genre.

2086   Tournis, A. "Liliani Cavani. " Jeune Cinéma (Paris)
            63(May-June, 1972):20-24.
            (See listing under "Film-makers. ")

2087   "The Tragic Mask of Bardolatry. " Cinema 1, 2(1963):
            27-29.
            A discussion of the career of Brigitte Bardot.

2088   Trecker, J. L. "Sex, Marriage and the Movies ...
            More of the Same. " Take One III, 5(July, 1972):
            12-15.
            A study of the discontentment and obsessions of
        marriage and sex as portrayed in American films.

2089   Trent, Paul. The Image Makers. New York: Mc-
            Graw-Hill, 1972.
            Subtitle: 60 Years of Hollywood Glamour. In-
        teresting text on the "stars" and their photographers.
        Heavily illustrated with portraits by these outstanding
        photographers. Discusses importance of fan magazines
        as a cheap source of photographs for fans, and easy
        advertising for studios. Later, candid shots became
        popular (during World War II). A few women still-
        photographers are mentioned--Charlotte Fairchild,
        Ruth Harriett Louise.

2090   Tuckman, Mitch. "Interview with Judy Smith. " Wo-
            men and Film No. 1(1972):30.
            (See listing under "Film-makers. ")

2091   Turim, Maureen. "Review of 'Lady Sings the Blues. '"
            Velvet Light Trap 8(1973):34.

2092   "Twelve Women Working to Make Things Better. "
            Mademoiselle 81(February, 1975):123.
            Jill Godmilow, film-maker, is one.

2093   "Two New Films on Women." Goodbye to All That
        23(December, 1971):7.

2094   Tyler, Parker. The Hollywood Hallucination. New
        York: Creative Age Press, Inc., 1944.

2095   _____. "The Lady Called 'A'; or, if Jules and Jim
        Had Only Lived at Marienbad." Film Culture No.
        25(1962):21.

2096   _____. Magic and Myth of the Movies. New York:
        Simon and Schuster, 1947. 2nd printing, 1970.
        "Unique view of the way in which one of our most
        significant cultural institutions actually works--or used
        to work--on us"--Richard Schickel, in the Introduction,
        1970. Shows how the movies expose attitudes, neu-
        roses, desires of makers and viewers. While the book
        is not specifically about women, Mr. Tyler seems to
        be an early perceiver of the effect of film on its au-
        dience--male and female.

2097   _____. Sex Psyche Etcetera in the Film. New
        York: Horizon Press, 1969.
        Chapters relevant to women: "Awful Fate of the
        Sex Goddess," "Revival of the Matriarchic Spirit."

2098   van Vranken, F. "Women's Work in Motion Pictures."
        Motion Picture Magazine 26(August, 1923):28-29, 89.

2099   Van Wert, William. "Love, Anarchy, and the Whole
        Damned Thing." Jump Cut No. 4(November-Dec-
        ember, 1974):8.
        A review of Lina Wertmuller's "Love and An-
        archy."

2100   Verdi, E. "Entretien avec Liliana Cavani." Cinema
        (Paris) 167(June, 1972):144-47.
        (See listing under "Film-makers.")

2101   Viotti, Sergio. "Vogues in Vamps." Films and Film-
        ing 1, 5(February, 1955):5
        Film vamps through the years.

2102   Wald, Jerry. "Don't Pity Working Girls." Films and
        Filming 6, 1(October, 1959):6, 29.
        A brief history of the working-girl on film. Re-
        fers to "The Best of Everything."

2103   Waldman, D. "The Eternal Return of Circe." Vel-
          vet Light Trap 9(Summer, 1973):49-51.
              Part II about "A Very Curious Girl." See Kay
       (entry 1920) for Part I.

2104   Walker, Alexander. The Celluloid Sacrifice: Aspects
          of Sex in the Movies. New York: Hawthorn Books,
          1967.
              Part One--The Goddesses: a kind of history of
       the development of images of women, "types" of stars,
       with chapters on Bara, Bow, Pickford, West, Dietrich,
       Garbo, Harlow, Monroe, Taylor. Part Two--Guar-
       dians (Censors). Part Three--Victims: examines fe-
       male sexuality, controls of sex drive as expressed in
       film, victimization of screen heroes by female dom-
       inance.

2105   Walker, Beverly. "From Novel to Film: Kubrick's
          'Clockwork Orange'." Women and Film No. 2(1972):4.
              An analysis of Kubrick's attitude toward women.

2106   _____. "Moral Tales: Eric Rohmer Reviewed and
          Interviewed." Women and Film 1, 3-4(1973):15.
              The writer candidly tells of her fascination with
       Rohmer's films which led, finally, to an interview with
       him.

2107   Ward, M. "The Making of 'An American Family,'"
          Film Comment 9, 6(November-December, 1973):24-
          31.
              (See entry under "Film-makers.")

2108   _____. "Pat Loud." Film Comment 9, 6(November-
          December, 1973):21-23.
              An interview. Pat Loud describes the effect on
       her and her family of being filmed for "An American
       Family," a 12-part TV film.

2109   Warner, A. "Yesterday's Hollywood: These Women
          Spell Danger." Films and Filming 18(December,
          1971):30-36.

2110   Weales, Gerald Clifford. The Film Heroine: Yester-
          day and Today. New York: U.S. Information Ser-
          vice, 1957.
              9 page booklet.

2111   Webb, Teena. "Bergman Without Options. " Jump
        Cut No. 5(January-February, 1975):1.
        A review of "Scenes from a Marriage. "

2112   _____ . "Myths, Women and Movies. " Women and
        Film No. 2(1972):66.

2113   _____ . "Reel Women and Real Women. " See 4
        (January, 1971):15-18.

2114   Weinberg, Herman G. "Hollywood, O Hollywood. "
        Film Culture 1, 3(May-June, 1955):7-11.
        The publicity still: sex which isn't there.

2115   _____ . "'A Woman of Paris' in 1973. " Take One
        3(January-February, 1972):18-20.
        A review of Chaplin's 1923 film, and a compari-
        son of it with Bertolucci's "Last Tango in Paris. "

2116   Weiss, Marion. "Interview with Eleanor Perry. " Wo-
        men and Film 2, 7(1975):44.

2117   Weller, Sheila. "Hollywood Double Feature. " Ms.
        3, 11(May, 1975):46.
        Reviews of two books about Hollywood: Bed/
        Time/Story by Jill Robinson and Eve's Hollywood by
        Eve Babitz.

2118   Wells, Walter. Tycoons and Locusts. Carbondale,
        Ill: So. Ill. U. Press, 1974.
        Studies Hollywood setting of eight popular novels
        of the 30's--the effect of environment on personality.

2119   White, David Manning and Richard Averson. Sight,
        Sound and Society: Motion Pictures and Television
        in America. Boston: Beacon Press, 1968.
        Another book of readings, a few of which have
        reference to women in film.

2120   Whitehall, Richard. "DD. " Films and Filming 9, 4
        (January, 1963):21-22.
        Diana Dors as a sex symbol.

2121   Wikarska, Carol. "San Francisco--FILMEX. " Women
        and Film 2, 7(1975):113.
        (See entry under "Film-makers. ")

2122   Williams/Douglas. "Film: The Emerging Woman. "
        Off Our Backs 4, 4(March, 1974):16.

2123   Williams, Robert. "Stereotypes of Negroes in Films. "
        Vision 1, 2(Summer, 1962):67-69.

2124   Wilmington, Mike. "Carnal Knowledge. "   The Velvet
        Light Trap No. 6(Fall, 1972):31.
            A review.

2125   Wise, Naomi. "The Hawksian Woman. "   Filmkritik
        (Germany) 17(May-June, 1973):256-64; and Take One
        3, 3(April, 1972):17-19.

2126   Wlaschin, K. "Liberated Women: Venice '71. "
        Films and Filming 18(November, 1971):26-30.

2127   Wolfenstein, Martha and Nathan Leites. Movies: A
        Psychological Study.   Glencoe, Ill. : Free Press,
        1950.   (Re-issued 1970, Arno Press.)
            An analysis of stereotyping of men and women
        in films from late 1945 to 50.   Authors believe people
        in common culture share common daydreams offered
        to them by "art. " The collective dreams are in part
        the source, in part the product of popular myths, sto-
        ries, plays, films.   The book examines recurrent
        daydreams which enter into consciousness of millions
        of moviegoers.   There is much in this book concern-
        ing women: the good-bad girl image, the heroine as
        mother.   The authors looked for typical themes in
        American, French, British films and guessed about
        movie makers and audiences to account for the emo-
        tional significance of recurrent themes.   One obser-
        vation: in American films nobody is weak, certainly
        not women.

2128   "A Woman's Place--Review of Film 'Antonia: A Por-
        trait of the Woman. '" Time 104, 17(October 21,
        1974):4.
            Antonia Brico in 1930, at age 28, the first wo-
        man to conduct the Berlin Philharmonic.   Today, at
        age 73, conductor of semiprofessional orchestra in
        Denver.   Documentary: remarkable woman scarred
        but not humbled by the problem of being a woman and
        an artist in America.   Conceived by Judy Collins, a
        former pupil (better known as a folk singer), and di-
        rected by Collins and Jill Godmilow.

2129   "Women and Film International Festival." Cinema
       Canada No. 8(June-July, 1973):9.

2130   "Women Disrupt Sick Flicks." Old Mole 1, 38(May 1,
       1970):2.

2131   "Women in Film." Film Library Quarterly 5, 1(Win-
       ter, 1971-72).
              (See listing under "Film-makers.")

2132   "Women in Film." Take One 3, 2(February, 1972):1-
       38.
              (See entry under "Film-makers.")

2133   Women in Media Collective. "The Berkeley Women
       and Media Conference." Women and Film 1, 5-6
       (1974):92.
              Conference is described and discussed by collec-
       tive.

2134   "Women on Women in Films." Take One 3, 2(Novem-
       ber-December, 1970):10-15.
              (See entry under "Film-makers.")

2135   "Women's Film Co-op." Off Our Backs 2, 2(October,
       1971):33.
              On films and film-makers.

2136   "Women's Liberation?" Film (Great Britain) No. 64
       (Winter, 1971):10-11.

2137   Young, Christopher. "June Allyson." Films in Re-
       view 19, 9(November, 1968):537-47.
              A filmography and career of "cute" Hollywood
       leading lady.

2138   Yurman, C. "Mae West Talks About the Gay Boys."
       Gay 24(July 20, 1970):3.

2139   Yvonne. "The Importance of Cicely Tyson." Ms. III,
       2(August, 1974):45.
              Effect of Cicely Tyson image on young black
       women. Discusses her role in "Sounder," a human-
       ized black mother, and the TV film, "The Autobio-
       graphy of Miss Jane Pittman."

2140   Zambrano, A. L. "'Women in Love': Counterpoint

on Film." Literature/Film Quarterly (Salisbury, Md.) 1, 1(1973):46-54.

2141   Zinman, David. 50 Classic Motion Pictures: The Stuff that Dreams Are Made Of. New York: Crown, 1970.
    Categories--one of which is "Dames." An arbitrary collection.

2142   Zwerdling, Shirley. Film and TV Festival Directory. New York: Back Stage Publications, Inc., 1970.
    World-wide history and full details of nearly 400 festivals in 50 countries. Does not mention any women's film festivals.

2143-9 [No entries]

Chapter 4

WOMEN COLUMNISTS AND CRITICS

2150   Adler, Renata. A Year in the Dark; Journal of a
        Film Critic 1968-69. New York: Random House,
        1968-69.
            130 film reviews and 50 essays which appeared
        in the New York Times from 1968-69. 14 months as
        a movie critic.

2151   "Alma Mabrey Talley: Obituary. " New York Times
        (June 26, 1970):41.
            A writer and film critic.

2152   Alpert, Hollis and Andrew Sarris. Film 68/69: An
        Anthology by the National Society of Film Critics.
        New York: Simon and Schuster, 1969.
            A collection of film reviews for 1968-69, includes
        contributions by Penelope Gilliatt, Pauline Kael.

2153   Alward, Jennifer. "Memoirs of a Censor. " Take One
        4, 10(March-April, 1974):14.
            TV Censor in Program Practices Department at
        CBS describes her work. (Also known as "executive
        editors. ")

2154   Amberg, George, et al. The Art of Cinema. 2 vols.
        New York: Arno Press, 1972.
            An anthology of essays on film aesthetics by ex-
        perimental film-maker and film aesthete Maya Deren;
        also other critics, a psychologist and scholar.

2155   "Authors and Editors. " Publishers Weekly 199(May
        24, 1971):31-32.
            Pauline Kael, film critic and author.

2156   Ayers, Richard. "Pauline Kael, the Film Critic with
        a Chip on Her Shoulder. " Cinéaste 1, 2(Fall, 1967):
        6-9.

2157   Bach, Margaret. "Parker Tyler Then and Now. "
         Cinema 6, 2(Fall, 1970):42-44.
             Critic Bach examines Tyler as a critic.

2158   Baker, Peter. "When Private Lives Are Public Prop-
         erty. " Films and Filming 3, 6(March, 1957):12.
         Hollywood and the scandal magazines.

2159   Barrett, Rona. Miss Rona. Freeport, N. Y. : Nash
         Pub. Corp. , 1974.
         Hollywood TV news and gossip columnist--auto-
         biography.

2160   Baxandall, Lee, ed. Radical Perspectives in the Arts.
         Baltimore: Penguin, 1972.
             Article: "Culture Is Not Neutral, Whom Does It
         Serve?" by Merideth Tax.

2161   Betts, Ernest. Inside Pictures. London: The Cres-
         set Press, 1960.
             British film critic and columnist turned scenario
         editor records his experiences on both sides of the
         screen. Includes: Chapter IX, 'Marlene Dietrich:
         the Anatomy of a Star, " p. 58. Chapter XV, "Genesis
         of the Film Critic, " p. 120. The book traces the
         history of film critics. "Kitty Kelly" (Andrie Alspro-
         ush) for Chicago Tribune--first independent motion
         picture critic, Iris Barry, C. A. Lejeune. Chapter
         XIII, "The High Cost of Being a Star. "

2162   "Beyond Theory of Film Practice: An Interview with
         Noel Burch. " Women and Film 1, 5-6(1974):20.
             The Marxist film critic and theorist is interview-
         ed and analyzed. He discusses his book, Theory of
         Film Practice, but writers question its applicability
         for feminist theory of film.

2163   Boyum, Joy G. and Adrienne Scott. Film as Film:
         Critical Responses to Film Art. Boston, Mass. :
         Allyn and Bacon, Inc. , 1971.

2164   Brée, G. 'Interviews with Two French Novelists. "
         Contemporary Literature 14(Spring, 1973):147-56.
             Interviews with Nathalie Sarraute, novelist, and
         Célie Bertin, novelist and film critic.

2165   Buscombe, Edward. "The Citizen Kane Book. "

Screen 13, 1(Spring, 1972):92.
A critical review of Pauline Kael's book.

2166   "Caroline Alice Lejeune: Obituary. " New York Times
        (April 2, 1973):38.
        English motion picture critic.

2167   Childs, J. "Penelope Gilliatt. " Film Comment 8, 2
        (Summer, 1972):22-26.
        (See listing under "Film-makers. ")

2168   Citron, Michelle. "Feminist Criticism. " The Velvet
        Light Trap No. 6(Fall, 1972):43.
        Definition of feminist criticism and suggestions
        for its future development.

2169   Cocks, Jay and David Denby, eds. Film 73/74. New
        York: Bobbs-Merrill Co. , Inc. , 1974.
        Includes reviews by Kael--"Last Tango in Paris";
        Gilliatt--"Memories of Underdevelopment"; Haskell--
        "Sleeper. "

2170   Cooke, Alistair, ed. Garbo and the Night Watchman:
        A Selection from the Writings of British and Amer-
        ican Film Critics. London: Cape, 1937.
        In 1937, film articles by people "who loved life
        and liked film. " Includes writings of Cecelia Ager,
        early feminist, whose special assignment was to judge
        only the women in films. C. A. Lejeune, also a film
        critic, is mentioned.

2171   "Correspondence and Controversy. " Film Quarterly
        17, 1(Fall, 1963):57-64.
        Ian Cameron, Pauline Kael and Andrew Sarris
        debate the auteur theory, and discuss the questionable
        merits of each other's criticism.

2172   Coulouris, George and Bernard Herrman. "The Ci-
        tizen Kane Book. " Sight and Sound 41, 2(Spring,
        1972):71-73.
        The actor and musical director of "Citizen Kane"
        answers Pauline Kael, arguing that Welles indeed was
        responsible for the development of "Citizen Kane. "

2173   Crist, Judith. The Private Eye, the Cowboy and the
        Very Naked Girl. Chicago: Holt, Rinehart and
        Winston, 1968.

Miss Crist's reviews from the New York Herald
Tribune and World Journal Tribune and other magazines have been collected in this anthology.

2174   "Critic and Superstar." Newsweek 82(December 24,
        1973):97.
            A portrait of Pauline Kael.

2175   "Critic Around the Clock." Newsweek 69(March 27,
        1967):95.
            On Judith Crist, critic.

2176   "The Critical Issue: A Discussion Between Paul
        Rotha, Basil Wright, Lindsay Anderson, Penelope
        Houston." Sight and Sound 27, 6(Autumn, 1958):
        271-75, 330.
            Trends in film criticism during the last 30
        years.

2177   de la Roche, Catherine. "Development of Soviet Cin-
        ema." Sight and Sound 14, 56(Winter, 1945-46):111-
        13.
            State of the industry in USSR.

2178   _____. "Escapism and Soviet Culture." Sight and
        Sound 15, 60(Winter, 1946-47):141-42.
            Soviet ideological censorship.

2179   _____. "Man with No Message." Films and Film-
        ing 1, 3(December, 1954):15.
            Critic discusses career of British director Carol
        Reed.

2180   _____. "Religion and the Cinema." Films and
        Filming 1, 12(September, 1955):13.
            An article on the propagandistic influence of re-
        ligious organizations on films' themes.

2181   _____. "The State Institute of Cinema and the Film
        Actors' Theatre in Moscow." Sight and Sound 17,
        66(Summer, 1948):101-02.

2182   Denby, David, ed. Film 70/71. New York: Simon
        and Schuster, 1971.
            Review by Gilliatt--"My Night at Maud's."

2183   _____. Film 71/72. New York: Simon and Schus-

ter, 1972.
Reviews by Gilliatt--"The Touch"; Kael--"Murmur
of the Heart"; Haskell--"King Lear. "

2184   Deren, Maya. An Anagram of Idea, Art Form and
Film.   Yonkers, N. Y. : Alicat Book Shop Press,
1945.

2185   _____. "Critic vs. Artist. " Village Voice 5, 38
(July 14, 1960):10-11.
The film-maker and critic discusses criticism.

2186   _____. "Movie Journal. " Village Voice 5, 39(July,
29, 1960):6, 8; 5, 44(August 25, 1960):6, 8; 6, 32
(June 1, 1961):9, 17.
Discusses directives to creativity.

2187   _____. "Notes, Essays, Letters. " Film Culture
39(Winter, 1964):1-86.
Bibliography.

2188   _____. "On a Film in Progress and a Statement. "
Film Culture 22, 23(Summer, 1961):160-63.
Discusses philosophical and haiku aspects of her
work.

2189   _____. "Reply to Farber's Article on Maya Der-
en. " New Republic 115(November 11, 1946):630.

2190   _____. "Tempo and Tension. " The Movies as
Medium.   Lewis Jacobs, ed. New York: Farrar,
Strauss and Giroux, 1970.
See pp. 144-62.

2191   Diamonstein, Barbaralee. Open Secrets. New York:
Viking, 1972.
"Judith Crist, " pp. 74-78.

2192   "Does She, or Doesn't She?" Newsweek 71(April 15,
1968):94.
Renata Adler, critic and author.

2193   "Dorothy Masters: Obituary. " New York Times (December 23, 1964):27.
Motion picture critic.

2194   Edwards, H. "Sheilah Graham. " Inter/View 24(Aug-

ust, 1972):22.
An interview. Sheilah Graham talks about her
work and that of other gossip columnists.

2195   Eells, George.   Hedda and Louella.   New York: Putnam, 1972.

2196   Eisner, Lotte.   "Film History."   Films in Review 2,
10(December, 1951):18-21.
Why film history is so difficult to write.

2197   Farber, M.   "Maya Deren's Silent Films: Criticism."
New Republic 115(October 28, 1946):555-56.

2198   "Four Stars for Baby."   Parents' Magazine 48(June,
1973):32-34.
A portrait of Judith Ripp, motion picture critic.

2199   Frank, S.   "Headaches of a Movie Censor."   Saturday
Evening Post 220(September 27, 1947):20-21+.
A portrait of Helen Tingley, motion picture cen-
sor.

2200   Geraghty, Christine.   "Film Culture: An Article."
Screen 15, 4(Winter, 1974-75):89.
One of several articles dealing with various aspects of film culture.   This one is concerned with
feminist criticism, and with the images or mythologies
of women as projected in articles in the journal, Women and Film.

2201   Gillette, D. C.   "Hollywood-image-wreckers."   Journal of the Producers Guild of America (Los Angeles)
15, 2(June, 1973):3-6, 17.
(See entry under "Images.")

2202   Gilliatt, Penelope.   Unholy Fools.   New York: Viking
Press, Inc., 1973.
A collection of Gilliatt's criticism and reviews
dealing primarily with her favorite subject, comedy.

2203   Graham, Sheilah.   College of One.   New York: Viking,
1967.

2204   _____.   Confessions of a Hollywood Columnist.
New York: Morrow and Co., 1969.
(See entry under "Actresses.")

2205   _____. The Rest of the Story. New York: Coward-
        McCann, 1964.
        Autobiography.

2206   _____ and Gerold Frank. Beloved Infidel. New
        York: Holt, 1958.
        Autobiography.

2207   Grant, Elspeth. "From Pearl White to Pearl Har-
        bour. " Sight and Sound 11,43(Winter, 1942):61-62.
        How she judges a film.

2208   Harman, J. "C. A. Lejeune. " Sight and Sound 42,3
        (Summer, 1973):150.
        Obituary. A tribute to the critic.

2209   Haskell, Molly. "Film: Orificial and Unexpurgated. "
        Village Voice 18(March 1, 1973):66.

2210   _____. "Unifying the Motley Threads. " Village
        Voice 18(February 22, 1973):62.

2211   Hine, A. "Hollywood Columnists. " Holiday 5(April,
        1949):8-9, 11+.

2212   Hinxman, Margaret. "Even a Fan Deserves an Honest
        Answer. " Films and Filming 5,10(July, 1959):15.
        What kind of criticism to expect from a fan ma-
        gazine.

2213   Hopper, Hedda. From Under My Hat. Garden City,
        N. J. : Doubleday, 1952.

2214   _____. The Whole Truth and Nothing But. New
        York: Doubleday, 1963.
        The autobiography of the Hollywood gossip colum-
        nist, but also talks of the "stars. " (See also entry
        under "Actresses. ")

2215   Houston, Penelope. "The Ambassadors. " Sight and
        Sound 23,4(April-June, 1954):176-80.
        Recent American-British collaborations in Eur-
        ope.

2216   _____. "Characteristics, Duties of the Film Cri-
        tic. " Sight and Sound 18, 69(Spring, 1949):42-43.

2217   . Contemporary Cinema. New York: Pen-
        guin, 1963.
        An account of films of late 1950's and early 60's.

2218   . "The Critical Question." Sight and Sound
        29, 4(Autumn, 1960):160-65.
        Characteristics of British critical writing.

2219   . "Critic's Notebook." Sight and Sound 30, 2
        (Spring, 1961):62-66.
        Good, bad and trends in criticism. Refers to
        her own reviews.

2220   . "Cukor and the Kanins." Sight and Sound
        24-4(Spring, 1955):186-91, 220.

2221   . "England, Their England." Sight and Sound
        35, 2(Spring, 1966):54-56.
        Discusses foreign products in Britain.

2222   . "The Figure in the Carpet." Sight and
        Sound 32, 4(Autumn, 1963):158-64.
        An analysis of Alfred Hitchcock's films.

2223   . "Hitchcockery." Sight and Sound 37, 4(Au-
        tumn, 1968):188-89.
        Truffaut's "Bride Wore Black" and Bogdanovich's
        "Targets" compared.

2224   . "Hollywood in the Age of Television."
        Sight and Sound 26, 4(Spring, 1957):175-79.
        TV has caused Hollywood to lose audience and
        money.

2225   . "The Horizontal Man." Sight and Sound
        38, 3(Summer, 1969):116-20.
        An analysis of the films of Miklós Jancsó, Polish
        director.

2226   . "Keeping Up with the Antonionis." Sight
        and Sound 33, 4(Autumn, 1964):163-68.
        Britain and the foreign production.

2227   . "Kramer and Company." Sight and Sound
        22, 1(July-September, 1952):20-23, 48.
        Critic Houston discusses producer Kramer's
        career.

2228 _____ . "Mr. Deeds and Willie Stork." Sight and
        Sound 19, 7(November, 1950):276-79, 285.
          Hollywood's assumptions in its picture of the na-
        tional scene: politics, foreign films, sociological
        films.

2229 _____ . "The Nature of the Evidence." Sight and
        Sound 36, 2(Spring, 1967):88-92.
          Questionable authenticity of stock footage used as
        evidence in documentaries.

2230 _____ . "'Shane' and George Stevens." Sight and
        Sound 23, 2(October-December, 1953):71-76.
          An analysis of his films.

2231 _____ . "Whose Crisis?" Sight and Sound 33, 1
        (Winter, 1963-64):26-28, 50.
          Is there an industry crisis?

2232 _____ . "007." Sight and Sound 34, 1(Winter, 1964-
        65):14-16.
          The James Bond character.

2233 _____ and John Gillett. "Blockbusting." Sight and
        Sound 32, 2(Spring, 1963):68-77.
          Reasons for formulas, subjects, etc. of epics.
        Refers to "King of Kings" by Nicholas Ray.

2234 _____ , _____ . "Conversations with Nicholas
        Ray and Joseph Losey." Sight and Sound 30, 4(Au-
        tumn, 1961):182-87.
          Critics interview, comment on the films, careers
        of Ray and Losey.

2235 _____ and Kenneth Cavander. "Interview with Carl
        Foreman." Sight and Sound 27, 5(Summer, 1958):
        220-23, 264.
          Discusses Foreman's scriptwriting career. Re-
        ference to "The Key," directed by Carol Reed, one of
        Britain's first Realists (and a male).

2236 Ibranyi-Kiss, A. "August-July: Interview with Alexa
        De Wiel and Sharon Smith." Cinema Canada No. 6
        (February-March, 1973):58-61.
          Women in film.

2237 "Interesting Women." McCall's 96(March, 1969):99.
        Renata Adler, critic.

2238   'Irene Thirer: Obituary." New York Times (Febru-
        ary 20, 1964):29.
        Motion picture editor and critic.

2239   'Iris Barry: Obituary." New York Times (December
        23, 1969):32.
        Museum director and film authority.

2240   Johnston, Claire. "Women's Cinema as Counter Cin-
        ema." British Film Institute publication.

2241   Kael, Pauline. "Circles and Squares." Film Quart-
        erly 16, 3(Spring, 1963):12-26.
            Negative interpretation of the "politique des au-
        teurs." Refers to Sarris as practitioner.

2242   _____. The Citizen Kane Book. Boston: Little,
        Brown, 1971.
            Pauline Kael's analysis of "Citizen Kane," her
        questioning of Welles' "authorship."

2243   _____. Deeper into Movies. Boston: Little,
        Brown, 1973.
        Motion picture reviews.

2244   _____. Going Steady. Boston: Little, Brown,
        1970.
            Movie reviews from New Yorker, January 1968
        to March, 1969.

2245   _____. I Lost It at the Movies. Boston: Little,
        Brown, 1965.
            Essays. Movie reviews by Pauline Kael. A
        careful reading of all will show her evolving film aes-
        thetic.

2246   _____. Kiss, Kiss. Bang! Bang! Boston: Lit-
        tle-Atlantic, 1968.
        Reviews.

2247   _____. "Morality Plays Right and Left." Sight
        and Sound 24, 2(October-December, 1954):67-73.
            Films as advertising ways of life. Reference
        to pro- and anti-communist propaganda.

2248   Kanfer, S. "Difficult but Triumphant." Time 98
        (September 27, 1971):82-83.

A portrait of Penelope Gilliatt.

2249   Kauffmann, Stanley with Bruce Henstell. American
       Film Criticism, from the Beginnings to Citizen
       Kane. New York: Liveright, 1972.

2250   "Kiss Kiss Bang Bang and Styles of Radical Will. "
       Screen 11, 3(1970):115-17.
       Reviews of two books on film criticism.

2251   Knepper, Max. "Hollywood's Barkers. " Sight and
       Sound 19, 9(January, 1951):359-62.
       Fan magazines.

2252   Lejeune, Caroline Alice. "Alexander Korda: A
       Sketch. " Sight and Sound 4, 13(Spring, 1935):5-6.
       Critic Lejeune discusses Korda.

2253   _____. Chestnuts in Her Lap, 1936-46. London:
       Phoenix House, 1947.
       "A collection of some of the reviews and film
       articles written for The Observer, " 1936-1946.

2254   _____. Cinema. London: Alexander Maclehose
       and Co. , 1931.
       A film critic analyzes her art. Articles on Mary
       Pickford and Nazimova.

2255   _____. "Films of the Quarter. " Sight and Sound
       2, 5(Spring, 1933):21-22.
       Economic depression and sound cause American
       film industry to founder, giving the English film in-
       dustry an opportunity to emerge.

2256   _____. "On Not Being Committed. " Films and
       Filming 5, 9(June, 1959):9.
       Discusses her own type of film criticism.

2257   _____. Thank You for Having Me. London: Hut-
       chinson, 1964.
       Pioneer English film critic for whom emotion
       was more important than film theory or aesthetics.
       Helped popularize films and film criticism in Eng-
       land. Speaks of film but also much on her person-
       al life.

2258   "Lejeune, Caroline Alice: Obituary. " Sight and Sound

42(Summer, 1973):150.
Obituary of the English motion picture critic.

2259 Lermon, L. "The Influentials. " Vogue 162(September, 1973):284-85.
Discussion includes film critic Pauline Kael.

2260 Lesage, Julia. "Feminist Film Criticism: Theory and Practice. " Women and Film 1, 5-6(1974):12.
Theoretical guidelines for feminist film criticism.

2261 "Liberated, All Liberated. " Vogue 155(June 1, 1970): 115.
A portrait of Renata Adler, film critic and author.

2262 Longguth, A. J. "Hollywood Since Louella. " Saturday Review Arts 1(March, 1973):33-36.

2263 McBride, Joseph. "Mr. MacDonald, Mr. Kauffmann, and Miss Kael. " Film Heritage 2, 4(Summer, 1967): 26-34.

2264 _____. "Rough Sledding with Pauline Kael. " Film Heritage 7, 1(Fall, 1971):13-16.
Contradicts Kael's New Yorker thesis that Mankiewicz, not Welles, shaped "Citizen Kane. " Comments--more irritated than enlightened by Pauline Kael's work.

2265 McCarthy, Todd and Charles Flynn. Kings of the B's. New York: E. P. Dutton and Co. , Inc. , 1975.
(See entry under "Film-makers. ")

2266 Macklin, F. A. "Editorial--The Perils of Pauline's Criticism. " Film Heritage 2, 1(Fall, 1966):1.
On Pauline Kael. Kael's reply: 2, 2(Winter, 1966): 43-44.

2267 _____. "Editorial. " Film Heritage 2, 4(Summer, 1967):1-2, 36-39.
On Susan Sontag and John Simon as critics.

2268 Martineau, Barbara Halpern. "Women vs. Cannes. " Cinema Canada 9(August-September, 1973):50-52.
(See entry under "Film-makers. ")

2269   . "Women's Film Daily. " <u>Women and Film</u>
         1, 5-6(1974):36.
         (See entry under "Film-makers. ")

2270   Michelson, Annette. "Film and the Radical Aspira-
         tion, " in <u>Film Culture Reader</u> P. Adams Sitney,
         ed. New York: Praeger Publishers, 1970.
           The author is advising editor to the book. Asks:
       can independent American cinema achieve ultimate ra-
       dical potential when the country is based on a war e-
       conomy?

2271   Montagu, Ivor. "Birmingham Sparrow: In Memoriam,
         Iris Barry. " <u>Sight and Sound</u> 39, 2(Spring, 1970):
         106-08.
           An article eulogizing Iris Barry, first film cri-
       tic in serious British journals; co-founder of the
       world's first "Film Society"; initiator of the first A-
       merican film archive, scholar and writer on literature
       and arts, especially film.

2272   Morgenstern, Joseph. "Perils of Pauline. " <u>Newsweek</u>
         71(May 20, 1968):101+ .
         On Pauline Kael.

2273   and Stefan Kanfer. <u>Film 69/70, an Anthol-
         ogy by the National Society of Film Critics.</u> New
         York: Simon and Schuster, 1970.
           A collection of film reviews for 1969-70, includes
       contributions by Penelope Gilliatt and Pauline Kael.

2274   Paletz, David. "Judith Crist: An Interview with a
         Big-Time Critic. " <u>Film Quarterly</u> 22, 1(Fall, 1968):
         27-36.
           The author discusses her type of criticism and
       what it's like being a professional critic.

2275   Parsons, Louella. <u>The Gay Illiterate.</u> Garden City,
         N. J. : Doubleday, Doran, 1944.
         (See entry under "Actresses. ")

2276   . <u>Tell It to Louella.</u> New York: G. P. Put-
         nam's Sons, 1961.
         (See entry under "Actresses. ")

2277   . <u>How to Write for the "Movies. "</u> Chicago:

A. C. McClurg and Co., 1915.

2278   "Pauline Kael. " Current Biography 35(March, 1974):
       15-18.
       A portrait of the author and film critic.

2279   "Pearls of Pauline. " Time 92(July 12, 1968):38-39.
       A portrait of Pauline Kael.

2280   "Peculiar Experience. " Newsweek 75(February 2,
       1970):80A+.
       A portrait of Renata Adler, critic.

2281   Peet, C. "Our Lady Censors. " Outlook 153(Decem-
       ber 25, 1929):645-47.

2282   Pelswick, Rose. "Confessions of a Movie Critic. "
       Photoplay 29(February, 1926):37, 141, and follow-
       ing issues.

2283   Penley, Constance. "Theory of Film Practice: Ana-
       lysis and Review. " Women and Film 1, 5-6(1974):
       32.
       Analyzes Noel Burch's Theory of Film Practice.

2284   "Perils of Pauline. " Newsweek 67(May 30, 1966):80+.
       A portrait of the film critic, Pauline Kael.

2285   Powell, Dilys. "Credo of a Critic. " Sight and Sound
       10, 38(Summer, 1941):26-27.
       How she judges films.

2286   "Replies to a Questionnaire. " Sight and Sound 23, 2
       (October-December, 1953):99-104, 112.
       (See listing under "Film-makers. ")

2287   "Replies to a Questionnaire. " Sight and Sound 26, 4
       (Spring, 1957):180-85.
       (See listing under "Film-makers. ")

2288   "Rigors of Criticism. " Time 90(December 1, 1967):
       38.
       Renata Adler, critic.

2289   Rosenheimer, A. , Jr. "Review: Maya Deren's Ana-
       gram of Ideas on Art, Form and Film. " Theatre
       Arts 31(January, 1947):68.

2290   Sabo, B. "On the Scene with Marvene Jones, Holly-
       wood Gossip Gal. " Inter/View 38(November, 1973):
       14-15.
          About Marvene Jones, the youngest Hollywood
       gossip columnist.

2291   Sarachild, Kathie. "Women's Films: The Artistic Is
       Political. " Feminist Art Journal 2, 2(Winter, 1973):
       6-8+ .

2292   Sarris, Andrew. "The Auteur Theory and the Perils
       of Pauline. " Film Quarterly 16, 4(Summer, 1963):
       26-33.
          On Pauline Kael.

2293   _____. The Primal Screen. New York: Simon
       and Schuster, 1973.
          Contains: "Citizen Kael vs. Citizen Kane, " p.
       111.

2294   Schickel, Richard and John Simon, eds. Film 67/68:
       An Anthology by the National Society of Film Cri-
       tics. New York: Simon and Schuster, 1968.
          A collection of film reviews that includes contri-
       butions by Pauline Kael.

2295   "The Screen Answers Back. " Films and Filming 8, 8
       (May, 1962):11-18, 44-45.
          An assortment of film people, including Kathleen
       Harrison, British character actress, and Susan Kohner,
       American actress. Answers to: What should a film
       critic do? Is your work influenced by critics? Which
       critics do you read? Is criticism getting better or
       worse? Includes listing of "Who's Who" of film cri-
       tics.

2296   Solomon, Stanley J. The Classic Cinema: Essay in
       Criticism. New York: Harcourt, Brace, Jovano-
       vich, 1974.
          A collection of essays including ones by Lillian
       Gish and Pauline Kael.

2297   Sontag, Susan. Against Interpretation. New York:
       Farrar, Straus and Giroux, 1966.

2298   _____. "A Note on Novels and Films. " In Against
       Interpretation and Other Essays, New York:
       Farrar, Straus & Giroux, 1966. pp. 242-45.

2299   _____. "Theatre and Film," in Styles of Radical
           Will. N.Y.: Farrar, Straus, and Giroux, 1969.
           pp. 99-120.

2230   "Third Journalist." Time 95(February 16, 1970):92+.
           Renata Adler, critic.

2301   "What Are the New Critics Saying?" Film Culture
           42(Fall, 1966):76-88.
           Includes reference to Annette Michelson.

2302   Woolf, Virginia. "The Cinema," in Collected Essays.
           Vol. 2. New York: Harcourt, Brace and World,
           1967. pp. 268-72.

"A to B" 2020
Abbagnato, Ornella 1070
Academy Award Winners 432,
    756, 961, 1244
Academy Awards 68, 69, 75,
    76, 966, 967
Achur, Giri 2020
Acting 125, 244, 279, 405,
    476, 517, 533, 613, 615,
    651, 664, 759, 817, 914,
    1034, 1070, 1090, 1264
Actresses 4, 13, 15, 16, 17,
    20, 21, 25, 34, 38, 49,
    52, 59, 67, 69, 70, 77,
    85, 87, 96, 99, 100,
    101, 106, 107, 110, 111,
    113, 114, 116, 117, 118,
    119, 122, 157, 266, 279,
    323, 330, 405, 460, 475,
    481, 498, 610, 675, 686,
    687, 689, 690, 822, 967,
    989, 1240
Actresses:
    Attitudes toward men 397
    Awards 759
    Failures 1240
    Independent 475
    Number of roles for 679,
        749, 1799, 2038
    Role models 2064
Acuna, Judith Shaw 1016
Adams, Edie 96
Adams, John 1193
Adams, Julie 96
Adams, Katherine 96
"Adam's Rib" 1245, 1877
Adaptations 1498
Adato, Perry Miller 2020
Addams, Dawn 96
Adler, Renata 2150, 2192,
    2237, 2261, 2280, 2288,
    2300

Adorée, Renee 96, 861
Adventure 81
Advertising 410, 1451, 1822,
    1846
Aesthetic 1264
"An Affair of the Skin" 331
Africa 1203, 1604
Age 122, 140, 164, 2031
Agents 97, 1114
Ager, Cecelia 2170
Aktaseva, Irina 1343
Alaimo, Louise 1016, 2020
Alberghetti, Anna Marie 96
Albertson, Lillian 1034
Albertson, Mabel 96
Albright, Lola 96
Alden, Mary 96, 126, 1035
Aldrich, Robert 1896, 1970
Alea, Thomas Gutierrez 1605
Alemann, Claudia 1304
"Alice Adams" 784
"Alice Doesn't Live Here Any-
    more" 1095, 1782, 1906
"Alice's Restaurant" 1752
All-man Legend 1878
Allasio, Marisa 96
Allbritton, Louise 96
Allen, Catherine 1305
Allen, Dede 1114, 1145, 1194,
    1443
Allen, Gracie 96
Allen, Jay Presson 1114
Allgood, Sara 96
Allison, May 96, 199
Allyson, June 96, 907, 1696,
    2137
Almanac 45, 919, 951
Alsproush, Andrie 2161
Alvarez, Carlos and Julia
    1112, 1326
Alward, Jennifer 2153
"The Amazing Equal Pay Show'
    1305

"An American Family" 1518,
   1630, 2018, 2107, 2108
American Film Manfacturing
   Co. 60, 960
"An American in Paris" 536
Ames, Adrienne 96
Anders, Evelyn 96
Anders, Merry 96
Anderson, Claire 96
Anderson, Donna 96
Anderson, Judith 96, 906
Anderson, Madeline 1041,
   1109, 1661, 2020
Anderson, Mary 96
Anderson, Mignon 96
Anderson, Sylvia 1042, 1666
Anderson, Thom 1508
Andersson, Bibi 96
Andresikova, Jana 495
Andress, Ursula 96, 770
Andrews, Julie 96, 301, 775,
   898
Andrews, Lois 96
Andrews Sisters (LaVerne,
   Maxine, Patty) 96
"Angela: Portrait of a Revolu-
   tionary" 1509, 2020
Angeli, Pier 96
Anholt, Edna 81
Anholt, Edward 81
Animal Trainer 1253
Animation 1071, 1408, 1586,
   1645
Ann-Margaret 96
Annabella 96
Annie Oakley 1922
Annuals 1, 3, 18, 922
Anson, Lura 96
Anspock, Susan 679
"Antonia: A Portrait of a Wo-
   man" 1189, 1653, 2128,
Antonioni, Michelangelo 1974
"Anything You Want to Be"
   2020
"Apotheosis" 1428, 1625
Arab Countries 982
"Arabesque for Kenneth Anger"
   1252
Archive 741, 1999, 2271
Arden, Eve 96, 207, 687
Arinbasarova, Natal'ja 139
Armstrong, Gillian 1305
Armstrong, Suzanne 1016

Art Director 92, 984, 1442,
   1782
Art of the film 50, 89, 93,
   279, 556, 587, 763, 948,
   953, 957, 986, 987, 1159,
   1160, 1161, 1162, 1163,
   1164, 1165, 1166, 1502,
   1527, 1594
Arthur, Jean 96, 807, 865
Arthur, Karen 1305
Arzner, Dorothy 35, 86, 97,
   961, 970, 978, 1051,
   1082, 1146, 1199, 1278,
   1295, 1323, 1331, 1332,
   1358, 1485, 1491, 1492,
   1493, 1573, 1574, 1603,
   1606, 1607, 1658, 1910,
   1923, 2000, 2005, 2015
"As Others See Us" 1178
Asseyer, Tamara 1114
Assistant Director (Co-Director)
   92, 984, 998, 1066, 1442,
   1458
Associate Directors/Stage Man-
   agers 1442
Associate Producers 1782
Astaire, Fred 311, 761, 762
Astor, Mary 96, 141, 142
Athletes 1729
"Attica" 1649
Aubier, Pascal 1281
Audran, Stephane 221
Audrey, Jacqueline 1658
Aunt Jemima 1775
Auslander, Leland and wife
   1053
Authors 97, 1233, 1241, 1242,
   1411, 1469, 1478, 1541
Autobiography 113, 115, 142,
   146, 154, 159, 242, 274,
   305, 306, 307, 313, 318,
   350, 351, 386, 406, 412,
   421, 429, 430, 432, 461,
   467, 480, 547, 548, 567,
   589, 634, 635, 657, 712,
   730, 755, 756, 833, 881,
   887, 902, 903, 909, 1131,
   1151, 1242, 1244, 1271,
   1371, 1412, 1622, 2205
"The Autobiography of Miss
   Jane Pittman" 2139
Avant-garde 964, 1142, 1214,
   1436, 1571, 1661

Awards 759, 901, 920, 974,
    1053, 1287, 1473, 1570,
    1578, 1613
Ayres, Agnes 96

Bacall, Lauren 96, 450
Bach, Margaret 2157
"Back Street" 2022
Baclanova, Olga 96
Bad 309, 1756
Baddeley, Hermione 96
Badham, Mary 96
Bailey, Pearl 96, 146
Bainter, Fay 96, 816
Baird, Leah 96
Baker, Carroll 96
Baker, Diane 96
Baldanello, Maria Grazia 1070
Balin, Ina 96
Ball, Lucille 96, 215, 246,
    458
Ball, Susan 96
Ballin, Mabel 96
Bancroft, Anne 96, 405
Bank, Mirra 2071
Bankhead, Tallulah 96, 154,
    422, 852
Banky, Vilma 96, 560
Bara, Theda 84, 94, 96, 155,
    204, 1774, 2104
Bardot, Brigitte 96, 127, 162,
    165, 262, 325, 357, 378,
    410, 607, 669, 670, 683,
    764, 795, 846, 1760,
    1826, 1846, 2058, 2087
Bari, Lynn 96, 342
Barkley, Deanne 1114
Barnes, Joanna 96
Barrett, Rona 2159
Barrie, Wendy 96
Barriscale, Bessie 96
Barry, Iris 2161, 2239, 2271
Barrymore, Diana 96, 159, 402
Barrymore, Ethel 96, 130,
    160, 161, 346, 375
Barrymore, John 198
Barrymore Family 96, 130
Bartalini, Isa 1070
Bartlett, Freude 2020
Barton, Peter 2020
Baskaya, Margarita 1199
Batchelor, Joy 1211, 1257, 1258,
    1408

Bates, Barbara 96, 156
Bates, Florence 96, 195
Bauchens, Anne 97, 1458
Baxley, Barbara 96
Baxter, Anne 96
Bayne, Beverly 96
Beasts 1915
"Beau Masque" 433
Beauty 174, 551, 1751, 1768,
    1915, 1936, 1972, 2031
Beavers, Louise 96
Beckett, Adam 1508
"Bed and Sofa" 2078
Beecher, Janet 96
"Behind the Green Door" 280
"Behind the Veil" 2009
Bel Geddes, Barbara 96
Bell, Tinker 839
Bellamy, Madge 96, 595
Belles 1855
Bennett, Charles 81
Bennett, Constance 96, 578,
    737, 1537
Bennett, Enid 96
Bennett, Joan 96, 173
Beranger, Clara 97, 1072,
    1110
Berenson, Marisa 284
Bergen, Candice 96
Bergen, Polly 96, 174, 1768
Berger, Senta 96
Bergman, Ingmar 476, 1890,
    1902, 1927, 1932, 1974,
    2007, 2042, 2074, 2111
Bergman, Ingrid 94, 96, 212,
    236, 386, 725, 813, 820,
    856, 2077
Bergman, Marilyn 1608
Bergman's Women 1890, 1927,
    1932, 1974
Bergner, Elizabeth 96
Berkeley, Busby 1924
Berlin, Abby 672
Bernard, Dorothy 96
Bernhardt, Sara 398
Bertin, Célia 2164
Bertolucci, Bernardo 144,
    1754, 1975, 1977, 2035,
    2115
Bertozzi, Patricia 1948
Bertsch, Marguerite 1075
Best Films 974
"The Best of Everything" 2102

Betti, Laura 842
Beulah 1744, 2001
Bibb, Porter 1540
Bibliography 299, 392, 645,
    867, 927, 936, 1001,
    1002, 1003, 1141, 1158,
    1163, 2049, 2187
"The Big Doll House" 1809
Billington, Francella 96
Binney, Constance 96
Biography 110, 111, 138,
    147, 158, 165, 172, 180,
    183, 235, 236, 262, 298,
    301, 303, 320, 327, 330,
    343, 352, 370, 402, 403,
    404, 407, 429, 444, 445,
    455, 458, 483, 496, 523,
    524, 527, 537, 545, 578,
    579, 584, 598, 621, 622,
    625, 638, 639, 658, 660,
    669, 688, 694, 695, 743,
    744, 758, 778, 780, 785,
    813, 814, 831, 841, 852
    864, 874, 880, 896, 897,
    898, 899, 915, 916, 917,
    1032, 1062, 1081, 1082,
    1110, 1146, 1173, 1184,
    1214, 1241, 1260, 1261,
    1276, 1303, 1346, 1353,
    1567, 1637
"Birth" 2020
"The Birth Film" 1092, 1780
"Birth of a Nation" 126
Bishop, Julie 96, 883
Bissett, Jacqueline 96, 679
Bitch 584, 1789, 1828, 1849
Björk, Anita 96, 243
Blaché see Guy-Blaché, Alice
Black/Blacks 57, 66, 73, 74,
    82, 89, 126, 146, 313,
    325, 326, 477, 481, 502,
    528, 768, 840, 1775,
    1776, 1784, 1845, 1870,
    1904, 1914, 1962, 1981,
    1983, 1992, 1993, 2057,
    2066, 2123, 2139
Black, Karen 679
"Black Bart" 765
"Black Girl" 2066
Blackman, Honor 96
Blaine, Vivian 96
Blair, Betsy 96
Blair, Janet 96

Blais, Marie-Claire 1599
Blake, Madge 96
Blanchard, Mari 608
Blandick, Clara 96
Blasetti, Mara 1070
Blondell, Joan 96, 209, 540
Blondes 104, 168, 440, 472,
    863, 1766, 1861
Bloom, Claire 61, 96, 151,
    447
Bloom, Vera 14
"The Blue Knight" 1473
"Blue Water, White Death"
    1239
Blyth, Ann 96
Blythe, Betty 96
Boardman, Eleanor 96, 192
Bodard, Mag 1507
Bogdanovich, Peter 2223
Boland, Mary 96, 617
Bondarčuk, Natalija 143, 649
Bondi, Beulah 96, 803
Booth, Clare see Clare Booth
    Luce
Booth, Karen 96
Booth, Margaret 1634
Booth, Shirley 96
Borden, Olive 96
Borer, Mary 1666
Borg, Veda Ann 96, 863
"Boris Godunov" 1361
Bostan, Elizabeta 1118, 1405,
    1406, 1560
Bouchier, Chili 227
Bouman, Suzanne 2020
Bow, Clara 96, 167, 662,
    689, 893, 1241, 2104
Box, Betty 1666
Box, Muriel 1101
Brackett, Leigh 1114, 1206,
    1778
Bradna, Olympe 96
Brady, Alice 96, 185, 220
Brakhage, Jane and Stan 1092,
    1780
Brand, Jane Warren 1016
Brando, Jocelyn 96
Brando, Marlon 121, 144
Brandon, Liane 1016, 1188,
    2020
Brady, Alice 184, 1394
Breamer, Sylvia 96
Brent, Evelyn 96

Brice, Fanny 523
Brice, Rosetta 96
"The Bride Wore Black" 2223
Brier, Robert 1589
Briscoe, Lottie 630
Britt, May 96
Britton, Barbara 96
Britton, Pamela 96
Brockwell, Gladys 96
Broderick, Helen 96
"Broken Goddess" 1849
Bronson, Betty 96
Brooks, Louise 96, 232, 233,
    234, 255, 591
Brown, Barbara 1016
Brown, Kay 1114
Brown, Vanessa 96
Brown, Winnie 96
Browne, Coral 96
Bruce, Virginia 96
Brunettes 440, 1861
Bryan, Jane 96
Buck, Marilyn 1466
Buck, Pearl 936
Bujold, Genevieve 376, 413,
    530
Bulca, Ioana 782
Bunin, Elinor 1155
Burch, Noel 2162, 2183
Burch, Ruth 1591
Burke, Billie 96, 178, 242
Burrill, Christine 1605
Burstyn, Ellen 679, 1782
Burton, Charlotte 96
"Bus Stop" 847
Busch, Mae 96, 828
Bush, Pauline 96
Bute, Mary Ellen 1064, 1065,
    1105, 1319, 1414, 1415,
    1586, 1638, 2015
Byington, Spring 96

"Cabaret" 705
"Cabin in the Sky" 464
"The Cabinet" 2020
Cagney, Jeanne 96
Calvert, Catherine 96
Calvert, Phyllis 96
Calvet, Corinne 96
Camera Assistant 1397
Campbell, Alan 81
Campbell, Susan 1432
Canfield, Marie Celine 1016

Cannes 1967
Cannibals 1781
Cannon, Dyan 251
Canova, Ann 14
Canova, Judy 14, 96, 691
Capote, Truman 1498
Caprice, June 96
Capucine 96
Cardinale, Claudia 96, 552,
    637, 2058
Carew, Ora 96
Carle, Gilles 541
Carlisle, Mary 96
"Carnal Knowledge" 1842,
    1851, 2124
Carné, Marcel 1743
Carol, Martine 96
Carol, Sue 96
Caron, Leslie 96, 279, 536,
    600
Carr, Catherine 1113
Carroll, Diahann 96, 840
Carroll, Madeleine 96
Carroll, Nancy 96, 648, 654,
    655, 805
Carse, Janet Wood 1314
Carson, Jeannie 96
Carson, Jo 1508
Carson, Robert 81
Carter, Helena 96
Carter, Janis 96
Cartoonists 1442, 1645
Carver, Louise 96
Carver, Lynne 96
Cash, Rosalind 477
Cass, Peggy 96
Cassavetes, John 2016, 2042
Casting Directors 1114, 1591
Castle, Irene and Vernon 270,
    808
Catalogue 1, 2
Caulfield, Joan 96
Cavagnac, Guy 1281
Cavanaugh, John 1432
Cavani, Liliana 1093, 1175,
    1468, 1609, 1620, 1781,
    2086, 2100
Censors
    Film 1036, 2153, 2199,
    2281
    Moral 2104
Censorship 61, 95, 1568,
    1817, 1987, 2054, 2083

Cesares, Maria 96
Chadwick, Helene 96
Chaffee, Joan 1337
Chambers, Marilyn 280, 1792
Champion, Marge 96
Chanel, Gabrielle 1454
Channing, Carol 96
Chaplin, Anne Morrison 136,
    1044
Chaplin, Charlie 2115
Chaplin, Geraldine 96, 386
Chapman, Marguerite 96
Character actors 863
    Awards 759
Charisma 2050
Charisse, Cyd 96
Charleson, Mary 96
Chase, Ilka 96
Chatterton, Ruth 96, 265,
    763
Chauvinist 1915, 2003
Cherrill, Virginia 96
Chevalier, Elizabeth 1633
Child stars 7, 96, 120, 165,
    559, 706, 755, 835
Childbirth 2013
"Children of Paradise" 1752
Childs, Abby and Jon 2020
"Chircales" 1418
Chopra, Joyce 1016, 1188,
    2020
Choreographers 1339, 1449,
    1461
"Choreography for Camera"
    1571
Christian, Linda 96, 274
Christians, Mady 96
Christie, Agatha 936
Christie, Julie 96, 121, 382
Christie Film Co. 187, 1126
"Christopher Strong" 1491
Christy, Ann 96
Churchill, Joan 1304, 1379
Chytilova, Vera 1252, 1278,
    1358, 1572, 1658
Cilento, Diane 96
"Cincales" 1243
Cinderella 1706
Cinema fashions 1948
Cinema verité 956, 1126,
    1313, 1511, 1692, 2013
Cinematographers 983, 984,
    992, 1239, 1325, 1458,
    1540

"Citizen Kane" 287, 310,
    2165, 2172, 2242
Clair, Ethlyne 55
Claire, Ina 96
"Claire's Knee" 1976
Clark, Edith 1127
Clark, Eleanor 1451
Clark, Marguerite 96, 181, 200
Clark, Petula 96, 706
Clarke, Mae 96
Clarke, Shirley 992, 1046,
    1073, 1097, 1126, 1128,
    1136, 1138, 1153, 1172,
    1193, 1201, 1207, 1224,
    1263, 1320, 1399, 1438,
    1439, 1444, 1503, 1531,
    1543, 1640, 1658, 1662,
    1670, 2015, 2027
Clayton, Ethel 96
Clayton, Marguerite 96
"Cleopatra Jones" 312, 2066,
"Clockwork Orange" 2105
Clyde, June 1766
Cocková, Helga 490
Cocteau, Jean 1130
"Coffee" 2066
Coffee, Lenore J. 1110, 1131
Colbert, Claudette 96, 682,
    689
Colby, Anita 96
Coleman, Nancy 96
"La Collectionneuse" 1976
Collier, Constance 96
Collins, Joan 96
Collins, Judy 1653, 2128
Comden, Betty 81, 1132, 1206
Comediennes 56, 64, 188, 207,
    215, 246, 425, 444, 458,
    576, 658, 691, 899
Comedy 22, 23, 56, 64, 81,
    98, 188, 246, 425, 990,
    2001
Comer, Anjanette 96
Coming of age 2055
Comingore, Dorothy 287, 310
Communist 1913
Companeez, Nina 1039, 1040,
    1094
Competition 481
Composers 14, 958, 962,
    983, 997, 1335
Compson, Betty 96, 187, 1090
Compton, Joyce 96
Compton, Juleen 1114, 1658

Conference 1663, 1762
Connell, Barbara 1575
Connor, Bruce 797
Consciousness Raising 959
Continuity 1150, 1481, 1539
"The Cool World" 1128, 1320,
    1399
Coolidge, Martha 1305, 1610,
    2071
Cooper, Gladys 96, 297, 298
Cooper, Miriam 298, 788
Copelan, Jodie 1570
Copyright 1018
Corbin, Gladys 96
Corda, Luciana 1070
Cornell, Katherine 405
Cortese, Valentina 367
Costello, Dolores 96, 198
Costello, Helene 96
Costume Designer 536, 1127,
    1269, 1270, 1271, 1341,
    1442, 1454, 1624, 1628
Costume Mistress 1196
Costumes 994, 1269, 1270,
    1271, 1394, 1476, 1510
Coulouris, George 2172
Counter Cinema 1908
"Coup pour Coup" 1544
Courtot, Marguerite 96
Cowgirls 1922
Cox, Nell 2020
Craig, Helen 96
Crain, Jeanne 96, 513, 582
Crawford, Joan 96, 208, 213,
    225, 267, 306, 307, 308,
    459, 518, 726, 727, 875,
    1798
Crawley, Judith Rosemary
    Sparks 1587
Crennan, Leoni 1305
Crews, Laura Hope 96
"Cries and Whispers" 1974,
    2007, 2033, 2074
Crime 81, 1814
Crimi, Marisa 1070
Crist, Judith 2173, 2175,
    2191, 2274
Cristal, Linda 96
Critics 1898, 2150, 2151,
    2155, 2156, 2157, 2161,
    2162, 2163, 2164, 2165,
    2166, 2167, 2168, 2169,
    2170, 2171, 2172, 2173,
    2174, 2175, 2176, 2177-
    2193, 2198, 2202,
    2207, 2208, 2209, 2210,
    2215-2235, 2237, 2238,
    2239, 2240, 2241-2247,
    2248, 2252-2258, 2259,
    2261, 2263, 2264, 2266,
    2267, 2268, 2270-2274,
    2278-2280, 2282-2288,
    2292-2296, 2300, 2301
"Crocodile Tears" 1540
"Crocus" 2020
Crowley, Pat 96
"Cuando quiero llorar no lloro"
    1192
Cukor, George 1245, 1292,
    1866
Cummings, Constance 96
Cummins, Peggy 96
Cunard, Grace 96, 1492
Cussler, Margaret 1147
Cute 2137
Cuts 61, 95
Cutters 97, 1110, 1146, 1377,
    1459, 1634

Dahl, Arlene 96
Dale, Esther 96
Daley, Cass 96
Dalton, Audrey 96
Dalton, Dorothy 96
Dames 15, 687, 1680, 2141
D'Amico, Suso Cecchi 1070
Damita, Lili 96
"The Damned" 273
Dana, Viola 96
Dance 1158, 1250
"Dance, Girl, Dance" 1331,
    1923
Dancers 104, 112, 270, 597,
    808, 1339, 1543, 1955
Dandridge, Dorothy 96, 205,
    313, 1775
Dangerous 2109
Daniels, Bebe 96, 186, 314,
    315
Dansereau, Mireille 1891
D'Arbanville, Patti 283
Darmond, Grace 96
Darnell, Linda 96, 745
Darrieux, Danielle 96, 177,
    891
Darwell, Jane 96

Davenport, Dorothy 1492
"David and Lisa" 1376
Davies, Marion 96, 132, 444,
    627, 742, 2032
D'Avino, Carmen 1210, 1589
Davis, Bette 94, 115, 149,
    175, 208, 257, 285, 296,
    309, 318, 463, 465, 473,
    549, 651, 660, 677, 681,
    724, 738, 750, 777, 864,
    875, 886
Davis, Frank 1230
Davis, Joan 96, 691
Davis, Nancy 96
Daw, Marjorie 96
Dawn, Hazel 96
Dawn, Isabel 503, 1309
Dawn, Marpessa 96
Day, Doris 96, 776, 2064
Day, Laraine 96
"Day Care: Children's Liber-
    ation" 2020
"Day for Night" 1930
Dazey, Agnes 1133
De Acosta, Mercedes 1151
Dean, Julie 96
Dean, Priscilla 96
Deaths, Accidental 859
    Airplane crashes 859
    Suicide 860
DeCamp, Rosemary 96
DeCarlo, Yvonne 96
Dee, Frances 96
Dee, Ruby 96, 322, 323
Dee, Sandra 96
DeHaven, Gloria 96
DeHavilland, Olivia 96, 258,
    324, 349, 1696
DeHirsch, Storm 1136, 1153,
    1252, 1416, 1430, 1437
Deitch, Donna 1305
de Kermadec, Liliane 1290
de la Motte, Marguerite 96
de la Roche, Catherine 1526,
    2177, 2178, 2179, 2180,
    2181
Delraux, Andre 1275
Del Rio, Dolores 96, 190
DeLuart, Yolande 1509, 2020
De Matteis, Maria 1070
Demetrakas, Joanna 1304
Demidova, Alla 418
de Mille, Beatrice 97

DeMille, Cecil B. 43, 97,
    384, 1628
Democratic Convention 1540
Demongeot, Mylene 96
Dempster, Carol 96, 345,
    788
Deneuve, Catherine 96, 645,
Dennis, Sandy 96
Depression 1769
Deren, Maya 1050, 1142,
    1158, 1159, 1160, 1161,
    1162, 1163, 1164, 1165,
    1166, 1195, 1210, 1252,
    1278, 1425, 1469, 1502,
    1548, 1571, 1589, 1601,
    1661, 2154, 2184-2190,
    2197, 2289
Design 1070
Destroyers 1931
Detective 1561
Deviants 1991
Devore, Dorothy 56
De Wiel, Alexa 2236
"Diary of a Mad Housewife"
    438, 1376, 1789
Dickinson, Angie 96
Dickson, Gloria 96
Dictionary 31, 36, 80, 92,
    241, 942, 945, 971, 972,
    974, 983, 984
Didion, Joan 1114, 1148,
    1167, 1168, 1169, 1541,
    1669, 2073
Didion's Women 2073
Dietrich, Marlene 96, 216,
    247, 267, 329, 334, 338,
    339, 390, 396, 404, 415,
    416, 443, 534, 537, 591,
    601, 659, 689, 780, 817,
    823, 889, 1151, 1233,
    1786, 1960, 1966, 2104
Dignes, Carlos 337
Diller, Phyllis 96, 691
Directors:
    Men (see specific names)
    Women 4, 86, 92, 299,
    628, 675, 732, 867, 924,
    963, 967, 970, 971, 978,
    983, 984, 988, 992, 997,
    998, 1031, 1032, 1034,
    1037, 1038, 1039, 1040,
    1041, 1042, 1046, 1050,
    1051, 1055, 1056, 1057,

1061, 1064, 1069, 1070,
1071, 1072, 1073, 1074,
1075, 1079, 1081, 1082,
1084, 1085, 1087, 1088,
1093, 1094, 1097, 1098,
1099, 1101, 1103, 1105,
1108, 1109, 1112, 1114,
1116, 1117, 1118, 1119,
1121, 1122, 1126, 1128,
1130, 1134, 1135, 1136,
1137, 1138, 1142, 1143,
1144, 1146, 1149, 1153,
1154, 1157, 1158, 1159,
1160, 1161, 1162, 1163,
1164, 1165, 1166, 1170,
1171, 1172, 1173, 1174,
1175, 1176, 1177, 1178,
1184, 1185, 1188, 1189,
1190, 1191, 1192, 1193
1195, 1197, 1199, 1200
1201, 1203, 1204, 1207,
1209, 1210, 1211, 1212,
1213, 1214, 1224, 1225,
1228, 1229, 1246, 1249,
1252, 1254, 1255, 1257,
1258, 1259, 1262, 1263,
1267, 1268, 1274, 1276,
1278, 1279, 1280, 1281,
1282, 1284, 1285, 1290,
1295, 1296, 1297, 1299,
1302, 1303, 1304, 1305,
1311, 1316, 1318, 1319,
1320, 1321, 1322, 1323,
1326, 1331, 1332, 1333,
1336, 1337, 1338, 1339,
1343, 1346, 1349, 1351,
1352, 1353, 1354, 1355,
1356, 1358, 1359, 1360,
1363, 1365, 1366, 1367,
1369, 1370, 1379, 1381,
1382, 1383, 1384, 1385,
1386, 1387, 1388, 1389,
1395, 1399, 1400, 1401,
1402, 1403, 1404, 1405,
1406, 1407, 1408, 1409,
1410, 1414, 1415, 1416,
1418, 1419, 1420, 1421,
1422, 1423, 1424, 1425,
1427, 1428, 1429, 1430,
1431, 1432, 1433, 1434,
1435, 1436, 1437, 1438,
1439, 1442, 1447, 1448,
1450, 1453, 1455, 1460,

1461, 1463, 1469, 1471,
1472, 1474, 1480, 1485,
1486, 1490, 1491, 1492,
1495, 1501, 1503, 1505,
1513, 1514, 1515, 1521,
1524, 1525, 1534, 1535,
1540, 1542, 1543, 1544,
1549, 1551, 1552, 1554,
1555, 1556, 1557, 1558,
1560, 1565, 1566, 1572,
1573, 1574, 1575, 1576,
1577, 1580, 1582, 1583,
1585, 1589, 1593, 1594,
1599, 1600, 1601, 1602,
1603, 1604, 1606, 1607,
1609, 1615, 1617, 1620,
1621, 1623, 1636, 1637,
1638, 1639, 1643, 1644,
1646, 1653, 1654, 1658,
1659, 1668, 1670, 1672,
1783, 1881, 1901, 1910,
Directory 992, 1029, 1674
"Dirty Mary" 1537
"Discreet Charm of the Bour-
    geoisie" 221
Disney, Walt 588, 839, 1645,
    2084
Distribution 1825, 2045
Distributors 1109, 1188, 1492
Ditvoorst, Adriaan 1173
Divided 1852
Dix, Beulah Marie 97, 1110
"Djamilja" 1419
Dobson, Tamara 312, 481
"Dr. No" 770
Documentary 924, 952, 956,
    963, 1100, 1119, 1126,
    1147, 1243, 1299, 1396,
    1418, 1511, 1514, 1518,
    1546, 1673, 1956, 1987,
    2013, 2229
Dodd, Claire 96, 276, 342,
"La Dolce Vita" 2024
Domergue, Faith 96
Donkoff, Judith 1509
Donner, Vyvyan 1627
Dope Films 2051
Doran, Ann 96
Dorleac, Francoise 96
Doro, Marie 96
Dors, Diana 96, 223, 472,
    890, 2058, 2120,
D'Orsay, Fifi 96

Dougherty, Ariel 1016
Douglas, Donna 96
Dove, Billie 96, 179
Dove, Linda 1305
Dovjenko, Mrs. Alexander
   1658
Dow, Peggy 96, 703
Dowd, Nancy Ellen 2020
Downs, Cathy 96
Drake, Betsy 96
Drake, Donna 96
Drama 1776
Dramatic Coach 1034
Dramatists 936, 1273, 1310,
   1362, 1567, 1624
Dreams 1807, 1834, 2011,
   2043, 2094, 2127, 2141,
   2228
Dress, Evelyne 433, 1857
Dress Designers 1288, 1341
Dress Unit Designer 536
Dresser, Louise 96
Dressler, Marie 96, 246,
   350, 351
Drew, Ellen 96
Drew, Mrs. Sidney 1658
Dru, Joanne 96
Ducey, Lilian 1658
Duck, Daisy 588
Duke, Patty 96
Dulac, Germaine 1142, 1199,
   1214, 1219, 1252, 1278,
   1366, 1618, 1661
Dumont, Margaret 96
Dunaway, Faye 96
Duncan, Catherine 1178
Duncan, Isadora 1955
Duncan, Mary 96
Dunham, Katherine 661, 1449
Dunne, Irene 96, 594
Dunnock, Mildred 96
Duprez, June 96, 520
Duras, Marguerite 1177, 1204,
   1227, 1420, 1515, 1550,
   1890, 1963, 2017
Durbin, Deanna 7, 96, 120
Duse, Eleanora 360, 731
Dvorak, Ann 96

Eagels, Jeanne 343
Earth Mother 799, 1845, 2069
"Earthquake" 1570, 1651
East, Mrs. Gale Henry 1253

Eastern Europe 39, 947
Eastman, Andrea 1114
Eastman, Carol 1069, 1114,
   1311
"Easy Rider" 2051
Eaton, Shirley 96
Eburne, Maude 96
Economics 1883, 2270
Eddy, Helen Jerome 96
Eddy, Nelson 535
"Edge of the City" 1904
Editing 1152, 1205, 1220,
   1517, 1570, 1588, 1630
Editors 92, 97, 536, 984,
   992, 997, 998, 1030,
   1052, 1074, 1113, 1114,
   1132, 1145, 1146, 1194,
   1220, 1308, 1313, 1314,
   1341, 1377, 1443, 1445,
   1452, 1458, 1473, 1492,
   1540, 1568, 1570, 1578,
   1588, 1616, 1627, 1633,
   1634, 1651, 1782, 2238
Educational Films 1055, 1180,
   1647
Edwards, Anne 1181
Eggar, Samantha 96
Eggleston, Katherine 1492
"8-1/2" 2024
Eilers, Sally 96
"Einleitung zu Arnold Schoen-
   bergs Begleitmusik zu
   einer Lichtspielscene"
   1045
Eisner, Lotte 2196
Ekberg, Anita 96, 134, 723
Eldridge, Florence 96
Elek, Judit 1183, 1673
Elg, Taina 96
Elliott, Maxine 28
Elliott, Polly 1666
Ellis, Patricia 699
Emerson, Faye 96
Emerson, Hope 96
Emerson, John 1186, 1187
Emshwiller, Ed 1589
Enchantress 239, 245, 1783,
   1785
Encyclopedia 112, 931
"The End of the Art World"
   1305
England 222, 227, 757, 2221,
   2226, 2255

Enigma 1751
Entertainers 1729, 2039
Ephron, Phoebe 1499
Epics 81, 2233
Epstein, Ed 1451
Erotic 1751, 1812, 1872,
    1898, 1958, 2026
Evans, Dale 96, 377
Evans, Edith 96
Evans, Joan 96
Evans, Madge 96
Evelyn, Judith 96
Everest, Barbara 96
Executives 115, 231, 1114,
    1324, 1368, 1613
"The Exorcist" 1757
Experimental 1389, 1427,
    1436, 1438, 1925
Exposition 1832
Extras 752, 904

Fabray, Nannette 96
"A Face in the Crowd" 653
Fairbanks, Douglas 831
Fairchild, Charlotte 2089
Falana, Lola 477
Falconetti, Marie 96
Fallen 1787
Family Films 1817
Famous Players 1075
Fan Magazines 27, 35, 58,
    2212, 2251, 2289
"Fanny" 600
Fantasy 81, 1864, 1880
Farley, Dot 96
Farmer, Frances 96, 387,
    400
Farnum, Dorothy 1492
Farr, Felicia 96, 380
Farrar, Geraldine 28
Farrell, Glenda 96
Farrington, Mrs. Frank 1196
Farrow, Mia 96, 251
Fashions 2083
"Fashions for Women" 1146
"Fat City" 529
"Faustine et le bel été" 1094
Faye, Alice 96, 643
Faye, Julia 96
Fazan, Adrienne 536, 1132
Fazenda, Louise 56, 96, 570
Fealy, Maude 96
"Fear Woman" 2020

Featured players 62
Fedosova, Nadezda 574
Feiffer, Judy 1114
Fellini, Federico 2024
Fellini's Women 2024
Female Imagery 1838
Female View 1233
Feminine Aesthetic 1264
Femininity 2064
Feminist 1765, 1814, 1864,
    1887
  cinema 1581, 1893, 1934
  criticism 1791, 1898,
    1930, 1931, 1944, 2168,
    2170, 2200, 2240, 2260
  movement 1764
"La Femme du Ganges" 1420,
    1515, 1963, 2017
Femme fatales 479
Ferguson, Elsie 96, 193, 767
Ferguson, Helen 96
Ferrer, José 568
Feudal 1978
Fiastri, Iaia 1070
Field, Betty 96
Field, Mary 1647
Field, Shirley Ann 96
Fields, Dorothy 14
Fields, Gracie 96
Fields, Mary 924
Fields, Verna 1114, 1452
Fields, W. C. 81
Fighting Lady 1840
"A Film About a Woman Who"
    1305, 1364
Film Conference 1663, 1762,
    2133
Film criticism 1161, 1526,
    1527, 2249, 2254, 2256,
    2285, 2288, 2295, 2296
Film Distribution 1193, 1492,
    1544
Film Exposition 1832, 2012
Film Festivals 393, 668,
    1023, 1049, 1053, 1078,
    1182, 1200, 1209, 1236,
    1248, 1252, 1256, 1262,
    1264, 1277, 1312, 1328,
    1329, 1334, 1358, 1421,
    1422, 1423, 1424, 1444,
    1508, 1509, 1545, 1559,
    1590, 1595, 1598, 1650,
    1654, 1674, 1818, 1830,

Film Festivals (cont.)
  1853, 1863, 1865, 1868,
  1881, 1898, 1916, 1917,
  1940, 1964, 1965, 1967,
  1968, 2046, 2121, 2129,
  2142, 2269
Film Industry Crises 2231,
  2255
Film Noir 961, 1828
"Film No. 4" 1479
"Film No. 5" 1479
Film Script 1185
Film Society 2271
Film writers/reviewers 963,
  1033, 1308, 1422, 1526
Filmmakers 983, 1009, 1011,
  1014, 1016, 1071, 1083,
  1087, 1105, 1109, 1111,
  1112, 1114, 1119, 1125,
  1137, 1153, 1157, 1158,
  1159, 1160, 1161, 1162,
  1163, 1164, 1165, 1166,
  1188, 1228, 1232, 1237,
  1238, 1264, 1265, 1469,
  1522
Filmmakers
  Black 1918
  children 1156
  teenagers 1546
Filmography 128, 131, 132,
  133, 134, 137, 156, 167,
  175, 176, 178, 179, 184,
  185, 187, 188, 189, 190,
  191, 192, 193, 195, 196,
  197, 198, 199, 200, 201,
  202, 203, 204, 207, 209,
  210, 211, 212, 214, 215,
  216, 217, 218, 224, 240,
  241, 254, 258, 261, 264,
  265, 276, 277, 286, 291,
  293, 294, 295, 299, 302,
  311, 319, 321, 327, 332,
  333, 334, 335, 336, 342,
  344, 345, 347, 348,
  349, 353, 355, 356,
  361, 364, 365, 367,
  368, 375, 380, 381, 382,
  383, 385, 392, 398, 401,
  434, 437, 439, 448, 449,
  450, 451, 497, 499, 500,
  504, 505, 507, 508, 509,
  510, 512, 513, 515, 516,
  534, 538, 555, 560, 562,

  566, 573, 581, 582, 583,
  592, 594, 595, 596, 608,
  609, 614, 617, 632, 638,
  640, 642, 643, 644, 648,
  654, 665, 666, 667, 680,
  682, 687, 689, 691, 692,
  699, 700, 701, 703, 706,
  707, 709, 717, 722, 724,
  725, 726, 727, 728, 734,
  735, 736, 737, 738, 739,
  740, 746, 748, 754, 769,
  779, 783, 798, 800, 803,
  806, 808, 811, 812, 815,
  816, 819, 836, 843, 844,
  853, 854, 858, 861, 862
  863, 865, 866, 869, 879,
  883, 891, 906, 907, 913,
  963, 1037, 1040, 1047,
  1056, 1088, 1110, 1125,
  1141, 1206, 1210, 1211,
  1278, 1281, 1302, 1307,
  1323, 1360, 1363, 1376,
  1389, 1414, 1415, 1471,
  1472, 1531, 1578, 1637,
  1640, 1662, 1774
Films 69, 73, 80, 82, 89,
  91, 99, 106, 293, 294,
  295, 345, 460, 535, 654,
  920, 929, 967, 984, 999,
  1000-1029, 1063, 1758
  for Children 1291
  for high school women 1770
Fine, Sylvia 14
"Finnegans Wake" 1319
Finney, Albert 606
Firestone, Cinda 1649
Fisher, Doris 14
Fisher, Morgan 1508
Fitzgerald, F. Scott 1233
Fitzgerald, Geraldine 96
Flaherty, Frances 924, 1100,
  1221, 1350
  Francis and Robert 1100
Flappers 893, 1233
Fleming, Rhonda 96
Fletcher, Adele W. 1288
"Fly" 1625
Foch, Nina 96, 536
"Fog Pumas" 1626
Fonch, Arnold 1255
Fonda, Henry 804
Fonda, Jane 32, 96, 144,
  237, 251, 316, 379, 527,

678, 804, 837, 1605
Fonda, Peter 251, 804
Fonda Family 288, 804
Fontaine, Joan 96, 258
Fontanne, Lynn 405, 917
Ford, Constance 96
Ford, John 241, 1950
Ford's Women 1950
Foreman, Carl 2235
Forrest, Ann 96
Forrest, Sally 96
Fortunes 773, 899
Fosse, Bob 664
Foster, Dianne 96
Foster, Edith 1180
Foster, Susanna 96
Fowler, Marjorie 1220, 1443,
    1473, 1578
Foxe, Cyrinda 253
France 11, 931, 985
"Francesco de' Assisi" 1093
Francis, Anne 96
Francis, Connie 96
Francis, Kay 96, 693
Frankenheimer, John 664
Franklin, Sidney 1317
Frederick, Pauline 28, 96,
    203, 370
Freeman, Mona 96, 632
Friedman, Bonnie 2020
Friedman, Roberta 1508
Fruchter, Norm 1466
"The Fugitive Kind" 1745
Fuller, Mary 96
Funicello, Annette 96
"Funny Face" 1997
Furness, Betty 176

Gablot, Ginette 1304
Gabor, Eva 96
Gabor, Zsa Zsa 96, 406, 558
Gaffer 1391, 1442
Gaierová, Nelly 486
"Galileo" 1093
Gam, Rita 96
"Game" 2020
Gance, Abel 1228
Garbo, Greta 32, 86, 94, 96,
    147, 148, 180, 194, 206,
    232, 239, 267, 293, 341,
    359, 372, 390, 392, 395,
    409, 497, 545, 586, 591,
    599, 633, 667, 685, 718,

760, 785, 849, 857, 875,
    894, 896, 915, 1151,
    1622, 1783, 1966, 2050,
    2104
Garden, Mary 28
Gardner, Ava 96, 455, 866
Gardner, Helen 96
Garland, Beverly 96, 500
Garland, Judy 96, 115, 120,
    229, 320, 402, 519, 592,
    638, 704, 754, 758, 762,
    814, 841
Garner, Peggy Ann 96
Garon, Pauline 96
Garrett, Betty 96, 879
Garson, Greer 96, 330, 573
Gates, Nancy 96
Gaynor, Janet 96, 264
Gaynor, Mitzi 96
Geddes, Barbara Bel 96
Geiger, Julie 1444
"Genesis 3:16" 2020
Genres 81, 1804, 2030, 2041,
    2051, 2065, 2085
Genta, Gabriella 1070
George, Gladys 96
"George of the Body" 1389
"Georgy Girl" 273
Geraghty, Carmelita 96
Germany 65, 964, 1254
"Gertrude Stein: When This
    You See Remember Me"
    2020
"Geschichtsunterricht" 1045,
    1549
Ghostley, Alice 96
Giang, Tra 895
"The Gibbous Moon" 2020
Gibson, Helen 421, 1235
Gibson, Hoot 421
Gifford, Frances 96
Gilliatt, Penelope 81, 1114,
    1123, 1139, 1226, 1237,
    1238, 1327, 2152, 2167,
    2182, 2183, 2202, 2248,
    2273
Gillmore, Margalo 96
Gilmore, Virginia 96, 869
Gilson, René 1281
Gimbel, Peter 1239
Gingold, Hermione 96, 427
"The Girl" 1358
Girlfriend 165

"The Girls" 1122, 1358, 1790
Gish, Dorothy 96, 191, 429,
    533, 788
Gish, Lillian 86, 96, 232,
    292, 429, 430, 431, 533,
    641, 675, 684, 772, 788,
    832, 844, 872, 875, 978,
    1658, 2296
Gish Sisters 84, 429
Glamorous 1889, 2083, 2089
Glaum, Louise 96
"Glimpse of the Garden" 1252
Glyn, Elinor 1241, 1242
Godard, Jean-Luc 363, 379,
    1530, 1819, 1827, 1931
Goddard, Paulette 96, 689
"The Goddess" 1730, 1856
Goddesses 17, 26, 245, 378,
    404, 474, 586, 591
    1694, 1813, 1826, 1882,
    1888, 1954, 1957, 1958,
    2097, 2104
Godmilow, Jill 1114, 1189,
    1614, 1653, 1823, 2092,
    2128
Godowsky, Dagmar 87, 96
Godoy, Armando Robles 1938
Gods 1694
"Going Places" 2040
Golddigger 540
Goldwyn, Samuel 28, 453,
    1869
Goldwyn Studios 1628
Gomez-Quinones, Ronda 1114
"Gone with the Wind" 1696
Good 687, 1695
Good-Bad Girl 2131
"The Good Earth" 1317
"Goodbye in the Mirror" 1416
Goodrich, Frances 990, 1206
Gordon, Mary 96
Gordon, Ruth 81, 96, 432,
    1244, 1245, 1292, 1477,
    2220
Gorin, Jean-Pierre 379, 1827
Gorrel, Philippe 1204
Gosselin, B. 1232
Gossip 423, 1854
Gossip Columnists 1854,
    2158, 2159, 2194, 2195,
    2201, 2203, 2204, 2205,
    2206, 2211, 2212, 2213,
    2214, 2262, 2275, 2276
    2290

Goudal, Jetta 96
Grable, Betty 26, 96, 330,
    434
Graham, Sheilah 2194, 2203,
    2204, 2205, 2206
Grahame, Gloria 96
Grandin, Ethel 96
Granger, Dorothy 96
Grant, Elspeth 2207
Grant, Katheryn 96
Grant, Lee 96, 671
Granville, Bonita 96
"The Grasshopper" 1789
Gray, Coleen 96
Gray, Dolores 96
Gray, Gilda 96, 832
Grayson, Kathryn 96
"The Great Man" 568
Green, Adolph 81, 1132
Green, Mitzi 96
"Green Mansions" 1449
"The Green Wall" 1938
Greenwood, Charlotte 96
Greenwood, Joan 96, 515
Greer, Jane 96
Greiner, Nancy 1016
Grenfell, Joyce 96
Grey, Lita 96
Grier, Pam 481, 528, 1115
Grierson, Ruby 924
Griffies, Ethel 61, 96
Griffith, Corinne 96
Griffith, D. W. 183, 266,
    345, 430, 788
Griffith, Linda (Mrs. D. W.)
    33, 943
Grimes, Tammy 96
Grips 1442
"Growing Up Female: As Six
    Become One" 1435,
    1973, 2020, 2022, 2070,
    2072
"Guess Who's Coming to Din-
    ner?" 656
Guild, Nancy 96
Guilds 1442
Guy-Blaché, Alice 970, 1084,
    1218, 1278, 1346, 1490,
    1492, 1577
Gwynne, Anne 96
Gyarmathy, Livia 1349, 1673

Haber, J. Alan 1608
Hackett, Albert 1206

Hackett, Florence 96
Hackett, Joan 96
Hagen, Jean 96
Halas, John 1257, 1258, 1408
Hale, Barbara 96
Hale, Georgia 96
Hale, Louise Closser 96
Hall, Juanita 96
Hamilton, Grace 14
Hammerstein, Elaine 96
Hampton, Hope 96
Handworth, Octavia 96
Hani, Susumu 1978
Hansen, Juanita 96
"Happiness" 256
Harding, Ann 96, 734
Harlow, Jean 96, 294, 591,
    619, 694, 695, 718, 778,
    2104
"Harold and Maude" 1884
Harpies 1828
Harrington, Curtis 1589
Harris, Barbara 96
Harris, Julie 96
Harris, Rosemary 96
Harrison, Edward 1193
Harrison, Joan 81, 1231,
    1446
Harrison, Kathleen 2295
Hart, Dolores 96
Hartman, Elizabeth 96
Hartman, Gretchen 96
Harvey, Lillian 96, 562, 717
Haskell, Molly 1877, 2169,
    2183, 2209, 2210
Hasso, Signe 779
Haver, June 96
Haver, Phyllis 96
Havoc, June 96, 461
Hawks, Howard 1652, 1837
Hawksian Woman 1778, 1779,
    1837, 1875, 2125
Hawley, Ormi 96
Hawley, Wanda 96
Hawn, Goldie 96
Haworth, Jill 96
Hayden, Linda 819
Hayden, Tom 1605
Hayes, Helen 96, 235, 347,
    405, 466, 467
Hayward, Susan 96, 580, 583,
    584
Hayworth, Rita 26, 94, 96,

330, 538, 586, 721, 812
Head, Edith 1269, 1270, 1271
Hearst, William Randolph 444,
    627
"The Heartbreak Kid" 1149
"Heat" 878, 1928
Heatherton, Joey 96
Heckart, Eileen 96, 687
Hedren, Tippi 96
Hegerliková, Antonie 489
"Helen: Queen of the Nautch
    Girls" 2009
Heller, Roselyn 1114
Hellman, Lillian 936, 1273
Helm, Brigitte 228
Helton, Peggy 96
Hemingway, Ernest 1233
Hendrix, Wanda 96
Hendry, Gloria 481
Henie, Sonja 96
Hennessey, Sharon 2020
Henning-Jensen, Astrid 1276
Henry, Gale 56
Hepburn, Audrey 96, 230,
    735, 868
Hepburn, Katherine 32, 94,
    96, 211, 304, 333, 424,
    471, 521, 618, 656, 784,
    821, 838, 843, 1245
Heroines 278, 1788, 1858,
    1903, 2085, 2110, 2131
Herrman, Bernard 2172
HerStory Films 1948
"Hester Street" 1544
Hidari, Sachiko 623, 1978
Hiller, Wendy 96
Hilliard, Harriet (Nelson, Har-
    riet) 96
"Hillstrom Chronicle" 961
"The Hired Hand" 1730
"Hiroshima, Mon Amour"
    1227, 1550, 1745, 1890
Hirsch, Tina 1114
Historian 2179, 2196, 2270
History 11, 12, 14, 19, 22,
    24, 27, 29, 37, 46, 47,
    51, 65, 66, 68, 75, 81,
    84, 91, 93, 246, 251,
    314, 840, 932, 937, 954,
    965, 979, 980, 981, 986,
    987, 1125, 2196
History--Silent (1900-1929) 4,
    9, 16, 33, 60, 84, 86,

102, 106, 122, 124, 126,
129, 130, 136, 138, 153,
154, 156, 168, 180-192,
194, 195, 197, 199-206,
220, 228, 231, 233, 234,
241, 246, 255, 265-267,
275-277, 286, 290-293,
298, 299, 305, 315, 318,
319, 341, 343, 345, 346,
350, 351, 354, 355, 356,
358, 362, 374, 375, 384,
387, 389, 392, 395, 416, 421,
429-431, 438, 441, 442,
444, 452, 453, 457, 468-
470, 496-498, 505, 533,
534, 545, 555, 556, 560,
563, 570-572, 576, 587,
597, 599, 601, 613, 627,
628, 630, 632, 634, 653,
657-659, 662, 663, 667, 675,
676, 684, 685, 694, 695, 710-
715, 718, 731, 741, 742,
752, 757, 760, 767, 771,
773, 779, 780, 785, 787-
789, 791, 800-802, 809,
817, 818, 828, 830-832,
834, 844, 848-851, 857,
872, 875, 877, 884, 887,
889, 892-894, 896, 897,
899, 900, 908, 913, 915,
930, 960, 978, 988, 991
History--Sound (30's-70's) 6,
6a, 8, 23, 30, 40, 44,
69, 105, 162, 251, 452,
925, 926, 928, 941, 944,
949, 967, 1440, 1801
Hitchcock, Alfred 195, 664,
2222, 2223
Hochberg, Victoria 1305
Hochman, Sandra 1540
Hoffman, Dustin 121
Holden, Fay 96
Holliday, Judy 96, 246
Hollister, Alice 96
Hollywood 90, 123, 251, 423,
478, 980, 989, 1412, 1934,
2047, 2094
  novels about 2117, 2118
Holm, Celeste 96, 709
Holmes, Helen 96
Holzer, Baby Jane 602
"Home" 1305
"Home Born Baby" 1511, 2013

"Home Sweet Home" 1290
Hope, Gloria 96
Hopkins, Miriam 96, 689
Hopper, Hedda 2195, 2213,
2214
Horne, Lena 96, 464, 480,
661, 744
Horror Films 1915, 2030,
2039
Horton, Clara Marie 96
Hoskins, Grace 1523
"The Hot Box" 1809
Hoteley, Mae 96
Houghton, Katherine 656
House Committe on Unamerican
Activities 61, 287, 1622
Houston, Penelope 2176, 2215-
2235
"How About You?" 2020
Howell, Alice 56
Howes, Sally Ann 96
Hubley, Faith 992
Hudson, Rochelle 96
Huff, Louise 96
Hughes, Mary Beth 853
Huillet, Danièle 1045, 1549,
1594
Hulette, Gladys 96
Hull, Josephine 96
Hultin, Jill Foreman 1016
Hume, Benita 96
Humiliated 1802
Hunt, Marsha 96, 614
Hunt, Martita 96
Hunter, Kim 96
Hunter, Marion 1948
Hurlock, Madeline 96
"Hurry, Hurry" 1252
Hussey, Olivia 96
Hussey, Ruth 96
Huston, Cindy 1397
Hutchins, Patricia 1299
Hutton, Betty 96
Huyck, Williard 1115
Hyams, Nessa 1114
Hyer, Martha 96, 811
Hyland, Peggy 96, 1300

"I Am Curious Blue" 476
"I Am Curious Yellow" 476
"I Am Somebody" 1661, 2020
"I Cannibali" 1093, 1609,
1620, 1781

"I'm No Angel" 1730
"Image in the Snow" 1389,
     1455
Image Wreckers 29, 1858
Images 5, 35, 82, 169, 239,
     245, 278, 308, 309, 399,
     423, 440, 443, 453, 477,
     478, 502, 557, 584, 586,
     616, 624, 626, 667, 679,
     799, 846, 927, 955, 990,
     1077, 1135, 1231, 1252,
     1578, 1595, 1675-2142,
Also see specific headings:
     All-man Legend
     Athletes
     Bad
     Beautiful/Beauty
     Belles
     Bergman's Women
     Beulah
     Bitch
     Black
     Blondes
     Brunettes
     Cannibals
     Charisma
     Cinderella
     Cowgirls
     Cute
     Dangerous
     Destroyers
     Deviants
     Didion's Women
     Divided
     Earth mother
     Enchantress
     Enigma
     Entertainers
     Erotic
     Fallen
     Fellini's Women
     Feminist
     Feudal
     Fighting Lady
     Flesh-peddlers
     Ford's Women
     Frauds
     Geniuses
     Girlfriend
     Glamorous
     Goddesses
     Good
     Good-Bad girl

     Harpies
     Has-Beens
     Hawksian Women
     Heroines
     Hopefuls
     Humiliated
     Independent
     Killers
     Kubrick's Women
     Leone's Woman
     Liberated women
     Lolita
     Love
     Maid
     Male fantasies
     Male-female relation-
        ship
     Mammies
     Marital relationship
     Martyr
     Matron
     Men-pleasers
     Men without women
     Money-makers
     Monsters
     Mother
     Mother-informer
     Moviemakers
     Mulattoes
     Myths/legends
     Negative
     New patterns
     Nongenue
     Nonwoman
     Odd couples
     Other woman
     Passionate
     Pin-up
     Political
     Poor-little rich girls
     Pornographic
     Positive
     Prostitutes
     Pure
     Puritanical
     Realistic
     Reckless
     Redheads
     Red-hot mamas
     Revered
     Revolutionary
     Roles
     Rules for behavior

Images (cont.)
  Run-away heiresses
  Sacrificing
  Scarlett O'Hara
  Scatterbrains
  Seductive
  Sex
  Sex symbols
  Sexism
  Sexual relationship
  Sexuality
  Sexually repressed
  Sirens
  Sisters
  Slut
  Sorceress
  Spiritual
  Stars
  Stereotypes
  Strong
  Tattered queens
  Vamp
  Venus
  Virgin
  Wife
  Woman and Manchild
  Women without men
  Women's place
  Working class
  Working girls
  Working women
"Imagine" 1318
"Imitation of Life" 1904,
  1926
Imrie, Kathy 477
Independent 475, 1207, 1304,
  1319, 1670, 2020
Index 73, 375, 648
Inescort, Frieda 96
Ingenue 387
Innocent 5, 200
Institution 93, 987
Interviews 121, 151, 162,
  166, 170, 193, 221, 226,
  252, 266, 281, 284, 285,
  337, 340, 353, 366, 376,
  388, 390, 394, 418, 447,
  463, 464, 465, 473, 478,
  530, 539, 540, 546, 558,
  569, 600, 606, 641, 656,
  663, 664, 671, 673, 674,
677, 679, 681, 705, 716,
729, 765, 783, 837, 855,
873, 886, 992, 1038,
1045, 1047, 1051, 1064,
1065, 1067, 1070, 1073,
1087, 1093, 1094, 1103,
1121, 1123, 1124, 1135,
1154, 1175, 1189, 1192,
1203, 1215, 1223, 1229,
1231, 1241, 1246, 1262,
1268, 1274, 1275, 1278,
1284, 1306, 1323, 1335,
1338, 1343, 1348, 1351,
1353, 1360, 1401, 1405,
1418, 1419, 1430, 1431,
1432, 1433, 1441, 1477,
1491, 1493, 1503, 1505,
1531, 1562, 1599, 1604,
1609, 1611, 1625, 1636,
1638, 1641, 1651, 1662,
1795, 1823, 1895, 1896,
1911, 1975, 1980, 1996,
2010, 2027, 2090, 2116,
2120, 2235, 2236, 2243-
2246, 2273
"Introduction to the Enemy"
  1605
Inventors 983, 1053
Irola, Judy 1305
Irwin, May 96
Irvine, Louva 1795, 2020
"Island in the Sun" 1904
"It" 1241
"It Happens to Us" 2020
"It Only Happens to Others"
  732, 1532, 1600, 2022
Ivan, Rosiland 96
Ivers, Julia Crawford 1658

Jackson, Anne 96
Jaffe, Patricia 1313
Jaffe, Rona 936
Jagger, Mick 247
Jakubowska, Wanda 1199, 1367
James, Monique 1114
Jancsó, Miklós 2225
"Janie's Janie" 2020
Janis, Elsie 1315
Janney, Honore 536
Janowska, Alina 511
Japan 623

"Jaune le Soleil" 1177
Jaworsky, Henry 1286
"Jaws" 1239
Jayston, Michael 389
Jean, Gloria 96, 559
Jeanmarie, Renée 96
Jeffreys, Anne 96
"Jemina, Daughter of the
    Mountains" 1304
Jennings, Talbot 1317
Jens, Salome 96
Jergens, Adele 96
Jergens, Diane 96
Jersey, Wm. C. 1575
Jewel, Betty 788
"Jezebel" 257
"Joana, a francesa" 337
Johns, Glynis 96
Johnson, Agnes Christine
    1110
Johnson, Celia 96
Johnson, Edith 96
Johnson, Katie 96
Johnson, Kay 96
Johnson, Rita 96
Jolson, Al 83
Jonas, Joan 1444
"Jonathan Livingston Seagull"
    1397
Jones, Carolyn 96
Jones, Jennifer 96, 348, 499
Jones, Marvene 2290
Jones, Peaches 1104
Jones, Shirley 96
Jordan, Dorothy 96
Journalists 1241
Joy, Leatrice 96
Joyce, Adrien 81
Joyce, Brenda 96
Joyce, Peggy Hopkins 96
"Joyce at 34" 2020
Judge, Arline 96
"Judy Chicago and the Califor-
    nia Girls" 1509
"Jules and Jim" 1752, 2095
"Juliet of the Spirits" 2024

Kael, Pauline 2152, 2155,
    2156, 2165, 2171, 2172,
    2174, 2183, 2241-2247,
    2259, 2263, 2264, 2266,

    2272, 2273, 2278, 2279,
    2284, 2292, 2293, 2294,
    2296
Kahn, Madeline 679, 765
Kalem 789
Kalmus, Natalie Mabel Dunfee
    1457
"Kamouraska" 376, 530
Kane, Gail 96
Kanin, Garson 81, 1245,
    1292, 2220
Kanin, Kay 1208, 1223, 1832
Kaplan, Nelly 1038, 1040,
    1228, 1249, 1262, 1358,
    1530, 1639
Karina, Anna 363, 1121, 1279,
    1819
Kashfi, Anna 96
"Kato pesen" 1343
Katz, Gloria 1114, 1115
Kaufmann, Christine 96
Kazan, Elia 652
Kedrova, Lila 96
Keeler, Ruby 96, 217, 1924
Kelly, Claire 96
Kelly, Dorothy 96
Kelly, Grace 96, 407, 439,
    524, 579
Kelly, Kitty 2161
Kelly, Nancy 96
Kelly, Patsy 96
Kelly, Paula 477
Kendall, Kay 96
Kenly, Bill 1193
Kennedy, Madge 96
Kenyon, Doris 96
Kern, Jerome 14
Kernochan, Sarah 1114
Kerr, Deborah 96, 222
Kerry, Margaret 96
Keser, Mirjana 1119
"The Key" 2235
Key, Kathleen 96
Keyes, Evelyn 96
Killers 1929, 1994
King, Andrea 96
King, Anita 96
King, Mollie 96
"King Kong" 2039
"King Lear" 2183
"King of Kings" 2233

"Kings Go Forth" 1904
Kingston, Winifred 96
Kirk, Lisa 96
Kirk, Phyllis 96, 707
Kitt, Eartha 744
Kleckner, Susan 1795, 2020
Klein, James 1016, 1188,
    1338, 1435, 1973, 2020
"Klute" 1842, 1852, 2076
Knef, Hildegard see Neff,
    Hildegarde
Knight, Shirley 96
Knox, Margot 1305
Knudson, Peggy 96
Kohner, Susan 96, 2295
Kokanova, Nevena 271, 272,
    647, 1788
Komorowska-Tyszkiewicz,
    Maja 522
Konjuhova, Tat'Jana 419
Korda, Alexander 2252
Kramer, Robert 1466
Kramer, Stanley 2227
Kraning, Susan Pitt 2020
Krasilovsky, Alexis 1305
Kriegel, Harriet 1016
Krzyżewska, Ewa 554
Kubota, Shigeka 1444
Kubrick, Stanley 1994, 2105
Kuz'mina, Elena 542
Kwan, Nancy 96
Kyo, Machiko 96

LaBadie, Florence 96
Labrecque, J. C. 1232
"The Lady Sings the Blues"
    2091
Lake, Alice 96
Lake, Veronica 96, 547
Lalonde, M. 1232
LaMarr, Barbara 96, 858
Lamarr, Hedy 96, 548
Lamour, Dorothy 96, 689
"L'Amour, l'après-midi" 300
Lanchester, Elsa 550
Lanctôt, Micheline 541
"The Land" 1616
Landi, Elissa 96
Landis, Carol 96. 260, 261
Landis, Jessie Royce 551
Lane, Adele 96
Lane, Lola 96
Lane, Priscilla 96

Lane, Rosemary 96
Lange, Hope 96
Langford, Frances 96
Lansbury, Angela 96, 133,
    426, 687
Lansing, Joi 96
LaRoy, Rita 96
"The Last Picture Show" 673,
    674, 2055
"The Last Supper" 282
"Last Tango in Paris" 1754,
    1918, 1977, 2035, 2115,
    2169
Laughton, Charles 550
Laurie, Piper 96
Lavi, Daliah 96
Laurence, Florence 84, 96
Lawrence, Barbara 96
Lawrence, Carol 96
Lawrence, Catalina 1591
Lawrence, Viola 1578
Leachman, Cloris 673, 679,
    1996
Learn, Bessie 96
Lebrun, Francoise 546
Lederer, Gretchen 96
Lee, Anna 96
Lee, Carolyn 96
Lee, Gypsy Rose 96
Lee, Harper 936
Lee, Jane 96
Lee, Joanna 1114
Lee, Lila 96
"Legacy" 1305
Legend see myth
"The Legend of Lizzie Borden"
    2081
"Legs" 1428
Lehman, Gladys 990
Leigh, Janet 96, 664
Leigh, Vivien 96, 158, 218,
    327, 353, 405, 743, 751
Leighton, Margaret 96
Lejeune, Caroline Alice 2161,
    2166, 2170, 2208, 2252-
    2258
Lennart, Isobel 1310
Lennon, John 1318, 1428,
    1625
Leonard, Marion 96
Leone, Sergio 2065
Leone's Women 2071
Leslie, Gladys 96

Leslie, Joan 96, 516
Leslie, Lilie 96
Lessing, Doris 1966
"The Letter" 257
"Letter from an Unknown Wo-
  man" 1945
"Letter to Jane" 316, 379,
  1827
Levine, Dorothy 1431, 1433
Levine, Naomi 1436, 1437,
Levy, Barbara 1305
Lewis, Diana 96
Liberated Women 1706, 1759,
  1928, 2024, 2126, 2136
"Life of Juanita" 1455
"Life Times Nine" 1156
Light, Allie 1305
Lightner, Winnie 96
"Lights" 1252
Lili, Barono Hatvany 1362
Lillie, Beatrice 96, 152, 425
Lindfors, Viveca 96, 879
Lindsay, Margaret 96
"Lions Lane" 1176
Lisi, Virna 96
Literary Consultant 536, 1341
"The Little Foxes" 257
Littlefield, Lucien 96
Littlewood, Joan 1057, 1098,
  1099, 1144, 1197, 1225,
  1296, 1369, 1480, 1542,
  1593, 1615, 1658
Littman, Lynne 1114
"Lives of Performers" 1339
Livingston, Margaret 96, 153
"The Lizards" 1358
Lloyd, Doris 96
Lockhart, Freda Brace 1526
Lockhart, June 96
Lockwood, Harold 199
Lockwood, Margaret 96, 227,
  567
Loden, Barbara 992, 1114,
  1267, 1401, 1441, 1556,
  1557, 1558, 1877, 1959,
  1980
Loff, Jeanette 96
Logan, Ella 96
"Lolita" 824, 1994
Lolita 165, 1760, 1994
Lollobrigida, Gina 96, 385
Lombard, Carole 96, 332,
  680, 689, 718

London, Julie 96, 568
"Look Back in Anger" 1745
Loos, Anita 87, 1043, 1110,
  1129, 1139, 1186, 1187,
  1231, 1371, 1372, 1373,
  1374, 1478, 1547, 1662,
  1666
"L'Opéra Mouffe" 732
Loren, Sophia 26, 32, 96,
  239, 326, 553, 798, 799,
  1783
Lorne, Marion 96
Lorring, Joan 96
Losey, Joseph 2234
Loud, Pat 876, 2108
Louise, Anita 96
Louise, Ruth Harriett 2089
Louise, Tina 96
"Louisiana Story" 1616
Love 1890
Love, Bessie 96, 354, 571,
  1076, 1375
"Love and Anarchy" 1190,
  1619, 1824, 2041, 2099
"The Lovers" 1745
Lovers 1691
Lovett, Josephine 1110, 1377
Loy, Myrna 96, 208, 226,
  393, 739, 1208, 1832
Lucas, Marcia 1114, 1782
Luce, Clare Booth 97, 936,
  1567
"Lucía" 1773, 1952, 2041,
  2080
Lunt, Alfred 917
Lupino, Ida 96, 961, 970,
  1114, 1117, 1171, 1185,
  1199, 1282, 1302, 1303,
  1333, 1382, 1383, 1384,
  1385, 1386, 1387, 1388,
  1447, 1450, 1453, 1460,
  1463, 1471, 1472, 1486,
  1492, 1552, 1555, 1621,
  1643, 1646, 1658, 1668,
  1820
Lutyens, Elisabeth 1335
Lyn, Evelyn 14
Lynley, Carol 96
Lynn, Diana 96, 632
Lynn, Sharon 96
Lyon, Ben 315
Lyon, Sue 96, 824
Lyricists 14, 20, 1608

Maas, Audrey 1114, 1429,
    1782
Maas, Willard 1389, 1434,
    1455
McAvoy, May 96, 201
McBain, Diane 96
"McCabe and Mrs. Miller"
    1842, 1851
McCambridge, Mercedes 96,
    451
McConnel, Lorraine 1016
McCord, Vera 1658
McCormack, Marnie 1304
McCormack, Patty 96
McCracken, Joan 96
McCue, Maureen 2020
McDaniel, Hattie 96, 205
    661, 697, 1775, 2001
MacDonald, Jeanette 96, 197,
    535
MacDonald, Katherine 96,
    384
McDonald, Marie 96
MacDougall, Elspeth 2020
McFarland, Olive 96
McGee, Vonetta 477, 481
MacGraw, Ali 96
McGuire, Dorothy 96, 692
Mack, Helen 96
MacKaill, Dorothy 96
MacKay, Tanya Ballantyne
    1662, 1666
McKenna, Siobhan 96
MacKenzie, Midge 2020
MacLaine, Shirley 96, 589,
    590, 855, 1544
MacLaren, Mary 96
McLean, Barbara 1443, 1568,
    1578
McLeod, Catherine 96
MacMahon, Aline 96, 815
McNamara, Maggie 96
Macpherson, Jeanie 97, 1110,
    1417
McQueen, Butterfly 96, 205,
    661, 826, 1775
"Madame Sin" 473
"Madeline Is" 1839
Madison, Cleo 96
Maedchen in Uniform" 1252,
    1358, 1563, 2053
Magazines 26, 96, 1392,
    1952, 2158

Fan magazines 27, 35, 58,
    2089, 2212, 2251
"Magic Beauty Kit" 2009
Magnani, Anna 96, 386, 531,
    640, 888
Maid 2057
Main, Marjorie 96, 644, 691
Maison, Edna 96
"Make a Face" 2022
Make-up 126, 1035, 1120,
    1300, 1340, 1394, 1510
Maldoror, Sarah 1203, 1274,
    1604
Male Fantasies 1880, 1985
    2055
Male-female relationship
    1839, 1875, 1952, 2042,
    2066, 2080
Mallory, Patricia 96
Malone, Dorothy 96
"La maman et la putain" 546
Mammies 205, 1775, 1845
Mangano, Silvana 96, 137
Manners, Diane 14
Manning, Irene 96
Manning, Mildred 96
Mansfield, Jayne 26, 96,
    564, 585, 604, 605,
    1943, 1951,
Mansfield, Martha 96
Mara, Adele 96
"Marco Polo" 1411
Marcorelles, L. 1172
Margo 96
Margolin, Janet 96
"Marilyn Times Five" 1692
Marion, Frances 86, 97, 970,
    978, 1088, 1110, 1206,
    1222, 1411, 1412, 1413,
    1492, 1658
Maris, Mona 96
Marital Relationship 1900,
    1902, 2018, 2088
"Marked Woman" 1815, 1921
Marker, Chris 1551
Markey, Enid 96
Marlow, Lucy 96
Marner, Eugene and Carol
    1108
Marsh, Mae 84, 86, 87, 96,
    241, 356, 596, 613, 788
Marshall, Brenda 96
Marten, Helen 96

Martin, Mary 96
Martin, Susan 1267, 1877
Martin, Vivian 96
Martineau, Barbara 1967-
    1972, 2268
Martinelli, Elsa 96
Martyr 1849
"Mary Poppins" 839, 2084
Masculine Power 1810
Masina, Giulietta 96
Maskell, Virginia 96
Mason, Marsha 679
Mason, Shirley 96
Massey, Ilona 96
"Master of the House" 2078
Masters, Dorothy 2193
"Match Girl" 797
Mathis, June 1110, 1199
Matriarchic Spirit 2097
Matrons 195, 617
Maurey, Nicole 96
Maurice, Mary 96
Maxwell, Marilyn 96
May, Doris 96
May, Edna 96
May, Elaine 96, 425, 867,
    1069, 1114, 1149, 1278,
    1311, 1623
May, Nina 96
Mayo, Edna 96
Mayo, Virginia 96
Meadows, Audrey 96
Meadows, Jayne 96
Medina, Patricia 96
Mei, Tsen 96
Mekas, Jonas 1172
"Melinda" 1845
Mellen, Joan 1939
"Memories of Underdevelop-
    ment" 1605, 2169
Men-Pleasers 1869
Men without Women 1808
Menken, Marie 1252, 1389,
    1409, 1410, 1429, 1434,
    1436, 1438, 1440, 1455,
    1640, 2015
Mercer, Beryl 96
Mercer, Frances 96
Mercer, Mae 477
Merchant, Vivien 96
Mercouri, Melina 96, 625
Meredyth, Bess 1110
Merkel, Una 96

Merman, Ethel 96
Merrill, Dina 96
Merrill, Gary 463
"Meshes in the Afternoon"
    1252
Messinger, Lilly 536
Meszáros, Márta 1081, 1349,
    1358
"Metroliner" 1305
Metzger, Radley 1796
MGM 77, 109, 536, 993,
    1476
Meyer, Andy 797
Meyer, Russ 539, 716, 1796,
    2010
Michael, Gertrude 96, 420
Michaels, Dolores 96
Michelena, Beatriz 96
Michelson, Annette 1488,
    2270, 2301
Mide, Robin 2020
Mihu, Iulian 1134
Milan, Lita 96
Milano, Susan 1444
"Mildred Pierce" 1804
Miles, Sarah 96
Miles, Sylvia 878
Miles, Vera 96, 666
Miller, Ann 96
Miller, Arthur 1502
Miller, Barbara 1114
Miller, Geri 248
Miller, Patsy 96
Miller, Walter 290
Millett, Kate 1137, 1530,
    1795, 2020
Mills, Hayley 96, 170
Mills, Juliet 96, 170, 383
Mills Family 170
Milotte, Elma and Alfred 1325
Mimieux, Yvette 96, 278
Minnelli, Liza 96, 688, 705,
    862
"Minnie and Moskowitz" 1884
Minter, Mary Miles 96, 131
Miranda, Carmen 96
"Mississippi Mermaid" 460,
    1876, 1903
"Mrs. Miniver" 1231
Mitchell, Rhea 96
Mitrani, Michel 1281
Mizer, Bob 2029
Mizraki, Moshe 1530

Mobley, Mary Ann 96
Modugno, Ludovica 1070
Monroe, Marilyn 26, 32, 94,
    96, 150, 172, 263, 295,
    358, 391, 403, 408, 445,
    454, 478, 483, 518, 543,
    586, 598, 603, 612, 615, 620,
    621, 622, 631, 646, 746,
    753, 786, 847, 873, 874,
    916, 1831, 1888, 2058,
    2064, 2104
Monsters 1828
Montez, Maria 96, 336, 557,
    792, 793, 1941
Montezuma, Magdalena 532
Monti, Maria 1070
Montiel, Sarita 642
Monty, Gloria 1170
"Mood Mondrian" 1252
Moore, Colleen 96, 533, 634,
    800, 893
Moore, Constance 96, 291
Moore, Grace 635
Moore, Lisa 477
Moore, Mary Tyler 96
Moore, Terry 96
Moorehead, Agnes 96, 210,
    636, 687
Moran, Dolores 96
Moran, Polly 96, 246
Moreau, Jeanne 96, 337, 386,
    514, 544, 565, 810
Morella, Joe 1451
Moreno, Rita 96
Morgan, Michele 96
Morison, Patricia 96, 700
Morley, Karen 96
Morra, Irene 1443, 1578
Morris, Mary 328
Morrissey, Paul 1928
Morrow, Jo 96
Morse, Dolly 14
Moseley, Lillian 768
Mother 1730, 1751, 1781,
    1789, 2071, 2139
"The Mother and the Whore"
    2041
Mother-Informer 1937
Movie Makers 90, 103, 651,
    980, 983, 2010, 2047
Mulatto 126, 205, 1775, 1845
Mulford, Marilyn 2020
Mulvey, Laura 1911

Munro, Janet 96
Munson, Ona 96
Murdoch, Iris 1527
Murfin, Jane 1206, 1231
"Murmur of the Heart" 1884,
    2183
Murphy, Edna 96
Murphy, Mary 96
Murphy, Robynne 1305
Murray, Don 847
Murray, Mae 28, 96, 138,
    597
Musante, Joan 1305
Music 958, 961, 973
Musicals 14, 24, 53, 63, 81,
    83, 104, 108, 112, 311,
    536, 600, 705, 761, 762,
    933, 939, 958, 1924,
    2003
"My Name is Oona" 1626
"My Night at Maud's" 1976,
    2182
Myers, Carmel 96
Myth/Legend 127, 163, 166,
    173, 249, 308, 359, 443,
    454, 471, 603, 667, 846,
    1538, 1746, 1753, 1798,
    1938, 2009, 2070, 2096,
    2112, 2113, 2131, 2200,
    2228

Nagel, Anne 96
Naldi, Nita 96
"Nana, Mom and Me" 1191,
    1825, 2071
Nansen, Betty 96
"Narcissus" 1455
Narghita 145
"Nashville" 1096
Nassiter, Marcia 1114
National Film Archive 741
Natwick, Mildred 96
Naumberg, Nancy 1458
"Nausicaa" 1176
Nazimova, Alla 84, 96, 202,
    556, 675, 1089, 1849,
    2254
Neagle, Anna 96, 302
Neal, Patricia 96, 652, 701
"Near the Big Chakra" 2020
Neff, Hildegarde 96, 414,
    569, 665
Negative 1730

Negri, Pola 28, 96, 468,
    850, 875, 892
Negroes 10, 44, 48, 57, 66,
    73, 74, 126, 146, 205a,
    322, 323, 369, 456, 626,
    661, 697, 744, 1184,
    1320, 1776, 1800, 1821,
    1870, 1905, 1992, 1993,
    2001, 2123
Nelson, Gunvor 1252, 1533,
    1626, 2020
Nelson, Harriet 96
Nelson, Lori 96
Nelson Family 96
Nesbitt, Cathleen 96
Nesbitt, Miriam 96, 1492
New American Cinema
    membership 1462
    statement 1462
New Day Films 1014, 1020,
    1188
New Patterns 2045
Newman, Eve 1443, 1578
Newmar, Julie 96
Newspapers
    Christian Science Monitor
    840
Newsreel Collective 1466,
    1512, 2020
Nicholas, Denise 477
"Nicholas and Alexandra" 389
Nichols, Barbara 96
Nickel, Gitta 1566
Nides, Tina 1114
Nielsen, Asta 96, 441, 563,
    572, 657, 900
"Night of the Quarter Moon"
    1904
"The Night Porter" 1468
Nilsson, Anna Q. 96, 848
Nin, Anaïs 1469
Nixon, Marian 96
Nixon, Marni 96
Nongenue 1745
Nonwoman 2064
Nordstrom, Frances 1658
Nordstrom, Kristina 1086
Normand, Mable 56, 86, 96,
    576
North, Sheree 96
North American Film Co.
    1113
"Notebook 1962-63" 1252

Novak, Jane 96
Novak, Kim 96, 249
Novelists 166, 265, 936, 1043,
    1054, 1067, 1133, 1148,
    1177, 1181, 1227, 1233,
    1241, 1242, 1307, 1376,
    1467, 1484, 1497, 1540,
    1541, 1561, 1633, 1642,
    2164
Novels
    on Hollywood 2122
    on women 2070
Nuyen, France 96
Nyberg, Mary Ann 536
Nyman, Lena 476

Oberon, Merle 96, 250
Obituaries 110, 136, 469,
    503, 531, 640, 672, 912,
    1180, 1221, 1222, 1272,
    1308, 1309, 1314, 1324,
    1409, 1457, 1467, 1499
    1627, 2151, 2166, 2208,
    2238, 2239, 2258
O'Brien, Edna 1054, 1671
O'Brien, Margaret 96
O'Connor, Una 96
O'Day, Dawn see Shirley,
    Anne
Odd-Couples: Woman and Man-
    child 1884, 1929, 2055
O'Donnell, Cathy 96
"Oedipus Rex" 137
O'Hara, Joyce 1324
O'Hara, Maureen 96, 399,
    1840
Ohmart, Carol 96
O'Kalemo, Helen 96
"Old-Fashioned Women" 1305,
    2071
Oliver, Edna May 96, 123,
    361, 470
Oliver, Susan 96
Olivier, Sir Laurence 158
"Olympia" 1061, 1284, 1535
Ondine, Jack Smithby 557
O'Neil, Nance 96
O'Neill, Pat 1508
Ono, Yoko 1318, 1428, 1479,
    1625
"L'Opéra-Mouffe" 1532
Ophuls, Max 1945
Osborn, Elodie 1193

O'Sullivan, Maureen 96
"The Other Half of the Sky"
    1544
Other Woman 342, 1706
Otto, Linda 1114
Our Gang 56
Ouspenskaya, Maria 96
Overman, Lynn 96
Owen, Ruth Bryan 1492
Owen, Seena 96
"The Owl and the Pussycat"
    259
Oxenberg, Jan 1016, 1087

Pace, Judy 477
Page, Anita 96
Page, Geraldine 96, 381
Page, Sheila 1016
Paget, Debra 96
Paige, Janis 96, 510
Paige, Sheila 2020
Paik, Nam Jun 1444
Palmer, Betsy 96
Palmer, Lilli 96
Papas, Irene 96
"Paper Moon" 765
Paramount 689, 1034
Parent, Gail 1114, 1484
Park, Ida May 970, 1157
Parker, Dorothy 81, 96
Parker, Eleanor 96, 581
Parker, Jean 96
Parker, Suzy 96
Parrish, Helen 96
Parsons, Harriet 1260, 1261
Parsons, Louella 1487, 2195,
    2262, 2275-2277
Pasolini, Pier Paolo 137
Passionate 1935
Pathé Studios 290
Patrichi, Gina 698, 781
Patrick, Gail 96
Patterson, Elizabeth 96
Pavan, Marisa 96
Paxinou, Katina 96
Payne, Freda 477
Payton, Barbara 96, 702
Pearce, Alice 96
Pearson, Beatrice 96
Pearson, Virginia 96
Pellicer, Pina 96
Pelswick, Rose 2282
"Penthesilea, Queen of the

Amazons" 1913
Pepper, Barbara 96
Performances
    Preserved 741
Periodicals 96, 372, 1392
Perkins, Millie 96
Perrault, P. 1232
Perreau, Gigi 96
Perry, Eleanor 438, 1114,
    1139, 1267, 1311, 1376,
    1426, 1496, 1497, 1498,
    1641, 1662, 1666, 1877,
    2116
Perry, Frank 1497, 1498
Peters, Jean 96, 512
Peters, Susan 96
Peterson, Dorothy 96
Petri Elio 144
Petrova, Olga 96, 676
Petrovická, Jirina 488
Philbin, Mary 96
Phillips, Julia 1114, 1311
    Julia and Mike 1115
Phillips, Mary Beams 1305
Phillips, Norma 96
Photographer 92
"Phyllis and Terry" 1108
Pickett, Elizabeth 1492
Pickford, Mary 5, 28, 46,
    84, 86, 94, 96, 200,
    275, 362, 437, 457, 468,
    555, 556, 658, 710, 711,
    712, 713, 714, 788, 801,
    831, 899, 2104
Pierreux, Jacqueline 1275,
    1351
"Pigs" 1435, 1973
Pin-up 26, 446, 1759
Piperno, Marina 1070
Piskov, Hristo 1343
Pitagora, Paola 1070
Pitts, Zasu 96, 851, 913
"Planas-testimonio de un etno-
    cidio" 1418
"Play It As It Lays" 1541,
    2036
Pleshette, Suzanne 96, 593
Plivová-Simkova, Vera 1297
"Plumb Line" 1305
Podesta, Rosanna 96
Pogonat, Margareta 783
"The Point Is to Change It"
    1304

"La pointe courte" 1176
Political 1754, 1803, 1809,
    1864, 2037, 2049, 2265,
    2291
  activity 144, 237, 288,
    482, 611, 795, 1177,
    1204, 1243, 1326, 1338,
    1541
  opinions 678, 837, 1177,
    1204, 1516, 1541, 1553
Poor Little Rich Girls 1706
Popa, Letitia 1154, 1268
Poplavskaja, Irina 1419
Pornographic 1793, 1859
Pornography 280, 428
Porter, Katherine Anne 936
Positive 1836, 1844, 1882,
    2031
Powell, Dilys 1526, 2285
Powell, Eleanor 96
Powell, Jane 96, 508
Power, Tyrone 274
Powers, Mala 96
Powers, Stefanie 96
Prentiss, Paula 96
Preobrashenskaia, Olga 1199
Presle, Micheline 96
Preston, Catherine Craig 720
Preston, Robert 720
Prevost, Marie 96
Pringle, Aileen 96
Printzlan, Olga 1110
"Private Property" 1745
Procházková, Alena 494
Producers 92, 97, 469, 676,
    737, 963, 967, 983, 984,
    992, 997, 1106, 1109,
    1114, 1115, 1147, 1155,
    1218, 1241, 1260, 1272,
    1275, 1311, 1446, 1467,
    1507, 1523, 1537, 1540,
    1544, 1587, 1596, 1647
  associate producers 1782
  co-producers 1782
Production 678, 1070, 1207,
    1251
Proletarian Films 1815
Propaganda 964, 1381, 1913,
    2247
Prostitutes 1729, 1842, 1921
Provine, Dorothy 96
Prowse, Juliet 96
"Proxy Hawks" 1839

Public Opinion 409, 586
Publicists 29, 410, 536, 586,
    1341, 1442, 1451
Publicity Still 2115
"The Pumpkin Eater" 1730
Pure 1792
Puritanical 1890
Purviance, Edna 96
"Put Yourself in My Place"
    1304

Queen Elizabeth II 1986
Quigley, Juanita 96

"Rachel, Rachel" 1730
Racial Themes 73, 656
Radical 2014
Rafelson, Toby 1782
Rafferty, Frances 96
Rainer, Luise 96, 231
Rainer, Yvonne 1305, 1339,
    1364, 1461, 1944
Raines, Ella 96, 364
Ralston, Esther 96, 374, 1146
Ralston, Jobyna 96
Ralston, Vera Hruba 96
Rambeau, Marjorie 96
Rampling, Charlotte 273
Ransohoff, Doris 1631
"Rape" 1428, 1479
Rape 1810, 1870, 2082
Ray, Allene 55, 96, 290
Ray, Nicholas 2233, 2234
Raye, Martha 96, 691
Raymond, Alan and Susan
    1518, 1630
Raymond, Paula 96
Read, Lillian 96
Realistic 1791, 1960, 2117
Reardon, Mildred 96
"Rebecca" 195, 1231
Reckless 2004
"The Red Detachment of Wo-
    men" 1763
Red Hot Mama 1845
Redgrave, Lynn 96
Redgrave, Vanessa 96, 244
Redgrave Family 96
Redheads 584
Reed, Carol 2181, 2235
Reed, Donna 96
Reed, Florence 96
Reference 4, 12, 13, 14, 18,

Reference (cont.)
  20, 21, 22, 32, 36, 45,
  69, 934, 967, 975, 976
Reichert, Julia 1016, 1109,
  1188, 1252, 1338, 1435,
  1973, 2020
Reid, Mrs. Wallace 1658
Reid, Peggy 96
Reiniger, Lotte 1213, 1278,
  1524
Remick, Lee 96, 436
Reminiscences 135
Resnais, Alain 1551
Revere, Anne 61, 96
Reviews
  Book 173, 665, 762, 1216,
    1217, 1330, 1357, 1548,
    1919, 1939, 1989, 2117,
    2118, 2165, 2250, 2283,
    2289
  Film 71, 256, 316, 331,
    784, 968, 1000, 1079, 1093,
    1094, 1095, 1108, 1122,
    1149, 1190, 1226, 1249,
    1274, 1304, 1305, 1339,
    1393, 1419, 1420, 1529,
    1530, 1540, 1593, 1597,
    1604, 1609, 1626, 1653,
    1662, 1692, 1764, 1774,
    1783, 1842, 1891, 1892,
    1893, 1894, 1906, 1918,
    1933, 1976, 2022, 2023,
    2028, 2040, 2042, 2061,
    2071, 2074, 2080, 2091,
    2111, 2114, 2124, 2128,
    2144, 2152, 2169, 2173,
    2177, 2178, 2202, 2219,
    2253, 2273, 2294
Revolutionary 1764
Reynolds, Adeline DeWalt 96
Reynolds, Debbie 96, 730
Reynolds, Joyce 96
Reynolds, Marjorie 96
Reynolds, Vera 96
Rhue, Madlyn 96
Rich, Irene 96
Rich, Lillian 96
Rich, Vivian 96
Richards, Ann 96
Riefenstahl, Leni 299, 628,
  924, 964, 1061, 1062, 1074,
  1130, 1141, 1199, 1215,
  1254, 1255, 1278, 1284,

1285, 1286, 1352, 1353,
  1354, 1359, 1363, 1381,
  1448, 1534, 1535, 1554,
  1636, 1637, 1644, 1658,
  2036
Rigg, Diana 96
Ripp, Judith 2198
Risdon, Elizabeth 96
Ritter, Thelma 96, 687, 748
RKO 692, 1034, 1787
Roberts, Allene 96
Roberts, Rachel 96
Robertson, John S. 1377
Robinson, Frances 401
Robson, Flora 96, 352
Robson, May 96
Robyns, Gwen 756
Rochefort, Christiane 1124,
  1307, 1530, 1895
Rockefeller 1816
Rodriguez, Martha 1243, 1418
Rogers, Ginger 96, 311, 335,
  462, 733, 761, 762
Rogers, Jean 96
Rohmer, Eric 1976, 2106
Rojas, Abigail 1192
Roland, Rita 1030, 1443
Roland, Ruth 55, 96, 97, 411,
  412
Roles 1844, 2070, 2077
  lack of roles in films 1799,
    1880, 1897, 2038
Roman, Ruth 96, 507
Romance 54, 81
Romantic 822, 990
  Drama 1777
Ronay, Esther 1304
"Room at the Top" 1745
Rosay, Francoise 96
Roscoe, Judith 1114
Rose, Alex 1114
Rose, Tonia 81, 96
Rose, William 81, 96
"Rosemary's Baby" 432, 1244
Rosenberg, Royanne 1838
Ross, Diana 477
Ross, Karen 1466
Ross, Katherine 96
Ross, Shirley 96
Rossellini, Roberto 2061
Rossi-Drago, Eleanora 96
Rosulkova, Marie 484

Roth, Lillian 755
Rothman, Marion 1114
Rothman, Stephanie 961, 1662, 1666, 2022
Rothschild, Amalie R. 1016, 1109, 1188, 1191, 1328, 1461, 1602, 2020, 2071
"Rotten to the Core" 273
Rowlands, Gina 96
Royce, Riza 788
Rubens, Alma 96
Rubin, Barbara 1432, 1436, 1437
Rubley, Faith and John 1016
Ruick, Barbara 96
Rule, Janice 96
Rules for Behavior 1887
Run-Away Heiress 1867
Rush, Barbara 96
Russell, Gail 96
Russell, Jane 96, 449
Russell, Ken 1835, 1928
Russell, Rosalind 96, 740, 827
Rutherford, Margaret 96, 526, 756
Ryan, Peggy 96

Sacrificing 1804, 1890
Safier, Gloria 1114
Sagan, Leontine 1199, 1252, 1563
Saint, Eva Marie 61, 96
St. James, Susan 829
St. John, Adela Rogers 97
St. John, Jill 96
"Une saison dans la vie d'Emmanuel" 1599
Sale, Virginia 96
"Salomé" 1849
"Sambizanga" 1203, 1274
Sands, Diana 96, 331, 477
Saunders, Jackie 96
Saunders, Mary Jane 96
Savage, Ann 96
"The Savage Eye" 1745
"Savage Messiah" 1928
Savel'Eva, Ljudmila 435
Savina, Ija 417
Scala, Gia 96
Scala, Katherine 990
Scandinavia 37, 946
Scarlett O'Hara 1767

Scatterbrains 242, 617
Scenarists 1289, 1294, 1315, 1489
"Scenes from a Marriage" 1902, 1927, 2111
Scenic Artists 1442
Schapiro, Sue 1596
Schell, Maria 96
Schlesinger, John 1237, 1238
Schlondörff, Volker 1348, 1505, 1562
"Schmeerguntz" 1626, 2020
Schneemann, Carolee 1305
Schneider, Romy 96
Schneider, Rosalind 1109
Schroeter, Werner 532
Scott, Evelyn F. 97
Scott, Lizabeth 96
Scott, Martha 96
Scott, Pippa 96
Screen Actors Guild 482, 1291
Screenplays 963, 1058, 1059, 1060, 1293, 1470, 1474, 1582, 1583, 1886
Screenwriters 81, 87, 92, 97, 136, 432, 436, 503, 676, 920, 962, 983, 984, 990, 992, 996, 997, 998, 1032, 1043, 1044, 1054, 1058, 1069, 1070, 1072, 1075, 1088, 1096, 1110, 1113, 1114, 1115, 1123, 1124, 1129, 1131, 1132, 1133, 1139, 1140, 1148, 1167, 1168, 1177, 1181, 1186, 1187, 1206, 1208, 1222, 1223, 1226, 1227, 1230, 1231, 1237, 1238, 1239, 1241, 1242, 1244, 1245, 1264, 1267, 1283, 1307, 1309, 1310, 1311, 1315, 1317, 1327, 1362, 1371, 1372, 1373, 1374, 1376, 1411, 1412, 1413, 1417, 1426, 1477, 1478, 1487, 1489, 1496, 1497, 1498, 1499, 1540, 1541, 1547, 1550, 1561, 1562, 1563, 1567, 1612, 1622, 1642, 1669, 1671
Script Girl 571, 1090, 1146, 1150, 1375
Script Supervisors 1442, 1591

Script timer 536, 1341
Scriptwriter 1146, 1151, 1342,
    1487, 1489, 1519, 1631,
    1778
Searchinger, Marian 1114
Sears, Heather 96
Sears, Zelda 1492
"The Seashell and the Clergy-
    man" 1252
Sebastian, Dorothy 96
Seberg, Wini 96
Secretaries 1234, 1635
Sedgwick, Edie 478
Sedgwick, Josie 96
Seductive 1928
Segal, Vivienne 96
Sejbalova, Jirina 491
"Self-Health" 1305
Selznick, Joyce 1114
Sennett, Mack 570
Serial Queens 102, 787, 789,
    809, 884, 887
Serials 55, 102, 290, 809,
    1907
"A 7-1/2 Minute Film" 1304
"Seven Women" 1950, 2056
Severson, Anne 2020
Sex 51, 280, 1784, 1796,
    1835, 1842, 1890, 1984,
    1987, 2039, 2048, 2076
    2083, 2088, 2097, 2104,
    2114
Sex Appeal 506, 650
Sex Symbols 49, 127, 165,
    239, 245, 249, 357, 391,
    552, 603, 624, 890,
    1691, 1811, 1826, 1831,
    1951, 1984, 2050, 2097,
    2120
Sexism 1841, 2003, 2059
Sexploitationists 1796
Sexual Politics 1836, 1842,
    1977
Sexual Relationships 1754,
    1902, 1930, 1979, 2108
Sexuality 1751, 1928, 1938,
    1979, 2104
Sexually Repressed 1730, 1842
Seymour, Anne 96
Seymour, Clarine 96, 788
Shaffer, Deborah 2020
"Shane" 2230
Shannon, Peggy 96

Sharoff, Irene 536
Shaw, Jean 1016
Shaw, Victoria 96
Shaw, Wini 87, 96
Shay, Dorothy 14
Shearer, Moira 96
Shearer, Norma 96, 505, 771
Shepherd, Cybill 674
Sheridan, Ann 96
"Sherriffed" 1458
Sherwood, Madeleine 96
Sherwood, Robert 1231, 1411
Shirley, Anne 96
Shore, Dinah 96
Short, Gertrude 96
"Shoulder to Shoulder" 1907
Sidney, Sylvia 96, 208, 689,
    719, 806
Signoret, Simone 96, 340,
    845
Silva, Jorge 1243, 1418
Silver, Joan Micklin 1544
Simmons, Jean 96, 609
Simms, Ginny 96
Simon, Simone 96
Singers 83, 112, 145, 300,
    477, 642, 706, 933
"Singin' in the Rain" 81, 1132
Singleton, Penny 96
Sirens 1855
Sirk, Douglas 1926
Sisters 1855
Sjöman, Vilgot 476
Skipworth, Allison 96
"Sleeper" 2169
Slesinger, Tess 1230, 1317
Slut 1789
Smejkalová, Jarmila 492
"The Smiling Madame Beudet"
    1252
Smith, Alexis 96, 321
Smith, Judy 1016, 1306, 1435,
    1611, 1973, 2020, 2090
Smith, Kate 794
Smith, Maggie 96, 244
Smith, Rose 1588
Smith, Sharon 2236
Snodgrass, Carrie 438
Snow, Marguerite 96
Soap Opera 1880, 1902, 2051
Society 1883, 2009, 2078,
    2080
Solanis, Valerie 611

Solas, Humberto 1773
Solax 1490
"Soljaris" 649
Solomon, Holly 1500
Solovej, Elena 796
"Something Different" 1252, 1358
"Something Wild" 1810
Sommer, Elke 96, 506
Sondergaard, Gale 96
Sontag, Susan 1209, 1336, 1582, 1583, 2267, 2297, 2298, 2299
Sorceress 1758, 2103
Sorrin, Ellen 1016, 2020
Sothern, Ann 61, 96
Sound 296, 379, 958, 961
"Sounder" 1845, 2139
Soviet 19, 935, 972
Spaak, Catherine 96
Spain, Fay 96
Spencer, Dorothy 1570, 1651
Sperling, Karen 1102
Spheeris, Penelope 1083
Spiritual 1696
Spring, Sylvia 1662, 1666, 1839
"Squaw Man" 384
Stag Movies 1855
"Les Stances à Sophie" 1307, 1530
Stanley, Kim 96
Stanwyck, Barbara 96, 736, 790
Stapleton, Maureen 96, 405
Starke, Pauline 96, 183
Starling, Lynn 990
Stars 52, 53, 55, 59, 70, 77, 85, 88, 94, 100, 101, 104, 105, 107, 110, 118, 163, 227, 231, 238, 239, 245, 249, 267, 269, 308, 330, 353, 395, 404, 468, 478, 498, 519, 538, 577, 610, 632, 650, 718, 817, 825, 875, 886, 1115, 1691, 1705, 2009, 2089, 2161
Steele, Barbara 96
Steiger, Rod 447
Sten, Anna 96
Stenographic Services 1251
Stereotypes 146, 169, 456, 626, 697, 768, 826, 1079, 1697, 1699, 1700, 1839, 1870, 1981, 1983, 2024, 2031, 2123, 2127
Sterling, Jan 96, 507
Sternberg, Janet 2020
Stevens, Connie 96
Stevens, George 2230
Stevens, Inger 96
Stevens, Stella 96, 1259
Stewart, Anita 96, 185, 675
Stewart, Elaine 96
Stickney, Dorothy 96
Still photographers 1442, 1457, 1458, 2089
Stonehouse, Ruth 96
Storey, Edith 96
Storm, Gale 96
"Stormy Weather" 464
Story Analyst 97, 1536
Strasberg, Susan 96
Straub, Jean-Marie 1045, 1549, 1594
Strauss, Helen 1114
Streisand, Barbra 32, 83, 96, 121, 259
Strich, Elaine 96
Strikes 88, 482, 1291
"Strohfeuer" 1348, 1562
Strong 1828, 2127
Strown, Linda May 961
Stroyevna, Vera 1199, 1361
Stuart, Gloria 96
Stuart, Iris 96
Studio Projectionists 1442
Studio Teachers 1442
Studios see specific name
"A Study in Choreography for Camera" 1252
Stunt people 241, 421, 1104, 1235, 1564
Suffragette 1063, 1390, 1758
"Sugar Cookies" 575
Sullavan, Margaret 96, 504, 825
"Summer of '42" 2055
"Summer Wishes, Winter Dreams" 1892
"Sunday, Bloody Sunday" 1123, 1226, 1237, 1238, 1851
Super-8 1464, 1465
Supporting Performers 62, 67, 110, 111, 114, 116, 401,

Supporting Performers (cont.)
  420, 432, 759
Suput, Tatjana 1119
Susann, Jacqueline 166, 1067
Suzman, Janet 389
Svilova, Yelizaveta 1445
Svorcová, Jirina 485
Swanson, Gloria 84, 94, 96,
  196, 267, 496, 663, 689,
  742, 791, 832, 834,
  2032
Swashbucklers 81
Sweet, Blanche 87, 96, 188,
  788, 830
Sword movie 2085
Sykes, Brenda 477
"Sylvia, Fran and Joy" 1304
"Sylvia Scarlet" 1866
Syms, Sylvia 96

Talbot, Linda 1365, 1437
Talent Scout 158
Taliaferro, Mabel 96, 818
Talley, Alma Mabrey 2151
Talmadge, Constance 96, 189
Talmadge, Norma 96, 675, 802
Talmadge sisters 28, 84, 831
Tandy, Jessica 96
Tapley, Rose 96
Tarasova, Alla 912
"Targets" 2223
Tashman, Lilyan, 96
Tate, Sharon 96, 251, 769
Tattered Queens 1806
Tax, Merideth 2160
"Taxi" 1458
Taylor, Delores 1114
Taylor, Elizabeth 26, 32, 94,
  96, 373, 833, 880, 2064,
  2104
Taylor, Estelle 96
Taylor, Laurette 256, 303
Taylor, Renee 1114
Taylor, Valerie and Ron 1239
Technicians 1442
Technology 937
Temple, Shirley 7, 96, 120,
  164, 835, 1816
Tennant, Barbara 629
Terry, Alice 28, 96
Terry, Ellen 305
Terry, John 1630
"Testimonio indigena sobre

Planas" 1243
Tetzel, Joan 96
Tewkesbury, Joan 1096, 1114,
  1115
Thanhouser Studio 1196
"Thank Heaven for Little Girls"
  2003
Thaxter, Phyllis 96, 708
Theby, Rosemary 96
Themes 460, 1079, 1896,
  2070
Theology 1890
Theorists 1469, 2154, 2160,
  2162, 2184, 2186, 2187,
  2188, 2189, 2190, 2297
"There's Always Tomorrow"
  1926
Thiess, Ursula 96
Third World 1604, 1605
Thirer, Irene 2238
Thomas, Dylan 1502
Thomas, Marlo 394
Thomas, Olive 96
Thompson, Kay 96
Thorburn, June 96
Thorndike, Sybil 96
"Three Lives" 1137, 1530,
  1795, 2020, 2022
"Three Weeks" 1242
Thrillers 81
Thulin, Ingrid 96, 279, 501
Thurman, Mary 96
Tierney, Gene 96, 774
Tiffin, Pamela 96
"A Time for Burning" 1575
Tincher, Fay 56, 96, 388
Tingley, Helen 2199
Tinker Bell 839, 2084
Titles 1347, 1442
Tobin, Genevieve 96
Todd, Ann 96
Todd, Thelma 96, 836
Tonceva, Doroteja 219
Torchia, Emily 536
Toren, Marta 96, 747
Torres, Raquel 96
Totter, Audrey 96
"The Touch" 1932, 1935, 2183
Towers, Constance 96
Toye, Wendy 1101
Tracy, Spencer 32, 424, 471,
  521, 1245
Traverse, Madlaine 96

"A Tree Grows in Brooklyn"
   1230
Treen, Mary 96
Tresgot, Annie 1281
Trevor, Claire 96, 448
Trintignant, Nadine 732, 1037,
   1040, 1267, 1532, 1600,
   1658, 1877
"Triumph of the Will" 964,
   1284
Truffaut, Francois 460, 1876,
   1903, 1929, 1930, 2223
"Tub Film" 1305
Tuchock, Wanda 1492
Tucker, Sophie 561
Tupper, Lois Ann 2020
Turnbull, Margaret 1489,
   1612
Turner, Florence 84, 96,
   715
Turner, Lana 96, 390, 639,
   728, 905
Tushingham, Rita 96
Tutin, Dorothy 244
TV 1264
Twelvetrees, Helen 96
Twentieth-Century Fox 158,
   686
"Two English Girls" 1903
"Two or Three Things I Know
   About Her" 1931
Tyler, Judy 96
Tyler, Parker 1502
Types 94, 146, 166, 169,
   194, 201, 227, 239, 245,
   342, 387, 399, 440, 453,
   456, 478, 538, 545, 584,
   759, 799, 863, 892, 893,
   955, 990, 1231, 1252
Týrlová, Hermína 1071
Tyrrell, Susan 529
Tyson, Cicely 477, 911, 2139
Tyszkiewicz, Beata 365, 577

Ullmann, Liv 566
Ulric, Lenore 96
Umeki, Miyoshi 96
Underground Film 977
Unions 88, 1208, 1345, 1379,
   1442
Unsell, Eve 97
"The Untouchables" 1453
Ure, Mary 96, 606

Urecal, Minerva 96
Ursianu, Malvina 1134

Valli, Alida 96
Valli, Virginia 96
Vamp 5, 155, 165, 387, 892,
   1774, 1814, 2025, 2101
Vance, Vivian 96
Vancurová, Marta 487
Van Dongen, Helen 1616
Van Doren, Mamie 96
Van Fleet, Jo 96
Van Upp, Virginia 990
Van Vooren, Monique 96, 281
Varda, Agnes 732, 1031, 1032,
   1135, 1176, 1246, 1252,
   1278, 1360, 1404, 1501,
   1532, 1551, 1658, 1793
Varden, Evelyn 96
Varsi, Diane 96
Vasulka, Woody and Stella
   1444
Vedrès, Nicole 1106, 1467,
   1514
Velez, Lupe 96, 788
Venable, Evelyn 96
Venus 1783, 1888
Vera-Ellen 96
Verdon, Gwen 96
"Veronica" 1405, 1560
"A Very Curious Girl" 1249,
   1358, 1920, 2103
Video 1078, 1202, 1444,
   1543, 1598, 1647, 1982
   Festival 1771, 2079
Vidor, Florence 96, 355
"La vie rêvée" 1891
Viertal, Salka 1206, 1622
Vinogradskaja, Katerina 1342
Violet, Ultra 282
"The VIP's" 756
Virgin 1789
"Virginia Woolf: the Moment
   Whole" 2020
"Visions of Eight" (20th Olym-
   pian Film) 1402, 1474
Vitagraph 277, 1075, 1300
Vitagraph Girl 715
Vitti, Monica 96, 729, 1070
Viva 525, 870
Vivas, Marta 1948
"Vivian" 797
"Vivre ensemble" 1121, 1279

"Vivre Sa Vie" 1530
Vlady, Marina 96
Vogel, Amos 1193
Volonti, Gian Maria 144
Voluntaru, Maria 871
Von Furstenberg, Betsy 96
von Praunheim, Rosa 1504
Von Sternberg, Josef 113,
    247, 396, 601, 664, 817,
    1960, 2025
von Trotta, Margarethe 1348,
    1505, 1562
"Voyage to Italy" 2061
"La vraie nature de Bernadette"
    541

Wackner, Sophie 1628
Walcamp, Marie 96
Walker, Beverly 1114
Walker, Cheryl 96
Walker, Helen 96
Walker, Lillian 96
Walker, Nancy 96
Wallace, Irene 96
Wallace, Jean 96
Wallerstein, Mauricio 1192
Walley, Deborah 96
Walsh, Raoul 1794
Walters, Polly 96
"Wanda" 1401, 1441, 1556,
    1557, 1692, 1980, 2022
War 81, 752, 1390, 2270
Ward, Fanny 28, 96
Wardrobe
    Dept. 1476
    Mistress 84, 1632
Ware, Margaret 477
Warhol, Andy 1435, 1455,
    1849, 1973
Warner, Jack L. 115
Warner Bros. 115, 1801,
    1815, 1991
Warren, Eda 1443, 1578
Waters, Ethyl 96, 661, 840,
    881
Watson, Debbie 96
Watson, Lucile 96
Wayne, Mabel 14
Weber, Lois 4, 96, 970,
    1055, 1085, 1116, 1199,
    1278, 1321, 1370, 1395,
    1403, 1492, 1495, 1523,
    1525, 1576, 1617, 1658,
    2015

Weidler, Virginia 96
Weill, Claudia 1016, 1109,
    1114, 1188, 1328, 1544,
    1613, 2020
Weinberger, Anielle 1304
Weiner, Ann 1016
Weinstein, Hannah 1114
Weintraub, Sandy 1114, 1782
Weisz, Claude 1599
Welch, Raquel 96, 251
Weld, Tuesday 96
Welles, Orson 664, 2172,
    2242
Wellman, William 233, 234
Wells, Jacqueline see Julie
    Bishop
Wertmuller, Lina 1103, 1190,
    1229, 1280, 1356, 1358,
    1619, 1672, 1824, 2099
West, Claire 1628
West, Claudia 1231, 1317
West, Mae 81, 96, 224, 289,
    558, 624, 668, 689, 696,
    854, 882, 885, 910, 1206,
    1658, 1988, 1995, 2104,
    2138
West, Jessamyn 1642
Westerns 81, 2065
Westover, Winifred 96
Wexler, Haskell 1259, 1605
Wharton Studio 809
"What I Want" 2020
"What's the Matter, Sally! The
    Roof Needs Mowing" 1305
"What's Up, Doc?" 259, 765
White, Alice 96, 128
White, Pearl 55, 86, 96,
    102, 317, 809, 884, 887
Whitty, May 96
Whores 479, 1847
Wieck, Dorothea 96
Wieland, Joyce 1047, 1143,
    1252, 1648, 1662, 1797
Wife 1762, 2020
"The Wild Party" 1358
Wiley, Dorothy 1252, 1533,
    1626, 2020
Williams, Cara 96, 254
Williams, Edy 539, 716, 2010
Williams, Esther 96
Williams, Kathlyn 96
"Willow Springs" 532
Wilson, Colin 1527
Wilson, Elsie Jane 1157

Wilson, Lois 96, 286
Wilson, Margery 96, 1658
Wilson, Marie 96, 722
Windsor, Claire 124
Windsor, Geri 1114
Windsor, Marie 96
Winham, Francine 1304
Winkler, Margaret J. 1492
Winn, Kitty 1267, 1877
Winston, Helen 469, 1272
Winter, Mrs. Thomas G.
    1368
Winters, Shelley 96, 240,
    405
Winton, Jane 96
"Witchcraft" 1489
Withers, Jane 96, 120
Witnesses 390
Wolff, Peggy 1508
Wollen, Peter 1911
Woman and Manchild 1884,
    1929, 2055
"A Woman of Paris" 2115
"Woman to Woman" 1305
"Woman Under the Influence"
    2016, 2042
"Womanhouse" 1304
Women
    Attitudes of 397, 1953,
        2060, 2080
        toward 1837, 1932,
            1953, 1978, 2040,
            2060
    Canadian 1521, 1522, 1839,
        1891, 2022
    Degradation of 1851, 1937,
        2008
    Filmmakers 938, 950, 992,
        1001, 1012, 1013, 1014,
        1022, 1024, 1025, 1026,
        1027, 1028, 1029, 1048,
        1077, 1079, 1083, 1103,
        1109, 1114, 1119, 1125,
        1182, 1200, 1208, 1212,
        1216, 1217, 1252, 1262,
        1264, 1265, 1266, 1298,
        1304, 1305, 1306, 1322,
        1358, 1379, 1393, 1408,
        1409, 1410, 1414, 1415,
        1416, 1421, 1422, 1423,
        1424, 1427, 1428, 1429,
        1432, 1433, 1434, 1435,
        1436, 1438, 1439, 1440,

        1455, 1461, 1468, 1469,
        1479, 1482, 1492, 1500,
        1504, 1509, 1520, 1521,
        1523, 1526, 1533, 1541,
        1543, 1544, 1545, 1559,
        1565, 1589, 1595, 1602,
        1610, 1611, 1613, 1614,
        1618, 1629, 1630, 1648,
        1650, 1653, 1654, 1660,
        1661, 1662, 1666, 1667,
        1670, 1673, 1833, 1838,
        1862, 1865, 1873, 2020
    Filmmaking 1209, 1247
    Freedom of 624
    History in Cinema 992,
        1125, 1174, 1252, 1390,
        1492, 1988
    in Danish Film 1494
    in Films 995, 999, 1000,
        1001, 1014, 1048, 1077,
        1198, 1230, 1252, 1301,
        1311, 1378, 1379, 1380,
        1393, 1398, 1450a, 1569,
        1579, 1595, 1661, 1662,
        1664, 1666, 1877, 1946,
        1947, 1948, 2019, 2134
    in Horror Films 1915,
        2030, 2039
    in Sweden 1122, 1209
    Objectification of 616, 624,
        1252, 1966
    Peruvian 1938
    Position in society 2080
    Power of 1107, 1344, 1937
    in Quebec 1232
    Rights of 1091, 1660
    Roles of 1844, 1880, 2009,
        2020, 2077
    Roles in the Media 2038,
        2063
    Treatment of 2085
"The Women" 826, 827, 1231,
    1730, 1834
"Women Against the Industrial
    Bill" 1304
"Women and Children at Large"
    2020
"Women in Cages" 1809
"Women in Love" 1933, 2140
"Women of the Rhondda" 1304
"Women Talking" 2020
Women without Men 1808
Women's Films 693, 940, 959,

Women's Films (cont.)
    995, 999, 1002, 1003,
    1007, 1008, 1012, 1014,
    1015, 1016, 1022, 1024,
    1025, 1027, 1028, 1029,
    1048, 1063, 1068, 1077,
    1079, 1095, 1103, 1179,
    1182, 1198, 1200, 1209,
    1212, 1236, 1265, 1304,
    1305, 1322, 1358, 1364,
    1390, 1393, 1394, 1396,
    1421, 1422, 1424, 1435,
    1509, 1520, 1533, 1544,
    1545, 1553, 1559, 1653,
    1654, 1661, 1662, 1667,
    1804, 1832, 1833, 1843,
    1865, 1880, 1949, 1969,
    2020, 2028
  Defining 1684, 1848, 2041,
    2051
Women's Oppression 2081
Women's Place 1795, 2085
"The Women's Film" 1435,
    1611, 1973, 2020
"The Women's Happy Time
    Commune" 2020
Wong, Anna May 96, 135
Wood, Audrey 1114
Wood, Natalie 7, 96
Wood, Peggy 96, 902, 903
Woodbury, Joan 904
Woodlawn, Holly 169, 1849
Woodruff, Eleanor 96
Woodward, Joanne 96
Woolf, Virginia 1233, 2302
"The Word Is Persistence"
    1570
Workers 1801
Working class 1729
Working girls 2102
Working Women 1801
"The World, the Flesh and the
    Devil" 1904
Woronov, Mary 575
Wray, Fay 96
Wright, Teresa 96
Writers Guild of America 482,
    1291
Wyatt, Jane 96, 344
Wycherly, Margaret 96
Wyler, William 257
Wyman, Jane 96, 509
Wymore, Patrice 96

Wynn, May 96
Wynter, Dana 96
Wynyard, Diana 96

Yahrans, Bill 1605
Yamaguchi, Shirley 96
Yearbook 1, 3, 18, 72, 85,
    921, 969
"Les yeux ne veulent pas en
    tout temps se fermer"
    1594
York, Susannah 96, 252, 366,
    368
Young, Clara Kimball 96, 182,
    277, 319, 587, 908
Young, Loretta 96, 214, 909
Young, Margaret Ann 1347
Youth 122, 140, 158, 164
"Yudie" 2078
Yurka, Blanche 96

Zaglen, Helen 1016
"Zazdrość i medycyna" 554
Zelenohorská, Jitka 493
"Zestrea" 1268
Zetterling, Mai 96, 914,
    1122, 1355, 1358, 1402,
    1474, 1658
Zivanović, Tatjana 1119
Zorina, Vera 96
Zouzou 300
Zuker, Adolph 46, 918
Zwerin, Charlotte 924